The Armenians

The Armenians considers how the Armenian people have constructed their identity through the accumulation of historical experience and shared collective memory. The book takes the reader through the complex and often bloody historical events that the people of Armenia have experienced and tracks the evolution of their culture and politics up to their current situation as a small post-communist country poised between Europe and the Middle East and linked to a kaleidoscope of emigrant Armenian communities spread across the globe.

The Armenians are one of the oldest nations in existence, privileged to have one of the world's most stable and persistent identities. The quality of 'Armenianness' has proved to be so resilient that it has endured for 2,000 years, even though in that time the Armenian people have been compelled to resist invasion, suffer persecution, tolerate alien rule and take desperate measures to escape, including several mass emigrations that led to global dispersion. They even managed to survive the twentieth century's first large-scale genocide. In *The Armenians* a distinguished international team of social scientists seeks to explain how such confidence in a national identity came about, how it crystallized, and what Armenians today feel that they have derived from their spectacular past. The book pays considerable attention to the 1990s and 2000s, when post-Soviet Armenia has been building its independence, its political system, and its new economy and society. The book ends with an analysis of how the Armenian self-image has responded to the many challenges and contradictions thrown up by this rich store of experience.

The Armenians provides a comprehensive introduction to both the historical forces and the recent social and political developments that have shaped today's Armenian people. With contributions from leading Armenian, American and European specialists, it sets out the themes and issues of contemporary research in the history and social science of this distinctive people. The authors include Richard G. Hovannisian, James R. Russell and Ronald G. Suny.

The editors: Edmund Herzig is a Senior Lecturer in Persian Studies at the University of Manchester. His research focuses on the history and politics of Iran, Central Asia and the Caucasian region. His many writings include a book on contemporary Armenia, Azerbaijan and Georgia, *The New Caucasus*, and a number of articles and book chapters on Armenian history and politics. **Marina Kurkchiyan** is a Fellow in Socio-legal Studies at the University of Oxford, specializing in the post-communist transition in Armenia, Russia and Ukraine. Her research focuses on post-communist legal culture, social policy and the second economy. Her publications include works on economic crime in Russia, the interplay between law and informal practices, welfare reforms and research methodology.

Caucasus World: *Peoples of the Caucasus*
Series editor: Nicholas Awde

This series of handbooks provides a ready introduction and practical guide to the many peoples and languages of the Caucasus. Each handbook includes chapters written by experts in the field, covering all aspects of the people, including their history, religion, politics, economy, culture, literature and media, plus pictures, chronologies and appendices of up-to-date statistics, maps and bibliographies. Each volume in the Peoples of the Caucasus series will be an indispensable resource to all those with an interest in the Caucasus.

The Abkhazians
Edited by George Hewitt

The Circassians
Amjad Jaimoukha

The Chechens
Edited by Amjad Jaimoukha

The Armenians
Edited by Edmund Herzig and Marina Kurkchiyan

The Hemshin
Edited by Hovann Simonian

The Kalmyks
David Lewis

Other books in Caucasus World include:

The Russian Conquest of the Caucasus
J. F. Baddeley, with a Preface by Moshe Gammer

Small Nations and Great Powers
Svante E. Cornell

Storm Over the Caucasus
Charles van der Leeuw

Oil and Gas in the Caucasus and Caspian
Charles van der Leeuw

After Atheism
David C. Lewis

Daghestan
Robert Chenciner

Madder Red
Robert Chenciner

Azerbaijan
Charles van der Leeuw

Georgia: In the Mountains of Poetry
Peter Nasmyth

The Literature of Georgia
Donald Rayfield

The Russo-Caucasians of the Iranian Left
Cosroe Chaqueri

Society, Politics and Eonomics in Mazadaran
M. A. Kazembeyki

The Armenian Kingdom of Cilicia during the Crusades
Jacob G. Ghazarian

The Kingdom of Armenia
M. Chahin

The Armenians

Past and present in the making
of national identity

**Edited by
Edmund Herzig and
Marina Kurkchiyan**

RoutledgeCurzon
Taylor & Francis Group

LONDON AND NEW YORK

First published 2005
by RoutledgeCurzon
2 Park Square, Milton Park, Abingdon, Oxon OX14 4RN

Simultaneously published in the USA and Canada
by RoutledgeCurzon
270 Madison Ave., New York, NY 10016

RoutledgeCurzon is an imprint of the Taylor & Francis Group

Typeset in Times by
Taylor & Francis Books
Printed and bound in Great Britain by
Antony Rowe Ltd, Chippenham, Wiltshire

British Library Cataloguing in Publication Data
A catalogue record for this book is available from the British Library

Library of Congress Cataloguing in Publication Data
A catalog record for this book has been requested

ISBN 0–700–70639–9

Contents

Maps

Contributors

Aram Arkun is Coordinator of the Krikor and Clara Zohrab Information Center, New York.

Mark Grigorian is a producer in the Central Asia and Caucasus Service of the BBC, London.

Edmund Herzig is a Senior Lecturer in Persian Studies at the University of Manchester.

Richard G. Hovannisian is Professor of Armenian and Near Eastern History and holder of the Armenian Educational Foundation Chair in Modern Armenian History at the University of California, Los Angeles.

Marina Kurkchiyan is the Paul Dodyk Fellow at the Centre for Socio-legal Studies and a Fellow of Wolfson College in the University of Oxford.

Astghik Mirzakhanyan is a project co-ordinator to the United Nations Development Programme, Armenian Office.

Razmik Panossian is an independent researcher specializing in Armenia, the diaspora and the South Caucasus.

Susan P. Pattie is a Senior Research Fellow, University College London.

James R. Russell is the Mashtots Professor of Armenian Studies, Harvard University.

Ronald Grigor Suny is Professor of Political Science and History at the University of Chicago.

Boghos Levon Zekiyan is Professor of Armenian Language and Literature in the Eurasian Studies Department of the University of Venice and at the Pontifical Oriental Institute in Rome.

Transliteration and names

Except in chapter 2, 'Early Armenian Civilization', Armenian words are transliterated according to a simplified version of the Society for Armenian Studies system, with the diacritic accents omitted. Where accepted English forms of Armenian words and names exist, these are preferred to transliterated forms (e.g. Yerevan).

Many of the territories, towns and cities mentioned have undergone successive name changes over the centuries, often as a result of political changes such as conquests and revolutions. In general, we have used the names that will be most readily identifiable to the modern reader, while being appropriate to the context. In some cases, the name that was current (among Armenians) in the period under consideration is preferred, provided that does not obscure the identity of the place for the modern reader. Thus, for the nineteenth century we use Tiflis (Tbilisi, today the capital of Georgia) and Transcaucasia (today more commonly referred to as the South Caucasus). The more familiar (Mountainous) Karabagh, however, is used rather than Armenian (Lernayin) Gharabagh or Russian (Nagornyi) Karabakh. In some cases, for the sake of clarity, alternative versions or names of places are given in parentheses, e.g. Alexandropol (Leninakan, Kumayri, Gyumri). The forms Yerevan and Etchmiadzin are used throughout.

Personal names are given in transliterated forms, except where there is a generally accepted English spelling.

Acknowledgements

We wish to thank our fellow contributors, who responded so constructively to the idea of producing a book that would take the reader on a journey into the past and present of the Armenian nation. In keeping with the book's subject, they are scattered across the world in small clusters in Armenia, Britain and the USA, but their willingness to respond to our editorial suggestions nevertheless converted them into a cooperative team. We are grateful for their contributions and for their patient collaboration through the various stages of preparation. If there is today such a thing as the Armenian mind, their collective efforts have helped us to move towards some understanding of it.

Thanks are due also to Vrezh Nersessian, who offered valuable advice when the book was still at the planning stage. Our greatest debt is to Nick Awde, who encouraged us to work on the book in the first place and whose maps do so much to help make sense of the long, tortuous and often terrible history of the Armenian people. The book is much better for his assistance, and it would not have existed at all without his initiative and drive.

We are grateful to Michael Banks for his steady insistence that the English language should never be knowingly abused. Whatever polish the book may now possess owes much to the professionalism of the publishing team at Routledge and in particular to Heidi Bagtazo and Emma Davis, who dealt briskly and successfully with a series of niggling practicalities over which we had done little more than fret. Finally, it is a pleasure to thank the members of the Saryan family, who gave us their permission to reproduce on the cover a beautiful drawing by Martiros Saryan, 'The Blessing of Old Men'. The picture celebrates traditional Armenian community values with characteristic style and wit, and for us it epitomizes what we hoped to achieve in this book.

1 Introduction

Armenia and the Armenians

Marina Kurkchiyan and Edmund Herzig

Once again, after the disintegration of the Soviet Union, the peoples of the Caucasus have re-emerged into international affairs. This book is about one of them, the Armenians, of whom a minority live in the homeland state and the majority in one or another of a scattered series of communities across the world that are collectively known as the diaspora.[1] The purpose here is to explain who these people are, where they come from, what has made them the way they are, what their concerns are, and how it feels to be Armenian at the beginning of the twenty-first century. The focus throughout is on the common thread that links these things together: identity. To explore this theme, the editors brought together contributions by specialists from Armenia itself as well as from Europe and North America. Each author was encouraged to try to provide a readable, fresh and up-to-date account, so that descriptions of a variety of topics ranging from early civilization and religion to contemporary politics and social problems all blend into a single holistic discussion. The aim is that the finished volume should open a window on to the world of the Armenians.

The world of the Armenians is unusually complex, and not only because they are one of the world's oldest nations. They live in many different states and cultures across the world because their homeland has an exceptionally troubled history of being repeatedly subjected to invasion, looting and massacre over a two-thousand-year period. The majority of the people now live far away from the lands between the Black Sea and the Caspian, in cities like Buenos Aires or Los Angeles, even though they continue to think of themselves as Armenians. Even those who still live in the ancient capital city, Yerevan, are cut off from the most emotive geographical symbol of the Armenian homeland, Mount Ararat. Any attempt at travel in that direction is stopped at a heavily guarded border with Turkey.

The complexity of the Armenian world is matched by its contentiousness. It is impossible to study any aspect of it without having to deal with both

---

1   For the geographical distribution of Armenians today and through history, see R.L. Hewsen, *A Historical Atlas of Armenia* (Chicago: University of Chicago Press, 2001).

the conflicts aroused by its history and the clashing interpretations of them. Specific debates go all the way back to a set of unanswered questions about the ancient origins of the society and culture, and continue all the way down to the present day through many centuries of difficult relations with each of the three most prominent neighbouring states, Russia, Iran and Turkey. Contested issues vary from the relatively minor, such as the current dependence of the entire economy upon the recent reactivation of a single nuclear power station, built in the Soviet era and long defunct, to spectacular and shocking episodes like the Genocide of 1915 or the Karabagh war with Azerbaijan in the 1990s. Controversies like these have provoked fierce academic exchanges between competing schools of thought. But this book makes no attempt to engage such partisan arguments in detail, preferring to stand away from them wherever possible in order to focus on what Armenians have in common rather than on their disagreements, and to identify the ideas and experiences that are significant to all of them.

At the beginning of the twenty-first century, there are generally believed to be approximately seven million Armenians in the world, linked in their shared identity by what sociologists call a 'web of significance'. *The Armenians* is intended to draw a picture of how that unifying web came into existence. It is not a history as such, although chapters 1–6 are arranged in chronological order and deal with history. Rather, it is designed to explore the different strands of Armenian identity and to highlight features, contemporary as well as historical, that might help an observer to see the world through Armenian eyes. As in all national communities, the Armenian web of significance is formed by the collective memory. Memory is not itself history; it is a 'socially constructed' selection from history that provides a shared account of where Armenians came from, the things that they did themselves and the things done to them by others, and how and why they came to be so widely dispersed today. Within the selection is a multiplicity of different strands, among them religion, language, culture, family, literature, music and art. For each member of the community, the single most tightly binding thread may be different from the one that links someone else into the weave, but the web as a whole is the stronger for its elaborateness.

Armenians have traditionally put the ancient period of their history at the core of their self-image. A quick glance at the record helps to explain why. They can, and do, legitimately claim descent from the oldest cultures and most prominent civilizations of the region. The land that later came to be called Armenia is known to have been inhabited in the Palaeolithic and Mesolithic eras, and from the fourth millennium BC onwards it was home to people demonstrating inventiveness in technology and vitality in art. From the ninth to the sixth century BC the Urartean Empire flourished in the region, and later Armenians inherited a great deal from Urartean culture.

However, as James R. Russell argues in his chapter 'Early Armenian Civilization', the Armenian language was probably not indigenous, but brought to the region some three millennia ago by migrants from southeast

Europe. The earliest known use of the terms 'Armenian' and 'the Armenians' occurred in the late sixth century BC. Russell describes how comparative linguistic analysis leads to the conclusion that present-day Armenian speakers are the descendants both of those migrants and of various other ethnic groups. Some of those were present earlier, such as Urarteans, while others such as the Parthians were later arrivals. After his scrutiny of ancient Armenian religion and mythology, Russell is able to expose the extraordinary heterogeneity of the people's origins. What appears today to be a uniform heritage was initially the product of cross-fertilization with other peoples right across Eurasia from Western Europe to India, with Iranian, Semitic and Caucasian peoples predominant among them.

Russell's chapter takes the reader through the sixth, fifth and fourth centuries BC, when Armenia was a part of the Medean and Achaemenian empires, and on to the reign of Tigran II the Great in the first century BC. In Armenian society ever since, that final century before the beginning of Christianity has been celebrated. Although it was brief compared to the much longer historical epochs in later history, it became crucially important to the national self-image. Under Tigran II Armenia enjoyed an independence that permitted the growth of wealth, culture and civilization, before the country became a long-term battleground for the Roman (later the Byzantine), Persian and, in the following millennium, the Russian and Turkish empires. But even as the Romans imposed their law and values on the country, the single most important turning point for the Armenian identity was reached: the official conversion of the entire people to Christianity. This took place early in the fourth century, in the year 301 AD according to the tradition of the Armenian Church. In the sixth century the church rejected the authority of the Council of Chalcedon and became the Armenian Apostolic (Gregorian) Church, an autonomous branch of the world church.

The culture laid heavy stress on these historical facts, so that the words 'Christian', 'first' and 'unique' are embedded in the core of Armenian mentality. Living on the edge of the Christian world among Muslim communities, Armenians used religion to set themselves apart symbolically from their neighbours. As the centuries passed, it was the Church, according to the Armenians' strong belief, that preserved the nation and its culture from assimilation into the societies of a succession of overbearing military conquerors. Within Armenia's 'web of significance', the Church was the one social institution that could resist one alien rulership after another, thereby preserving the psychological identity and cultural integrity of the scattered local communities both inside the homeland and abroad.

The chapter by Boghos Levon Zekiyan reflects upon the significance of Christianity in Armenian history for the formation of the national ideology and the integrated perception, world-wide, of a single identity. Armenians themselves tend to assume that their early conversion to Christianity determined an irreversible, permanent orientation to the West. But as Zekiyan points out, being between West and East is a more complex matter than one of merely choosing an affiliation in a bi-polar world, because everyone, everywhere, has to deal realistically with their neighbours. In practice, therefore, the relationship has always been three-dimensional: Armenia and Armenians have continually functioned as a channel and intermediary, adapting, assimilating and transmitting among the great diversity of peoples and cultures with which they came into contact. The distinctive Armenian culture and identity emerged from that process of synthesis.

The adoption of Christianity was quickly followed by a second key moment in the evolution of a distinct Armenian identity: the invention (*circa* 400) of the Armenian alphabet and the subsequent development of an Armenian literary tradition. Even though the pivotal events took place a millennium and a half ago, Armenian society still recalls with pride the 'Golden Age' of the fifth to the seventh centuries, with its ground-breaking contributions to religion, philosophy and the arts made at a very early stage.

The flowering of Armenia ended with the devastating Arab invasion in the seventh century. Despite alien rule over the following centuries, Armenians recall the Bagratuni (from the ninth to the eleventh centuries) and the Cilician Armenian kingdoms (from the eleventh to the fourteenth centuries) as possessing limited political autonomy that permitted a second flowering of artistic and cultural expression. The result was the temporary emergence of splendid architecture and miniature painting encouraged by royal and ecclesiastical patronage. But with the loss of the last bastion of self-government in Cilicia, Armenia for many centuries ceased to function as a politically organized structure and survived in the homeland only as a cultural community. Living on territory divided between great powers that were frequently engaged in fighting each other and repeatedly smashing whatever stood in their way, Armenians were sustained by little more than their language, their religion and their memories. Not surprisingly, it became the custom to express Armenian identity in terms of conflict with foreign aggressors and struggle to preserve the nation's character despite alien, infidel domination.

Invasions by the Seljuks (in the eleventh century), the Mongols (thirteenth century) and the Emir Timur (fourteenth century) were followed by the Ottoman–Safavid wars of the sixteenth and early seventeenth centuries. Caught up in the appalling conduct of the successive waves of marauding soldiers, many Armenians simply fled, became political refugees, and tried to build new lives wherever they could. Their global wanderings precipitated the formation of an Armenian diaspora, with colonies scattered, by the end of the seventeenth century, across the Mediterranean, Western and Eastern Europe, the Middle East, South Asia and the Indian Ocean.

In the diaspora, Armenians were forced into a distinctive social situation. They lived locally, but they were not native; they belonged, but they were also foreign. They acquired a status 'betwixt and between' nations and cultures, which meant that they were often called upon to act as cross-cultural brokers in economic and other dealings. Many of them became long-distance merchants. Of necessity they became mobile, adaptable and pragmatic. The effect was an early and successful encounter with modernity, in the form of the humanist and rationalist culture of the European Enlightenment. The early adoption of printing, the foundation of the Uniate order of the Mekhitarists in Constantinople in 1700, and the publication of the first Armenian periodical in India, where Armenian merchant colonies were under strong British influence, all mark a decisive engagement with West European intellectualism. As the new ideas spread around the world during the eighteenth and early nineteenth centuries, permeating one scattered pocket of Armenians after another, communities were first reinvigorated and then inspired to build stronger mutual links both with one another and with the ancestral homeland. The cultural surge that followed is sometimes described as the *veratznund*, the rebirth.

Even so, Armenians stepped into the nineteenth century a divided people. Each group was stamped with the culture, language and lifestyle of their particular overlords or, in the case of the many living in the diaspora, their hosts. Western Armenia, the main part of the historical homeland, was Ottoman, or Turkish; Eastern Armenia was initially Persian, although most of it subsequently became Russian as the Tsars expanded their conquests in the region. As the rulers of the imperial powers played out their barbaric 'great game' in the South Caucasus, the Armenians and other people who happened to live on their chessboard suffered the real sacrifice as each piece was won or lost. Property was systematically looted, lives were ruined or abruptly ended, local economies were carelessly wrecked, residential neighbourhoods were smashed apart, self-reliant people were turned into pathetic asylum seekers.

Meanwhile, the industrial revolution in Western Europe brought about an even more rapid acceleration of political and social change across the world as the nineteenth century developed. Democratic theories of government and the modern conception of nationhood were rapidly spread by new communications technology. Such progressive ideas flourished even while the colonial empires subjugated much of Asia and Africa and industrial capitalism reduced newly urbanized peasants to the deepest poverty. The contradictory trends reached into the lives of people all over the world. The chapter by Aram Arkun assesses the impact of these changes, focusing on the way in which the world around them between 1800 and 1913 affected the lives of the homeland Armenians and triggered the formation of a new identity.

All three ruling elites of the Caucasus – Ottoman, Persian and Russian – found during the nineteenth century that they had to respond to the even more energetic imperialists of Western Europe by modernizing themselves. This they did with varying degrees of success by reforming and adapting their military, political and economic structures to allow them to compete in the modern world. Throughout their empires, they began to build up centralized institutions and more effective administrative procedures. For the subject peoples this reform meant more direct intervention from central government. The impact was more often malign than benign and bore down most heavily on marginal, disadvantaged and vulnerable groups, among them Christian Armenians living next to often hostile Muslim communities. In his account of the condition of Armenian groups in the homeland in this period, Arkun shows that although there were substantial differences in respect of political status and living conditions between the Ottoman, Persian and Russian empires, and between the urban middle class and the rural poor, Armenians everywhere continued to experience discrimination and hardship even if the extent of it varied. Among Armenian historians the nineteenth century has been viewed as a dark period in Armenian political, social and economic history, at least for homeland Armenians.

At the same time, however, the nineteenth century is known as a time of awakening, a *zartonk*. Arkun argues that even though the homeland population was profoundly divided by the militarized frontiers that separated the imperial powers, it nevertheless managed to retain and even to promote its own cultural unity. The foundation for this achievement was the shared written language. Wherever Armenians lived, they managed to teach it to their children by one means or another, and for everyone it was sustained and continually renewed in vernacular books and newspapers. By the second half of the century, newspapers in the national language became available in virtually all Armenian communities. For the first time ever it became possible to exchange information, to disseminate new political ideas, and to hold a genuine national debate. The eventual result was the formation of a consensual understanding of national identity, complete with modern political aspirations of territorial sovereignty and economic hopes for government-led prosperity. This reconstruction of the Armenian identity is interpreted by Arkun as a transformation in the character of the national myth. Armenian identity, formerly a cultural romanticism, became a realistic nationalist project, calling for political action. His chapter 'Into the Modern Age, 1800–1913' describes the difficult, multifaceted and painful process whereby an Armenian nation in the modern sense was formed. As he points out, it is a remarkable story. Nearly two thousand years of fragmentation and subjugation did not prevent the Armenian people from entering the twentieth century with a surviving language, religion and culture, an organized political movement, a coherent national ideology and a drive to be united and independent.

The human cost of all the attempts to bring such ambitions to life was very high. The story of the Armenians in the nineteenth century is a sequence of different acts of desperation. There were attempts to find allies, only to be deceived by all of them. There were uprisings followed immediately by reprisals and subsequently by long periods of repression. And there were waves of massacres, the most serious of which took place in the eastern provinces of the Ottoman Empire between 1895 and 1909. As many as

200,000 people were killed in a terrifying series of assaults, and it is generally agreed by historians that between 60,000 and 100,000 people who managed to dodge the knives and bullets took the radical decision to emigrate.

The dreadful human cost notwithstanding, the uprisings of the late nineteenth century did produce significant political gains. By 1900 a new diplomatic catchphrase, 'the Armenian Question', had been added to the factors determining each round of the ongoing game played by the imperial powers with the lives, land and property of the peoples of the Caucasus. Henceforth it would always be understood that the Armenians should no longer be treated as uncomplaining pawns in the game. They were still losers, but they had become troublesome. That meant that a decision would have to be made about the future political status of the Armenian-populated territories. Finding themselves entangled perforce in the high politics of great-power rivalry in the closing years of the nineteenth century and the early years of the twentieth, the Armenians placed their trust and hope in the governments of Western Europe and Russia. These soon proved to be misplaced. In 1915 the world watched almost in silence the first genocide of the century, the mass murder of the Armenians of Ottoman Turkey. In the space of a few months, approximately one-and-a-half million Armenians were killed and the rest of the population was forcibly expelled, most of them southward towards Syria. It was one of the most horrific instances of ethnic cleansing in recent history. It instantly became the most significant factor in Armenian identity in the twentieth century, and in the longer term it caused general immiseration, mass displacement and emigration even from non-Ottoman parts of the Caucasus, and the loss of a huge part of the homeland under the terms of the eventual political settlement.

The Genocide's psychological and social effects on the generations of Armenians after the First World War were similar to those of the Nazi holocaust on the generations of Jews that came after the Second World War. The immediate impact on the surviving population consisted of traumatic emotional distress. Over time this became a sense of having been victimized, combined with a strong sensitivity to issues of morality and justice. Ethnic identity, which had been gradually declining in importance as mental horizons expanded in the eighteenth and nineteenth centuries, was forced violently back into the centre of self-consciousness for all those who called themselves Armenians. That process created a social boundary around the group, sharply defined, and giving a heightened importance to the distinction between 'us' and 'them'. In relation to both these issues – identity and identification – strong forms of social pressure emerged spontaneously, and as time passed they became generally accepted and firmly noted. Children were told the hideous story of the Genocide, and repeatedly retold it. As the event became generally known in all parts of the diaspora, the Genocide became the main integrating force for the Armenian nation and continued in that role throughout the twentieth century.

The 1915 Genocide also shaped the Armenian nation's continuing imagery of the world immediately surrounding it. The Turks were constructed as an enemy group, forever dangerous, with their state pictured as an oppressive, backward-looking power regardless of the transformation brought about by revolution in the years following the Great War. In order to balance this negative image, it was cognitively necessary that Russia, Turkey's historic adversary, should be seen positively. The empirical contradictions produced by the mental logic were, and are, consciously tolerated. Although some political parties, such as the Armenian Revolutionary Federation, never accepted the seventy years of Soviet rule over Armenia, they nevertheless shared the widely held belief that Moscow could be relied upon for protection. Armenians were apt to point out that the Russians possessed a similar religious tradition to their own. And if that were not sufficient to produce political harmony, Russian strategic logic could always be expected to persuade them to see Armenians as the natural guardians of their southern frontier.

The seven years between 1914 and 1921 brought an intense sequence of profound events for Armenians, covered in this book by Richard Hovannisian. Asking first what happened to the Armenian people under the shadow of the First World War, and then how it happened and why, he sets out the historical logic, political circumstances and ramifications of the Genocide and the Russian Revolution. The chapter takes the reader through the labyrinthine politics of the many states involved in the region's affairs. Defeated by the Allied armies the Ottoman Empire collapsed, to be replaced in the 1920s by the secular nationalist Republic of Turkey. Tsarist Russia itself, all but beaten by the German army, was falling apart as it unsuccessfully fought the revolutionaries in the domestic arena. Nevertheless, the armies of both powers continued to lay waste to the Caucasus in spite of their domestic distractions. At the same time, the United States, Great Britain and France, victorious and powerful, intervened in the region almost casually, with vacillating policies and actions conceived on the basis of shifting perceptions and inconsistent promises.

In the midst of all these self-interested outsiders, Armenian politicians persisted in efforts to seize control of events. They were united in their aspiration to gain independence, but they were divided on every other issue and faced a chronic lack of resources. The clashes of the various outside forces were having a devastating effect on the people on the ground. In the short time between 1914 and 1921 ethnic Armenians were swept completely out of the main territories of their historical home, suffering massive human and material losses in the process. Hundreds of thousands were driven out, eventually to join the refugee diaspora that by then was already spread all over the world.

The Russian revolution of 1917 forced the Tsarist army to withdraw from the region, opening a window of opportunity through which an independent Republic of Armenia could be proclaimed. Leaders of the surviving

Armenians gathered in Yerevan and did just that, in 1918. Initially, Armenia's first government for more than a thousand years was able to assume control of a substantial territory. They combined the Russian part of Eastern Armenia with the eastern half of Turkish Armenia, because since 1916 that region had been under Russian army control. But the fledgling state could deploy only ramshackle defences, both military and diplomatic. Faltering against Turkish army attacks and the cynical manoeuvrings of Western diplomacy, Armenian jurisdiction was gradually reduced to a small, landlocked zone at the very eastern reaches of the ancient homeland. In 1920 it was yet again reconquered, this time by triumphant Communists from Russia who had formed a tactical alliance with the 'Young Turk' government in Istanbul. Armenia's self-governing regime gave way to the Bolsheviks, and the border was redrawn around a small land area that significantly excluded the ethnic enclave of mountainous Karabagh to the east.

The account of all these events by Richard Hovannisian opens up all the complexities of the brief period of independent government and its impact on Armenian identity. He argues that the Armenians living in the diaspora saw it quite differently from the people who actually lived in Armenia, a difference that has persisted since. The diaspora was made up of people who migrated in the aftermath of the massacres of 1894–1909, together with survivors of the 1915 Genocide and a steady flow of economic migrants from Western Armenia. For all these people, the homeland meant the Armenia of the Ottoman Empire, around the biblical Mount Ararat and Lake Van. Few Western Armenians saw the Russian part of Eastern Armenia as a homeland that they could identify with.

But for Armenians who lived in Armenia, the declaration of the First Republic was the fulfilment of the dreams of centuries, however tiny the new state might be. The newly elected government quickly created a new judicial system, introduced a national currency and a progressive income tax, and despite all its financial, social and military problems it managed to launch an educational infrastructure designed to resemble Western models of universal and secular education. An example was the foundation of the nation's first university, based on the most advanced principles, including gender equality.

Despite the short lifespan of the independent republic, its two years of freedom exerted a disproportionate impact on Armenia's identity. Henceforth the self-image was to be that of a modern progressive nation with a mature political consensus, which could and should establish its own institutions of government on the basis of democracy and civil society. These assumptions were given a second chance to come true in the late 1980s, when Armenia once again took the path to independence, this time from the Soviet Communist regime. In the spirited debates on constitution-building and public policy, the vivid memory of the stillborn achievements of the first Republic of Armenia became a source of inspiration and ambition for masses of the homeland's people.

In his chapter on Soviet Armenia, Ronald Grigor Suny argues that, given the pitiful condition of the surviving homeland, Armenians in 1920 faced a stark choice between Soviet control and emigration. By that time 30 per cent of the population of the republic had been lost to migration and premature death, and half of the remaining 60 per cent were themselves refugees. The country was without an organized middle class and it lacked a mature set of economic, political and social institutions. Armenia therefore entered its Soviet period as a society thrown back to its pre-capitalist agrarian economy. Inevitably it became a dependent republic on the periphery of the big empire ruled from Moscow.

In broad outline, Armenia's seventy-year Soviet experience between 1921 and 1991 was necessarily similar to that of all the other nations in the Union. Lenin's inaugural policy of War Communism eased into the more moderate New Economic Policy but then gave way to Stalin's brutality, displayed first in his collectivization programme and then in the terror known as the Great Purges. There followed the Second World War, in which Hitler's savage army was halted, at profound cost, at Stalingrad just north of the Caucasus. With the war over, the Soviet economy began to boom and Stalinism eventually passed away. A post-Stalin thaw marked the USSR at its peak of success under Khrushchev, although his regime gave way to a generation of stagnant leadership from Brezhnev. Finally, Mikhail Gorbachev's unsuccessful attempt to modernize the Communist system in its final decade ended with the inward collapse of the federal authority in 1991. From beginning to end, the regime's ideological extremism made it authoritarian, militaristic, rigid, arbitrary and often cruel, even though it always attempted in its ponderous fashion to implement intellectual, scientific, socialist and other civilized values.

However, a conventionally critical account such as this understates the many positive aspects of the Soviet Union's seventy-year impact on the human, social and economic affairs of the world's largest country. In nearly all its regions, Soviet rule brought four successive generations of rapid economic growth. As wealth expanded, entire new cities and industries were created, massive infrastructure facilities were constructed, and a large proportion of the people were educated to world-class levels. At the same time, new libraries, museums, galleries and concert halls were provided free of charge, and literature, the arts and the sciences were actively promoted. Impressive strides were also made in such fields as health care and technological innovation.

Despite the uniformity in overall Soviet policy towards the republics, they retained and in some ways actively cultivated their own individuality. In the chapter 'Soviet Armenia, 1921–91' Ronald Suny reflects on the particular Armenian experience of Soviet rule, surveying its outcome and assessing its impact on the national mentality of the people living in Soviet Armenia. He argues that although the Soviet regime was temperamentally anti-nationalist, its choice of policy actually gave rise to a strong feeling of territorial nationalism. The various nations were encouraged to cultivate a 'self' while simultaneously keeping all political, ideological and social issues entirely separate from it. Precisely because they were forbidden as Soviet citizens to draw on anything current or politically sensitive when choosing what to do to celebrate their 'national day' and similar events, the people of each nation searched in their past, real or imagined, for ways to keep their collective self-image alive. They developed a taste for talk of ethnic origin, traditional religion, past golden ages, and their love of their geographical homeland.

In the case of Armenia this focus on history provided the most efficient choice of fuel for a nationalist fire. That fire was intensified for teenagers by the impact of schools that taught in the medium of the Armenian language, and for older students by the cultural activities of the many higher educational establishments. When the relaxed period of the 1960s arrived, many of the picturesque old Armenian churches were restored. In their new splendour they had to be regarded as heritage sites rather than as buildings for worship, but even so they helped to contribute to a growing cultural self-awareness.

These things were sufficiently subsidized by the USSR in order to provide for its assortment of national cultures and to keep each one pure and distinct. Nationalism of this culture-oriented, non-political kind is very different from the assertion of sovereignty-as-citizenship that characterizes nationalism in democracies. Concerned as it is with 'blood and belonging', it brushes aside all the differences of thought and diversities of taste within a group, in favour of raw feelings. As a result, when Armenia rebelled against the Soviet regime in 1988, culture and territory became the rallying-cry for the masses, whose nationalist passions were at their strongest in relation to the ethnic enclave of Mountainous Karabagh.

For a whole generation, Soviet policy on the issue of the lost lands of Western Armenia was subordinated to broader foreign policy interests. Lenin supported the Young Turk government, which meant that the Armenian territorial claim had to be brushed aside. The 1921 Treaties of Kars and Moscow formalized the loss. The uncompromising strictness of the USSR's early policy meant not only that mention of Western Armenia was erased from international diplomacy, but also that both the Armenian Question and even the Genocide became taboo within the USSR. Censorship ensured not just that school textbooks ignored these topics, but that all other publications did so as well. From the 1920s until the 1950s, anyone who dared to speak out in public was labelled an 'enemy of the people', then eliminated. An entire generation of Armenians grew up under these conditions between the two world wars, knowing little about what had happened in Western Armenia only two decades earlier. The Soviet propaganda machine had successfully engineered their historical and social understanding. Their ignorance of their own people's very recent history made Western Armenia seem remote, and the Genocide seem like a minor event. Both became peripheral to the national self-image of people in Armenia.

However, the warmth of the relationship between Moscow and Istanbul did not last long and cooled to freezing point during the Second World War. In 1945 the Soviet government formally declared a claim to historic Armenian lands and demanded a revision of the Soviet–Turkish border. This U-turn in foreign policy was quickly followed by a corresponding U-turn in domestic policy. Genocide was inserted into the history textbooks, academic publications were granted permission to tackle the subject (provided they did not question the self-serving official line on the Russian role in events) and in subsequent decades a handful of prominent writers duly took up the subject. A better-informed generation grew up, sufficiently numerous and confident by 1965 to crowd the streets of Yerevan in the first-ever demonstration demanding that the USSR should make an issue of the Armenian Question in its foreign policy. That event signalled the beginning of a new phase in Armenian nationalism. From then on, the self-image of the people of the homeland compelled them to seek ways to take action on the linked issues of Genocide recognition and land restoration.

A different pattern had been formed among Armenian families who had settled in other countries. In her chapter on the diaspora, Susan Pattie examines the outlook of the distant Armenians today, and explains why it is that many of them have remained emotionally tied to the national idea to such an extent that each generation cannot avoid transmitting an equal fervour to its children. That might seem paradoxical when nearly all of these people live in different countries and owe loyalty to the governments of those countries. They have diverse lifestyles and speak other languages primarily or exclusively. Some even conduct all their relationships within networks that do not contain other Armenians. Pattie argues that the emotional link between all these disparate individuals was created by the 1915 Genocide, and she describes the social fabric of the communities that they have established since that time. Although by 1915 some of the communities had already been established in countries like Syria, Iran and India for over seventeen hundred years, the ethnic cleansings of the late nineteenth century and especially during the Great War threw up a tidal wave of refugees. The wave flooded the established diaspora with new arrivals, who then changed the way that the older residents thought about themselves.

Since that time nearly every Armenian family outside the homeland has either itself experienced a first-hand memory of a politically motivated death, loss or trauma, or knows others who have. That consciousness of the 1915 killings and related horrors, universally shared, has held together the group identity; it is now the essence of 'Armenianness'. Given that shared consciousness, the logical implication has been to assert demands for international recognition of the fact that the Genocide actually took place and for apologies to be made by those who can speak for the perpetrators. Sometimes there have also been additional demands for compensation for the families of the victims, and restitution of the stolen lands. Regardless of whether or not a campaign for such goals can have a realistic prospect of success, it does have a powerful role in maintaining the group identity.

The short-term trauma of the Genocide was followed for a much longer period by the sense of vulnerability that always afflicts people on the move. Before most survivors finally settle down, they will have made three or four unsuccessful attempts to find a secure environment elsewhere. The practical uncertainty of refugee life has provoked a generalized anxiety in the minds of the expatriates, causing them to feel as if they are constantly threatened, even in the many countries where they are in fact secure. For even, say, the Parisians or Californians among them, it is a source of reassurance to be constantly in touch with fellow exiles whose situation is similar, which means that an ongoing community life has to be cultivated and serviced. The chapter 'Armenians in Diaspora' describes how that is done, through family ties, the Church, political parties, cultural organizations, and clubs and social networks.

To keep a community going in a foreign environment, Armenians have had to constantly redefine the group boundaries and adjust them to changing circumstances, such as the gradual assimilation of the younger generation into the host culture. The effect is that, in the diaspora, questions that can be taken for granted in Armenia itself, such as who belongs and what it is that they belong to, become matters of endless debate. In response, as Pattie observes, the definition of 'Armenianness' has undergone a sequence of transformations. At first it was thought to be objective, a matter of blood lines or inherited genes: if you or your parents were born Armenian, you were perforce Armenian. Then the stress moved to the culture, in the form of things that could be taught and learned. If people really belonged, they would speak the language, they would know their country's history, and above all their lives would be devoted to their extended families. That phase evolved into an ideological choice. It became sufficient that Armenianness be demonstrated by taking part in community activities and attending the Church. And in the most recent past, the emphasis has moved on to entirely subjective factors, removing altogether any need for external evidence. To be an Armenian now, it is enough that one be conscious that one is. In the pithy phrase of Anny Bakalian, cited in the chapter, identity has shifted from a matter of *being* Armenian to *feeling* Armenian.

This succession of changes has been less marked in the settlements of the Middle East, where Armenians have always been noticeably different from everyone else because religion remained a key marker of difference between communities. It is in the Western countries, with their long-standing traditions of individualism and of actively integrating the foreign-born into a secular unity of politics and culture, that the progressive evolution in how the group is defined has been so noticeable.

The meaning of the 'homeland' proved to be similarly controversial in the diaspora communities, especially during the forty-year Cold War after 1945.

For most Armenians, the sight of a dependent republic that had virtually disappeared into the mighty USSR signalled an end to their hope of returning one day to the independent state they dreamed about, united within its traditional borders. For others, whatever the political regime and however uninspiring the current circumstances, their duty remained: they must support their land of origin and keep in close touch with it. But even for those who stayed loyal to their identity throughout the history of the USSR, the Soviet Union's version of Armenia was perceived less as the nation's true heartland than as a poor relation in need of handouts and protection.

However, the 1991 formation of an independent state brought drastic change to the Armenian identity, both at home and abroad. With the collapse of the Soviet Union coinciding with the end of the Cold War, a truly independent homeland became available to all Armenians whether they were living in the territory or not. For the second time in the twentieth century, they had to reshape their mental world to take that into account. The last six chapters of this volume examine how that reshaping was done, with each contributor examining a different aspect of the experience of the new state's first, critical, decade of self-reliance. Unexpectedly, the initial ten years of freedom turned out to be harsh, difficult and violent – a circumstance that was vividly reflected in the startling growth of the diaspora. The global expatriate Armenian community expanded faster through emigration from the homeland in the 1990s than at any time since the First World War.

The many crises that independence brought to the new Armenia actually began years before Gorbachev and Yeltsin orchestrated the death throes of the Soviet Union. The first one was provoked by intense nationalism. As the rigid grip of central government was progressively relaxed, an emotional wave of feeling about 'correcting the error of history' swept through Armenia. This slogan referred to a 1921 decision of the Soviet rulers in Moscow to include Karabagh within the borders of Azerbaijan, regardless of the fact that most of its population was ethnic Armenian. Feeling gave rise to action, and in February 1988 the Karabagh Movement held a mass demonstration that filled the streets of central Yerevan in spite of the winter cold. The assembly was the largest in the history of the USSR, the demonstrators all wanting to give support to the claims of the Armenian people of the mountainous Karabagh region of Azerbaijan to 'self-determination', by which they meant irredentism: separation from Azerbaijan followed by unification with Armenia.

The Karabagh Movement met immediate resistance from both Azerbaijan and the Soviet Union, resistance that caused it to add a new goal and thereby change its nature: it became a political campaign against the Soviet regime. The movement's leaders took control of Armenia in 1990, declared independence from Moscow rule in 1991, and assumed command of the Armenian troops that became involved in violent conflict with Azeri forces in and around Karabagh itself between 1992 and 1994. The result was that the new Armenian state was born into both political and popular confusion. The campaign for a free Karabagh had become intermingled with the campaign for a free Armenia to such a degree that it was difficult for ordinary people to distinguish one from the other. The Karabagh issue brought war; the Armenian issue brought the transition: a massive programme of state-building, economic transformation, social change, ideological reversals and, along with all of that, intense societal pain. Ordinary people were left to deal with everything on the list at the same time.

The chapter by Marina Kurkchiyan is specifically focused on the Karabagh issue. She sets out the historical background and shows how the conflict escalated from a domestic dispute between citizens of the same state upwards to diplomatic confrontation between sovereign governments and then on to active warfare. In 1994 Karabagh was liberated by volunteer fighters who succeeded not only in ejecting the Azeri authorities both from the province itself and from a strip of territory known as the Lachin Corridor linking it to Armenia, but also in conquering a substantial area of Azerbaijani territory. Their victory was made possible by unstinting, although strictly unofficial, supplies of personnel and equipment from Armenia.

The war ended in a fragile ceasefire in 1994 followed by protracted negotiations that dragged on; they had not reached a settlement by early 2004. The ceasefire froze the conflict in favour of the Armenians, who were left in control of the Karabagh district and a substantial part of Azerbaijan. The cost to Armenia was relatively light in immediate military terms, but crippling in terms of the wider economic perspective. The government in Baku secured the collaboration of Turkey in imposing a total blockade on their respective Armenian borders. The closure of roads, railways, gas pipelines and electricity supplies across the two major borders not only made the country unduly dependent on the few remaining transport links that ran through Georgia, but also directly intensified the already severe economic hardships being caused by the transition. Meanwhile, Karabagh declared its independence, a symbolic gesture which did not lead to recognition by any state, even Armenia itself. The leadership in Stepanakert nevertheless set about constructing the official institutions of a national capital and by 1995 its presidency and parliament presided over an elaborate, if flimsy, national administration.

The military struggle over Karabagh made a powerful impression on the Armenian self-image. The earliest calls for self-determination in 1988 had provoked a hostile public reaction in Azerbaijan, rapidly expressed in a pogrom against the community of ethnic Armenians living in the Caspian industrial town of Sumgait. Several lesser incidents followed in Baku and elsewhere, and many families fled to Armenia. The news was flashed to Armenia and, as reports spread across the country, the perceived danger of a second genocide moved towards the ideological centre of the national movement. It was Turks, not Azeris, who had long been bogeymen in the

Armenian popular mind on the basis of past experience. But in reaction to Sumgait, Azeris were labelled 'Turks' and the distinctions between different Turkish-speaking nations were forgotten. Although the Sumgait atrocity was localized, it was nevertheless savage. That fact led to its being readily portrayed as a renewal of the massacres in Western Armenia of seventy years earlier. In Stepanakert, Yerevan and expatriate communities around the world ancient feelings of vulnerability once again took hold.

However, on this occasion the sense of victimization lasted for only a short time. It subsided progressively in the early 1990s with Armenian successes on the battlefield. The post-Sumgait righteousness faded in parallel. Initial black-and-white assumptions about Armenians and Azeris blurred into grey as it became ever more apparent that soldiers on both sides were equally capable of committing horrific acts. When the eventual cease-fire left them not just in full control of Karabagh but also in military occupation of Azerbaijani land well beyond it, Armenians found themselves in a novel position: they were being called aggressors. This left no room in their self-image for the role of victim. Among the Armenians of the Caucasus, though not for those of the diaspora, that self-empowerment removed the symbolism of the Genocide. The great tragedy of 1915 was still seen as a horrific act that should be apologised for by the Turkish government and acknowledged by the world, and for that reason it continued to be stressed in Armenia's foreign policy. But the victory over Karabagh took away its emotional significance as a component of identity. Armenians were no longer losers; from now on, they were winners. Within the homeland, the rallying-cry of 'victim' could no longer serve to whip up popular feelings, even though its appeal remained as strong as ever in communities abroad.

It was not only the successful prosecution of the war with Azerbaijan that altered the composition of the self-image of the people of Armenia in the 1990s; the act of gaining independence itself also had a major impact. The achievement enabled the Armenian nation to see itself as an independent agent, capable of making a significant mark on the world in the here and now. That constituted a profound shift from the previous self-perceptions, all of which had looked backwards and encouraged contemporary Armenians to think of themselves as passive curators of memory and material heritage. The emphasis had always been placed on their guardianship of an ancient culture, their martyrdom in defence of a classic religion, their sufferings in the archetypal Genocide of the twentieth century, their unassertive compliance as objects of Moscow rule. But from 1988 onwards Armenians were transformed into a forward-looking group, fully capable of making their own decisions and implementing them. The people understood that they had first mobilized themselves along ethnic lines to achieve national unity, then they had demanded their sovereignty, then they had secured it, then they had successfully asserted it.

Domestically, the immediate impact of the shift in self-image was to raise expectations to an unrealistic level. People wanted a decent, comfortable and prosperous life, and they assumed that, with the diversions and waste of the Cold War out of the way, these things could be provided. In the early years this unqualified optimism empowered the leadership to undertake radical policies, even when sacrifice would be necessary if the desired improvement was to be achieved. However, public confidence in firm leadership had a dual implication. Freedom to act boldly was certainly one, but the other was that in an independent Armenia performance would form a basis for judgement. Furthermore, a full-scale national self-evaluation could take place even while those responsible for any shortcomings were still in office. In other words, Moscow was not running the country now; Yerevan was. Henceforth, all the power so eagerly granted to the local politicians would necessarily be held to account.

From the early 1990s onwards, the people began to pass judgement on their nation's independent record. Disillusionment immediately set in. People began to understand that many of their supposed romantic heroes were exhibiting crudely self-interested conduct; that corruption and hypocrisy were common in high places; and that, worst of all, actual performance was dismal – in every field of domestic policy. Emotionally, such negative features of real life could not be reconciled with the romantic image that had served as the psychological foundation of the national movement. The result was the widespread depression, pessimism, cynicism and apathy that dominated the social and political climate of homeland Armenia from the mid-1990s onwards. Enthusiastic commitment degenerated into cynical alienation.

In his analysis of Armenian politics in its first decade, Edmund Herzig looks closely at the way in which morale in the country declined from its high point around 1990. He examines the few successes and many failures of the political leadership, and explores the circumstances that turned well-regarded public figures into political bankrupts. His chapter outlines the major political events in Armenia between 1991 and 2004: the controversial parliamentary and presidential elections, the constitutional referendum, and the presidential resignation of 1997. He describes the political turbulence in 1999–2000 provoked by the assassination of prominent politicians when gunmen stormed the parliament in October 1999. Tracing the course of political development in post-Soviet Armenia, he comes to the conclusion that although there had been some progress towards democracy by the turn of the century, overall the record was a disappointment to Armenia's citizens. Civil society remained undeveloped, there was no mature political structure to represent the interests of party supporters, and members of the public were not protected from arbitrary actions by the government. Ordinary people felt just as much distrust of the politicians as they had in the Soviet period.

Progress in building democratic institutions in contemporary Armenia is further scrutinized in Mark Grigorian's chapter on the media and democracy. He assesses how deeply tolerance and democratic values have become embedded in Armenian national ideology and political life by focusing on the history, development and current state of the country's news and entertainment media. He suggests that the 'golden age' of freedom of expression occurred between 1990 and 1992, when the popular interest in the media's output was at its height. The beginning of the decade saw a peak in the activity of the unregistered press that had been triggered by the Karabagh movement from 1988 onwards. Many uncensored publications appeared, driven by the urge to 'tell the truth' in contrast to the carefully managed news that was put out in the official Soviet press. Known as *samizdat*, this unofficial press could certainly be called independent, and it gave an authentic voice to nationalist feelings. Being a genuine voice of the people, it could also be called democratic. However, it was far from being democratic in its lack of respect for the voices of minority opinion or for such values as tolerance.

In 1989 the laws that had imposed controls on the media were relaxed, and soon afterwards the Communists were defeated. The Armenian media was then free to turn itself into a viable, professional and independent voice. But that could not be done overnight, and each problem that the society as a whole went through caused difficulties for radio, TV and the newspapers. The blockade caused newsprint shortages and the 1992–4 energy crisis caused an electricity shortage, damaging both printing and broadcasting. After 1995 political pressures got worse, particularly in the run-up to each election. Nevertheless, the general standard of journalism did improve year by year, even though progress was slow. Things were a little better by the start of the new century than they had been in 1988, but there was still a long way to go towards full professionalism, editorial freedom and financial independence.

However, Grigorian does point to one area of firm ground for optimism. In the 1990s the Armenian public had greater access than ever before to a variety of news sources, even though most of them were both low quality and biased. The availability of such a wide range of interpretation and opinion forced people to choose, and in doing so they unconsciously cultivated a new and more sophisticated understanding of public affairs and even developed some tolerance of diversity. To reach a fully mature understanding of democracy would take a much longer time, but a start was made. Despite their poverty and the weakness of their democratic institutions, the Armenian people began to realize that the national interest was itself a pluralist concept, capable of being interpreted differently by separate social groups without posing any threat to the fundamental unity of the nation.

Even more important than the press to Armenian politics and national identity in the post-independence period was the state of the economy. In this book its recent vicissitudes are described by Astghik Mirzakhanyan. After reviewing both the modernizing achievements and the bureaucratic inefficiencies of the Soviet period, she points out that by the late 1980s Armenia was considered to be one of the most developed republics in the

Soviet Union despite its lack of natural resources. It had advanced technology, good infrastructure and a workforce that even by world standards was skilled and well educated. Not surprisingly, Armenians were feeling confident when they stepped on to the path towards a free market. They could justifiably assume that theirs was an advanced nation, capable of raising its standard of living to match that of the developed world within a short time.

In the event, the opposite happened. Very quickly, in the years following 1990, the country fell into destitution. Mirzakhanyan considers both why the economy was devastated and what attempts were made to revive it. She argues that an unfortunate coincidence of factors was responsible for the disaster. In addition to the problems common to all post-Soviet countries, such as the shock of privatization and the severance of links to the tightly integrated Soviet system, Armenia suffered first from a massive earthquake in 1988 and then from an economic blockade imposed by neighbouring Azerbaijan and Turkey. The consequences were so destructive that it became impossible to recover, at least within the first decade. Mirzakhanyan uses statistics and survey data to draw a picture of the hardship and poverty that settled across the country in the 1990s. She shows that despite some measure of success in restructuring the economy and in establishing macroeconomic stability during the first half of that period, by 2004 the new government had failed to make any tangible improvement in the living standards of ordinary people.

Faced with the extreme privation of the 1990s, how did people cope? What did they find they had to do in order to feed, clothe and shelter themselves and their families, and how did they manage when they became ill or incapacitated? Did the ways in which people were forced to respond to the prolonged crisis alter the social structure of the country? To what extent did such critical circumstances alter the national self-image? In her chapter on the nature of Armenian society in transition, Marina Kurkchiyan attempts to answer these questions. She argues that history came to the aid of the people by suggesting ways that could help them to bear the burden. Over the centuries Armenians had built up a tradition of mutual support known as networking. This was not founded upon altruism or charity or even goodwill. Rather, it was built upon a businesslike reciprocity developed so extensively that it enabled society to continue to function even under conditions that in a different culture might well have reduced normal life to chaos, despair and collapse.

Reciprocity, or networking, originated in the prolonged subjection of the homeland to foreign rule. Through successive centuries of governance by aliens who frequently exploited them, Armenians had learned the need to distrust authority in all its forms. They never had enough power to confront officialdom with any hope of success, so they cultivated instead ways of ignoring it, avoiding it, deceiving it, or working round it wherever they could. Rather than cooperate actively with officials like police officers, department managers, property inspectors and military commanders, they made sure that their energies were more constructively directed. They cultivated members of their extended family, their friends, their close colleagues and anyone else that they knew they could trust. All of these could be relied upon to accept a favour and be prepared to return it whenever called upon to do so. At different periods informal networking enabled the people to minimize the impact of Ottoman agricultural tithes, Tsarist business levies, Persian religious decrees and all the other miseries imposed by whichever imperial power was the overlord at the time. Supposedly omnipotent governments struggled to enforce their laws in the face of widespread noncooperation, while an alternative social structure and informal economy functioned invisibly below the deceptively passive surface of Armenian society.

The seventy years of the Soviet regime changed none of this. The central government's grand plans, construction projects, resource allocations and output targets all proceeded along at the official level, but sluggishly, while informal networking enabled food to be supplied to needy families, leaking taps to be repaired, and essential surgical procedures to be carried out. When the official system collapsed entirely in 1990, in effect the unofficial system took its place as the principal means of running what little there was of a new economy. The desperation felt by most people during the end-of-century years of war, blockade and transition served only to strengthen their old habits of informal networking. The higher the personal stakes, the more important trustworthiness and reliability became.

The overwhelming dominance of the private sphere over the public sphere in the 1990s had both positive and negative effects. On the positive side, the thick social texture woven by the continual flow of personalized exchanges worked to absorb the shock when all the supportive public services, such as social security, pensions, health care and education, collapsed. Informal networking provided social stability, just as it had centuries before when marauding armies were laying waste to the country. But on the negative side the vigour of the networking practices in the 1990s encouraged the growth of an informal economy characterized by tax evasion, embezzlement and corruption.

That informal economy encouraged, in turn, an explosion of inequality. In the space of just a few years after 1990, the economic collapse and the transition from planned economy to free market combined to destroy the egalitarianism of the former society and replace it with a polarized structure. The malign conjunction of rising unemployment and collapsing welfare services ruined most of the people who lived in the country, whereas a handful of the lucky, the well-connected and the unscrupulous were at the same time growing sufficiently rich to enjoy a Western standard of living complete with luxury cars, private houses and expensive consumer goods. Conscious that the privileges of the new elite had nothing to do with hard work or personal integrity, but much to do with cheating, corruption and theft, the majority began to think of the so-called 'new Armenians' as 'them', not 'us'.

From that moment, the romantic nationalism of the Karabagh movement began to crumble away, and with it both the emotional unity and the political self-confidence of the people. An optimistic national self-image could not be sustained once people had taken the mental step of classifying some of their fellow citizens as not being proper and worthy Armenians. Clearly a new test was being applied to decide who are the 'we' among 'we Armenians'. It was a test of something more subtle and less crude than mere ethnicity. The significance of this was that within a decade of achieving true independence, homeland Armenians were once again forced by circumstances to re-examine their national self-image, and doing so on this occasion shook their self-belief to its foundations.

Against all expectations at the time of the USSR's collapse, it was not a case of Armenians from the diaspora pouring into the liberated homeland in the hundreds of thousands; the flow was the other way round. In the ten years after 1990 a million people – a third of the population of independent Armenia – headed abroad in search of a job and a new home. Kurkchiyan argues that the emigrants forming this new outward wave were driven away not only by economic hardship, but also by disappointment, frustration and a sense of alienation. In principle, their sudden disillusionment could be reversed, but that could only happen in response to positive trends in Armenian politics and the active cultivation of an atmosphere of trust between the people and their rulers. And as Herzig points out in chapter 9, the tendencies in the first decade were rather for Armenian politics to move the other way, towards authoritarianism, and for trust in the leadership to decline.

How did the members of the diaspora feel about the newly independent Armenia? And how did the relationship between the two evolve and develop in the eventful years after the homeland was opened up to direct access by the diaspora? In the final chapter of this book Razmik Panossian reflects on the complexity of the homeland–diaspora interaction and probes into the core meaning of 'Armenianness' as revealed by the twin perspectives of the two branches of the split nation. In analysing the politics of the relationship between the Armenian leadership and the diaspora leaders during the first decade of independence, he demonstrates that the differences between the collective identities of the two entities proved to be much greater than had been expected. As he puts it, initial contact between them after 1990 was 'a reluctant embrace, much like distant relations who had become strangers'.

Each side, homeland and expatriate, had cherished an idealized image of the other throughout the long years of Cold War isolation without any necessity to put the expectation to the test. The lifting of the Soviet Union's solid barriers to free communication also lifted away the illusion. Disillusion meant that sometimes the pendulum swung to the other extreme – to an unsympathetic focus on the other's faults and failures. As soon as untrammelled contact between homeland and diaspora was permitted, it exposed the conflicts of interest, clashing expectations and incompatible values of the two communities, rather than reinforcing any sentimental notions of brotherhood. The result was that, as the twentieth century came to a close, the umbrella of Armenianness began to leak.

Panossian sets out to explore this situation more thoroughly. He looks back into history, where he discovers evidence that the sources of the recent division between the two groups are long-standing. He points out that, as far back as the early nineteenth century, Armenians were organized around two different centres that competed with each other in terms of both culture and ideology. The Western trend, based in Constantinople, now Istanbul, was stimulated by French and Italian liberalism to acquire a reformist ideology laced with pragmatism and realism. The Eastern trend was based in Tiflis, now Tbilisi, and was shaped by the romanticism of Russian and German schools of thought and in particular by their revolutionary ideas. The two identities, Western and Eastern, were divided by geography and evolved separately as parallel rather than integrated leadership groups. By the beginning of the twentieth century, the distinction between the two sides had become evident in the cultural and nationalist literature of Armenia, both in respect of the language used and the distinctive political agendas formed on either side of the division. After the 1915 Genocide and the consequent mass emigration from Western Armenia, the Western aspect of Armenian identity became the dominant self-image of the diaspora, whereas the Eastern shoot put down roots in Soviet Armenia. The subsequent isolation during the Soviet period pushed the two groups even further apart.

Turning to the contemporary identity differences between the homeland and the diaspora, Panossian comes to the conclusion that the concept of Armenianness carries different meanings for people in Armenia from those it holds for residents of the diaspora. Today the two are recognisably distinct cultural entities despite being united by the collective memory of belonging to the same nation with its rich and extensive history. This situation poses serious questions about the future. Is the gap between diaspora and homeland likely to widen over time, or might an ongoing interplay between the two parts of the nation lead eventually to their being reunited? Is the Republic of Armenia capable of gaining the legitimacy of a genuine homeland so that it can either convince its lost citizens to come back or unite them on the basis of its own agenda? Will the diaspora continue to sustain its internal communications and articulate its own ideological programme, or will its members slowly become assimilated into other nations and lose interest in Armenia's cause? More deeply, is nationalism, ethnic or otherwise, Armenian or any other, on the way to becoming out of date and fading into the past of an increasingly globalized world? These are open questions, to be decided by history.

2 Early Armenian civilization

James R. Russell

Introduction

It would be fair to suggest that every nation has an identity, a variety of geographic, linguistic, political, religious, cultural, and often physical features by which it defines itself, or through which others perceive it; and its history is bound up to some degree with the effort to preserve that identity, in the context of contacts with others. But to the same extent no self-defined nation, with perhaps the rare exception of peoples living in insular isolation, is homogeneous – national identity evolves, and changes, as a result of diverse influences and interactions with others. The Armenians today are no exception, though they are in some respects anomalous: their language and culture are perhaps the last surviving relic of the ancient Anatolian civilizations; and they are an east Christian island in a Muslim ocean.

The Armenian plateau, which forms the highest western rampart of the tectonically active mountain system stretching from the Balkans to the Himalayas, is divided by mountain ranges that run mostly on an east–west line, with the Taurus and Antitaurus rising over Syria and Cilicia to the south, towards the Mediterranean, and the Pontic range between Armenia and the Black Sea to the north. Because of this, the country, despite its temperate latitudes, has a harsh, continental climate of long winters with heavy snow in the mountains, being cut off from the temperate climate of the Mediterranean. There is little rainfall; all arable areas require irrigation. Of the large valleys of Armenia, the plain of Ararat, where modern Yerevan stands, is the lowest and is relatively warm and fertile. Though the Tigris and Euphrates both rise in the Armenian highlands, even these rivers, like the others, are fast-flowing mountain torrents, not navigable through most of the country.

There are many native grains: both wheat and barley. Xenophon drank beer during his winter sojourn in Armenia, to be mentioned below. There are also grapes and wine: tradition held that a vine at the little church of Akoṙi on Mt. Ararat, buried in the earthquake of 1840, was the one planted by Noah when he alighted from the Ark. (Mediaeval

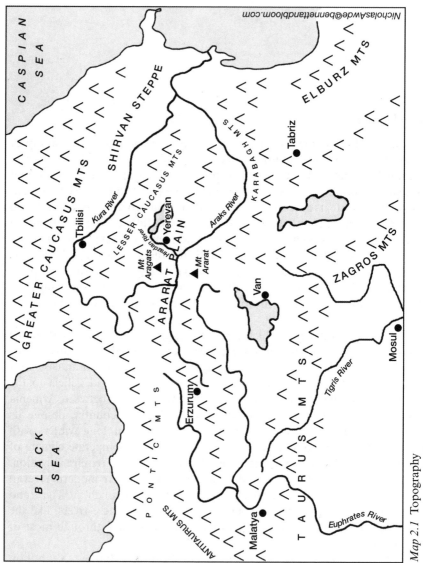

Map 2.1 Topography

tradition held Mt. Cudi, far to the southwest, to be the biblical mountain where angels gave St. James of Nisibis a piece of the wood from the Ark.) The country is good for herding sheep, for both meat and wool. And there are other food animals. Ancient Armenians ate a great deal of pork. The Urarteans, somewhat oddly, decorated some of their war-helmets with hammered reliefs of chickens; the Romans, who got this fowl from an Armenia that was allied to Parthia, called it the 'Parthian bird'. Through Armenia the apricot, too, came to Rome. The ancient Armenians were good warriors and cavalrymen: in Achaemenian times Armenia offered 20,000 foals to the Persian court every year. Armenia has gold and silver mines, and fine marble and the masonry stone tufa; the Romans imported red *sandix* pigment from the country, and Armenia exported the famous red dye extracted from the *vordan karmir* worm. Carpets and textiles were produced in antiquity, and Armenia is still famed for them.

For all their rugged and isolating features, the Armenian highlands stand athwart the busiest crossroads of world history: between the powers of the West (Greece, then Rome, then Byzantium, and now Turkey) and the East (Achaemenian, Parthian, Sasanian, and Islamic Iran); and between those of the North (Scythian, Cimmerian, Alan, and other Caucasian peoples, and now Russia) and the South (Assyria and later Mesopotamia, and then the Arabs). Armenia has been assaulted incessantly and conquered often, espe-cially, given the prevailing layout of its mountain ranges, by the great powers to the West and East, though raids by Caucasian tribes are a constant through antiquity as well. Armenia's geography and history together militate against centralized rule, and Armenians have rarely enjoyed full political independence. The threat and reality of invasion and of foreign, often oppressive, rule is a constant in Armenian history, from ancient to modern times. It is to be expected, then, that Armenian identity is a vital issue, a political matter, sharply defined and generally contrasted to a world around it perceived to be threatening.

Armenian tradition expresses identity mainly in terms of conflict, enshrining at its core a struggle, ostensibly extending over millennia, to maintain and protect the nation's distinct character. The struggle is expressed in mythical, religious, and historical terms – very different sets of metaphors and events, through all of which, however, a continuity is perceived. This chapter will consider many of these formative narratives and images; but it will be concerned still more with the diverse heterogeneous factors, the influences that anciently shaped an Armenian people. Many of these – especially certain Anatolian and Iranian components – might be considered alien from the standpoint of the present, but would not have been so regarded then. Reflection on what is and is not considered alien leads to another issue. The balance of the evidence suggests that the Armenian language was introduced into eastern Anatolia from southeastern Europe some three millennia ago; its present-day speakers are the descendants of those migrants and of various ethnic groups, some of which were present earlier (e.g., the Urarteans), others subsequent arrivals (e.g., the Parthians, an Iranian people).

Armenian origins: myth, language and archaeology

Human beings lived in the river valleys of the Armenian plateau in the Palaeolithic and Mesolithic eras. In the fourth to third millennia BC arose the Kura/Araxes and Trialeti cultures, which practised metallurgy and developed sophisticated techniques of animal husbandry, but did not evolve urban systems of settlement. In general, Armenia did not have large cities in antiquity; where there were such towns, most of the inhabitants were foreigners, either immigrants or exiles brought in to develop trade. The hilltop settlements of Elar, north of Yerevan, and Šengavit', on the Hrazdan River that flows through the modern capital, date from the fourth and third millennia BC: circular houses, and elaborate stone altars and sanctuaries have been found there, with figurines of cattle and women that perhaps were employed magically for fertility. At Vardenis, from the second millennium, was found a disk divided into four, with human figures – perhaps a seasonal calendar; at Lčašen, fourteenth century BC, was excavated a huge wheeled carriage used for burial, with bronze bird- and steer-finials, sun disks, and portrayals of helmeted charioteers. A strange sanctuary of the first millennium BC, with what look like multiple bowls and candelabra, was excavated at Metsamor. The Armenian mountains abound in indecipherable petroglyphs and drawings: the overall picture is of uninterrupted population, inventive technology, and a vital artistic and spiritual culture from the dawn of humanity to the present. Like other peoples, Armenians see themselves as the inheritors of the most ancient culture of their land, and doubtless the descendants of that culture's bearers were eventually assimilated and became Armenians. But the Armenian language – and thus, we may safely presume, a significant part of the Armenians' ancestry – came from elsewhere.

The vocabulary of the Armenian language consists largely of loan-words from Parthian, a Middle Iranian language. From the reign of the Medes (*c.* 685 BC) to the fall of the Sasanians (651 AD), Armenia was steeped in the political and religious culture of Zoroastrian (or Mazdean) Iran. The linguistic influence is so pervasive that, until the late nineteenth century, Armenian was thought to be an Iranian language. However, the great linguist Heinrich Hübschmann demonstrated that the core vocabulary of Armenian developed from proto-Indo-European according to sound laws profoundly different from those of Iranian. Armenian thus belongs to a separate branch of the *satəm* group of Indo-European: the mostly Eastern tongues that form the word for a hundred (reconstructed proto-Indo-European **kwomtom*) with an s, not a k (Russian *sto*; but Latin *centum*, etc.).

The Classical Greek historian Herodotus, writing in Ionia in the early Achaemenian period, describes the Armenians as Phrygian colonists who in their speech resemble Phrygians; and linguists assign Armenian to the Thraco-Phrygian branch of that hypothetical construction, the Indo-European linguistic tree. Thrace is at the tip of southeastern Europe, facing Anatolia, and of its older languages only a remote descendant, Albanian, survives. The Phrygians, a people whose language is long extinct, and who inhabited Northwestern Anatolia in ancient times, were descended from settlers from Europe. By the mid-first millennium AD their language had been replaced by Byzantine Greek. Of the indigenous languages of Anatolia, Armenian alone survived Hellenization or Islamization. The Phrygians have left few inscriptions – though they wrote their language in a script derived from Greek that is not hard to decipher – and these are almost all epitaphs, so the content is very limited. But from these, a very few words that are closely cognate to Classical Armenian have been found. For example, *nise-moun*, the dative of the demonstrative pronoun, meaning 'to this', is so close to Armenian *smin*, which means the same thing, that it is a firm indication that the languages may indeed be closely related. Phrygian *soubros*, 'pure, holy', has cognates in various Indo-European languages, including, most closely, Armenian *surb*. Herodotus reports a somewhat fanciful story about an Egyptian pharaoh who performed an experiment designed to discover the world's oldest language, which, the king supposed, would be the one a baby would speak of its own accord if not instructed otherwise. He had an infant isolated from all speech, till it pointed to a piece of bread and said '*Bekos!*', which, Herodotus explains, means 'bread' in Phrygian. Prof. De Lamberterie connects the word to Armenian *bek-anem*, 'I break', from which he suggests the Phrygian term is cognate to Armenian and means 'a piece, something broken off'. The Armenians probably had other cultural similarities to the Phrygians. For instance, the latter worshipped a rock-born god, Agdistis, while the Armenian oral epic cycle of Sasun begins with the rock-birth of the first generation of heroes, an episode probably derived from old Anatolian traditions, if not specifically Phrygian ones.

The first speakers of Armenian would thus have to have migrated east-wards across the vast Anatolian peninsula, probably in the mid- to late second millennium BC. There is evidence in place names for such migra-tions: the Muški, related to the Phrygians, gave their name to Mazaca (Armenian Mažak, Latin Caesarea, Turkish Kayseri) in Cappadocia, for instance; and a Greek reference to the Armenians as Melitenioi, i.e., people of Melitene (Hittite Melid, modern Turkish Malatya) still farther east, on the Euphrates, would place the proto-Armenian speakers even closer to the Van region, which, with the plain of Ararat to the northeast as a later centre, was to become the centre of historical Armenia. The lowlands around Van were called simply Hayoc' Jor, 'Valley of the Armenians', a name that survived the 1915 Genocide and is still echoed in the Kurdish name of the place, Khavazor.

Professors Gamkrelidze and Ivanov dispute the hypothesis of Armenian migration, which is presented in greatest detail by Igor Diakonoff in his

Pre-history of the Armenian People, and argue instead that Armenian – and indeed proto-Indo-European itself – is native to eastern Anatolia. Their suggestion, which is perhaps understandably attractive to people anxious to prove the legitimacy of Armenian territorial claims back to remotest times, has not gained general scholarly acceptance for many reasons. It would seem from the numerous and far-reaching sound-changes of Armenian that the language developed in relative isolation from other speakers of Indo-European and in proximity to non-Indo-European speakers, particularly the Urarteans and speakers of Kartvelian languages (i.e., early Georgian, Mingrelian, etc.). Armenian *erku*, 'two', derives from a proto-form **duo-*, but through two stages of sound change; *ji*, 'horse', corresponds to a poetic term attested in Sanskrit for a steed 'impelled' swiftly forward, *hayah-*; but the Armenian form of the base **ekwos-*, which also means 'fast', is *ēš*, 'ass'. Indo-Europeans and horses are always found together: the Armenian development might mean that Armenian speakers migrating from an earlier place where there were horses found themselves in a place where horses had not yet been introduced, or at least were still very uncommon and gradually came to use the standard word for horse for the only equid they found there: the donkey. Conversely, the first Mesopotamians to encounter horses called them *anshukurra*, 'mountain asses'.

However, the very survival of a poetic term for a noble steed in Armenian and across Indo-European poetic language indicates that the Armenians retained an early layer of Indo-European culture – oral poetry, mythology, and religious belief – which, with the application of suitable methods, one can recover. Armenia is more or less midway between the Hellenic and Indic spheres of Indo-European culture. In Greece much of the mythological material we now possess underwent a transformation of expression and purpose in the Classical period, becoming social and political metaphor. In India the same mythological stock material becomes part of religious story-telling and metaphysical theory. So, for instance, the Centaur, a mythical creature associated with sex and with the passions, appears in Greek mythology as the disruptive wedding-guest to be defeated by the founders of Athens. Marriage and political order control and sublimate the lubriciously chaotic power of the horse-man. In India, on the other hand, the probably cognate Gandharva is a divine musician who appears also as a kind of third power in human conception, the essence of the passion that generates a child. Armenia, in between, presents the myth through two layers at least: Iranian, then Christian. The rather dangerous creature who makes tempting music is identified with an Iranian mythical being that is part fairy, part randy ibex, the *yuškaparik*. Movsēs Xorenacʻi, an Armenian historian who probably wrote in the eighth or ninth century but whose oral, mythological sources are often of immemorial antiquity, has no hesitation in identifying the yuškaparik with the Centaurs of Greek mythology; and a later medi-aeval text goes further in identifying the siren-like creature and its song not only with the impulse to promiscuous sex, but with the origins of heresy – the Centaur has been Christianized.

The same array of divergent interpretations from West to East of a common mythological figure or archaic antiquity can perhaps explain an enigmatic Armenian myth. Peasant women make offerings in ruined Christian chapels in various parts of Armenia to a being called the *t'ux manuk*, the Black Youth. Folk songs describe him coming down out of the wild mountain forests along the course of streams to seduce girls at the village well. P. Vidal-Naquet, in his study *The Black Hunter*, considers a mythological figure named Melanthos, the Black One, who also lurks at the edge of settlements: his story is worked into the Athenian Apaturia ritual, which marks the socialization of the impulses of adolescent sexuality. In India the Black Youth is of course the Black god himself, Krishna, whose love-play with the cowgirls on the riverbank becomes the durable prototype of mystical love.

A third case is that of the legendary Armenian king Ara *gelec'ik*, 'the Beautiful'. According to Movsēs Xorenac'i, the Assyrian queen Šamiram (i.e., Šammuramat, Semiramis) fell in love with him, but he refused her advances. She ordered her armies to invade Armenia and capture him alive; but he was killed in battle, and the queen ordered his corpse placed in an upper room, where supernatural 'Ara-licking' (*aralēz*) dogs would come down from the sky to revive him. But, the Christian historiographer adds scornfully, the corpse decayed; so Semiramis dressed up a courtier and presented him to the credulous common folk as the risen Ara. Behind the Christian narrative one perceives the ancient mythological type of the beautiful youth, slain by reason of the lust of a powerful woman and lover (sometimes his mother or stepmother), who is then resurrected. This is the type of the Phrygian divine pair Attis and Cybele; in Greece, it becomes the complex tragedy, with political overtones, of Hippolytos and Phaidra. The Persian tale of Siyāvōš in the *Šāh-nāme* of Ferdōsī is a reflex of the same type. But there is also the added element of an other-world journey, in which the man dies, journeys to heaven and hell, and returns to life, bringing knowledge of divine retribution and reward, in the *Katha Upanishad* in India and the *Arda Viraz Namag* in Zoroastrian Iran. There is evidence to suggest that Armenian myth, midway between, combined this latter gnostic theme of the *Himmelsreise der Seele* – the heaven-journey of the soul – with the Hippolytos myth: the tenth book of the *Republic* of Plato, early fourth century BC, contains the myth of one Er, son of Armenios the Pamphylian, who is slain on the battlefield but returns to life and reports the reality of divine justice. Er is obviously none other than Ara. So in this third case as well, one must look behind various strata of later culture and ideology, and with judicious comparison – a kind of triangulation among surrounding, kindred Indo-European cultures – discover the Indo-European myth still present in Armenian tradition after at least three millennia of other accretions and colorations.

Much religious terminology still in use in Armenian comes from the Iranian vocabulary of Zoroastrianism: *patarag*, 'divine liturgy', is the

Parthian word for an offering; *hrašakert*, 'miracle', is Avestan *frašō.kərəti*, the renovation of the world after the defeat of evil. The pre-Christian Armenians used Iranian *bag* – 'god' in toponyms: Bagawan, Bagaran, Bagayařič, etc. But the chief term for 'God' still used, *Astuac*, is most likely native Armenian, of proto-Indo-European derivation. Prof. De Lamberterie has argued that it be connected to *ast-em* 'wed' and *hast-em* 'create', with cognates in Germanic. Mediaeval Armenian folk-etymology of *Astuac* as *hast-oł*, 'creator', is thus likely to be right, if not for sound scientific reasons.

It is important to stress here that Indo-European is a term used of a language and cultural group that was, even at its early stages, probably large and widespread enough to be physically diverse; and over the centuries of migration, in which fairly small numbers of Indo-Europeans, moving in different directions, mingled with other populations of the same size or larger, this diversity was greatly augmented. To the extent that archaeology provides evidence, the migrations were peaceful and gradual, without evidence of mass destruction or of radical or sudden change. The image of the racially homogeneous, fair-haired and blue-eyed Aryan conquerors is a pernicious fantasy reflecting the imperialist attitudes of nineteenth-century Europeans, not a valid historical model. Correspondingly, the migrant speakers of proto-Armenian were probably comparatively few; and they intermarried over the centuries with the peoples of eastern Anatolia, Syria and Mesopotamia, and the South Caucasus. To this day, some Armenians are fair-haired, but most are dark: there is no single Armenian type. When at the end of the fifth century BC Xenophon's mercenary army crossed the Armenian highlands to the sea in the retreat that their general chronicles in his *Anabasis*, there were various ethnic groups and building styles in Armenia. Roman historians centuries later knew of a score of languages spoken in the country, upon which Artaxias I imposed linguistic unity – by which is meant, most likely, the use of Armenian as an official language – only after 190 BC. Early Armenia was, undoubtedly, a country ethnically and linguistically heterogeneous.

The beginnings of Armenian history

Armenians call themselves *hay*, a word of unknown derivation: the country was called in ancient times simply by the plural form *(Mec) Hayk'*, '(Greater) Armenia'; or else, with the Iranian toponymical suffix still used, *Hayastan*. *Hay-* has been connected to the place Hayasa-Azzi, but this province lay too far north of Van, and west of Ararat, it is argued, for its name to have been so important. And the *-asa* ending cannot simply be made to go away. So a better explanation must be sought. In Armenian forms of Indo-European root words the intervocalic -t- is lost and the initial p- becomes h- or is elided entirely: this is why the Armenian equivalent of Latin *pater* is *hayr*, 'father', and of Greek *poda*, 'foot', *otn* or *het*. So *hay* could come from a boastful **potiyos*-, 'ruler, master'; or it might derive from

Hatti, for the proto-Armenians had to traverse the lands of the once-mighty Hittite Empire, and Hatti is the name the Hittites used of themselves. As for the word 'Armenian', it is first attested in the Old Persian version of the inscription of the Persian king Darius the Great of 518 BC on the rock at Behistun above the main road from Media to Babylon, where he records his victories over the various rebellious chiefs of the satrapies of the kingdom, including Haldita and Arkha of the *armina-*. There is a bas-relief of the captives before the king on the rock, too; and a sealing with the same scene was found recently at a site that may have been the Achaemenian satrapal residence, near Gyumri (formerly Leninakan, Kumayri, Alexandropol) in the Republic of Armenia. Igor Diakonoff thought the latter term derived from the place name Arme-Šupria, from whose second half would come *som-ekhi*, the Georgian word for an Armenian. Another possibility would be a derivation from the base *arm-* of Armenian *armat*, 'root', meaning 'native, indigenous', in which case the term might originally have been applied by Armenian speakers to the majority of the population, which consisted of non-Armenian speakers; and by outsiders to the country as a whole. In the Babylonian text of the Behistun inscription, the equivalent of Armenia is Uraštu, better known from the Assyrian form Urartu, or Hebrew Ararat (which properly denoted the whole mountainous country where Noah's Ark came to land, not, as in later usage, its highest peak). And indeed the Urarteans were the people indigenous to the land that became Armenia.

The Urarteans called their country Biain-ili; and this name survives in Armenian Van (the city, which the Urarteans called Tušpa; the latter persisted in Tosp, the Armenian name of the district around Van city). Assyria was Urartu's main rival: Šalmaneser III (861–51 BC) depicts on the Balawat gates the capture of Arzašku, on the northeast shore of lake Van, and the flight of the defeated Urarteans into the mountains. Under Sarduri, Menua, and Argišti I, Urartu expanded, reaching the zenith of its power around 750 BC. The country's political fortunes waned thereafter, under the successive blows of Tiglath Pileser (744–27) and Sargon II (721–05). Subsequently, Urartu was invaded by the Scythians, and in 585 it fell to the Medes, whose capital, Ecbatana, is today the city of Hamadan on the western edge of the Iranian plateau. Thereafter, Armenia's development was bound up with Iran. But the Urartean component in Armenian identity is significant. Not only do very many Urartean toponyms survive in Armenian form (Biaina>Van, Tušpa>Tosp, Erebuni>Yerevan, Arzašku>Arčēš, etc.), but also, it would seem, do some proper names. One of the *armina-* conspirators against Darius I was named Khaldita, a name which contains the name of the chief divinity of the Urartean pantheon, Khaldi. The very common Armenian name Aram is probably a form of Urartean Aramu, the name of a king who reigned 860–40 BC. The regal dynastic clan Arcruni of the Vaspurakan region believed themselves to be descended from an eagle (Armenian *arciw, arcui*). The latter bird-name in Armenian probably is a loan from Indo-Iranian (cf. Sanskrit *rjipya-*, Avestan *ərəzifya-*), but it is

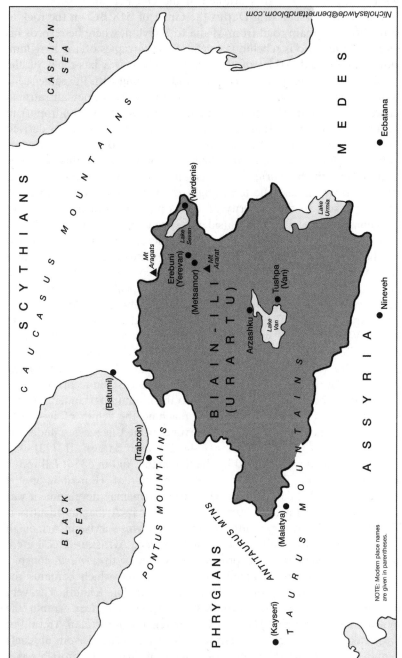

Figure 2.2 Urartu *circa* 750 BC

possible that it may have entered the language *via* Urartean, where Artsibi, meaning 'eagle', is attested as the name of a swift, royal steed (the swiftness of the bird of prey is the poetic cliché: Artašēs in an epic fragment rides a black steed swift as an eagle – the blackness is itself potent, for there is an Urartean fresco of a splendid black horse, and one recalls that the name of the Iranian hero Siyāvōš, attested in Armenian as Šawarš, means 'black stallion'). And there was a noble clan called Artsiuniuni in Urartu. Urartu began as a confederation of 'the forty kings of Nairi', of whom this family had been one. These were probably clan-based dynasts, and this decentralized form of power, well suited to a country broken by mountains into cantons isolated by the harsh winter snows, carried on into the high Middle Ages in Armenia with the institution of the *naxarar*.

Naxarar is itself a well-attested Parthian term from Old Iranian **naxwadāra-*, literally, 'holder of the foremost (rank)'; so the pre-existing institution acquired the name known to us from texts, in either the Artaxiad (190 BC to the early decades of the first century AD) or Arsacid (*c.* 50–429 AD) dynasties. Its importance to Armenian society cannot be overestimated. The Mamikonean *naxarars* were the hereditary commanders-in-chief of the Armenian forces; so the great Christian warrior-saint and martyr of the fifth century, Vardan, was of this charismatic clan. The Bagratunis, hereditary vassals of the Arsacids, claimed descent first from Tork' Angeł (a divinity of dark and vast powers derived from Tarhundas, the Anatolian weather-god, whom Armenians syncretized with Nergal, the Mesopotamian lord of the underworld), and then, after conversion to Christianity, from the house of David: their name comes from Iranian *baga-dāta-*, 'God-given'. After the final eclipse of the Mamikoneans in the uprising against Muslim Arab occupation that culminated in the battle of Bagrewand in 775, it was the Bagratunis who forged new Armenian kingdoms in the north-central part of the country and built the great metropolis of Ani. The patriarchs of the Armenian Church, from St. Gregory the Illuminator in the early fourth century down to St. Nersēs Šnorhali ('the Graceful') in the twelfth, traced their lineal descent back to the Parthian noble clans of the Surēns and Pahlawunis.

Aspects of Armenian material and spiritual culture can be traced to Urartu. The Armenian word *cov*, 'sea, lake', is most plausibly from Urartean *tsue*, 'idem'. The words for mulberry, plum, and apple (*t'ut'*, *salor*, *xnjor*) derive from Urartean. Down to recent times, Armenian farmers used an Urartean irrigation canal at Artamet (Turkish Edremit, near Van) whose construction they attributed to queen Šamiram. The craft of the Armenian mason, characterized by finely joined, smoothly dressed stone façades, is probably an inheritance from Urartean work. The Armenians, long famed for their metalwork, learnt this skill, too, from the Urarteans: metallurgy on the Armenian plateau can be traced back to the Kura/Araxes and Trialeti cultures. The Urarteans, like other ancient Near Eastern peoples, often employed in their art the symbol of the Tree of Life: the latter figures prominently in mediaeval Armenian songs and folk nuptial rites, of course with an overlay of Christian symbolism. There are Urartean metal figurines of harpies; and these creatures, often with additional Iranian features, are ubiquitous in Armenian sculpture and manuscript painting. The early inhabitants of the Armenian plateau carved cigar-shaped stones with sinuous figures of serpents and other creatures, apparently in connection with cultic observances connected with rivers. The Armenians call these stones *višap* – a Middle Iranian word for a poisonous aquatic monster – and tell stories about abductions of maidens by river-dragons. And their ancestors, carving the Holy Sign upon the stones, rechristened them as *xač'k'ar*s, the 'Cross-stones' that dot the Armenian landscape, to which blood sacrifices are still offered. Steles inscribed with Urartean cuneiform were pressed into service as *xač'k'ars*, as well.

In the Van area there are a number of blind portals carved into the living rock, which the Urarteans called Gates of God, believing that the god dwelt in the rock behind. In Armenian epic and folk-lore it is still believed that Mher, i.e., the Zoroastrian god Mithra, guided by a raven, zodiacal circle in hand, waits till the end of time behind one of these, the *Mheri duṙn* ('Gate of Mithra', Turkish *Meher kapisi*) at Van. On Ascension Eve, when Heaven is believed to open, so does the god's portal; and then he can be seen on horseback, covered with hair from head to toe like the Promethean wild-man of Caucasian lore. The Mher of folk epic is banished, and called Cain; but behind the Christian deprecation of the ancient divinity, who assumes the features of Antichrist (a feature the anti-clerical Bolsheviks eagerly adopted: in early Communist propaganda, it was proclaimed that Mher was loose at last and ravening for joy), one can easily discern the main features of the Mithraic cult that was diffused across the Black Sea and over Anatolia to the Roman Empire. Mithra is an apocalyptic being in Iran; and the Roman Mithras is born of rock, a tell-tale Anatolian feature. In Armenian epic recitations, Mher's great-grandfather is rock-born.

The Iranian Medes destroyed Nineveh, capital of Assyria, in 612 BC. They overran Urartu – and thus Armenia – in 585. Memory of the conquest in Armenia is filtered through the Persian legends of the rebellion of Cyrus against the Mede Astyages. The name of the latter means 'spearcaster' (*Rštivaiga); but to the Persians, for whom he was a tyrant, it sounded like that of a mythical monster of the Avesta, half-man, half-dragon, Aži Dahāka; and the Armenians remembered Astyages by the Middle Iranian form of the monster's name, Aždahak. Media (*Māda-) becomes in Armenian *Mar-k'*, by a change of intervocalic -d- to -r-, but Armenian fabulists heard in this term Persian *mār*, which means 'snake', so the Medes become the *višapazunk'*, 'progeny of the Dragon', and the Armenian hero Tigran (the name is Middle Iranian) in a surviving fragment of oral epic easily assumes the standard Indo-European and Iranian role of the hero fighting the dragon to release a captive maiden (in this case his own sister Tigranuhi). Xenophon in his *Cyropaideia*, 'The Education of

Cyrus', mentions one Armenian, Tigranēs in Greek (from Old Persian *Tiɣrāna-*, presumably), as a childhood companion of the Achaemenian, so it is possible that by Xenophon's time, at least, there were Armenian noblemen who bore Iranian names and attended at the Achaemenian royal court.

Alexander the Great bypassed the Armenian mountains in his haste to conquer the retreating armies of Darius III; and the Orontid (Armenian Eruandakan) satrapal house became vassals of the Seleucids. At Armawir in the plain of Ararat there were large inscribed stones with excerpts from Greek drama and the *Works and Days* of Hesiod, and mention is made of Pharnaces and Mithras, both common Irano-Greek dynastic names of Pontus. But there is little other evidence of Greek influence. After the Romans crippled Seleucid power in Anatolia at the battle of Magnesia (190 BC), two Orontid *stratēgoi*, Artaxias (Artašēs) and Zariadris (Zareh), shook off Seleucid suzerainty and founded independent kingdoms in Greater Armenia and Sophene. Xorenac'i refers to boundary-markers of estates (a common feature of Hellenistic society) of Artašēs, and some have been found, with his name in Aramaic inscriptions. He founded the city of Artaxata (Artašat, literally 'Joy of Artašēs') on the gentle hills of the valley of the Araxes at the foot of Mt. Ararat, which, classical authors report, the fleeing Hannibal helped him to design; and a medal has been found with a Greek legend, *dēmos Artaxisatōn*: 'municipality of the people of Artaxata'. Artašēs also brought Greek statues of the gods for the temples: for each Zoroastrian *yazata*, Xorenac'i lists one or more Greek equivalents. These have not been found, but other evidence from the area would seem to corroborate the veracity of Xorenac'i's report.

In the first century BC the Orontid king Antiochus of Commagene, a cousin of the Armenian royal house, erected two open-air shrines with altars and statues of the gods on Nemrut Dagh, where there was also his sacred tomb (*hierothēsion*). Each statue is identified in a Greek inscription: Artagnes, i.e., the Iranian Vərəthraɣna, Armenian Vahagn, corresponds to Herakles, just as in Xorenac'i's text; and a Greek bronze of Herakles found in Parthian Mesene has a later Parthian inscription on its thigh identifying the figure as the same Iranian divinity. The chief divinity of the pre-Christian Armenian religion was Aramazd, i.e., Ahura Mazdā, the Lord Wisdom of Zoroastrianism. His evil opponent, Angra Mainyu, the Frightful Spirit, is attested in Armenian as Haramani or, in a later form, Arhmn. There are various references, mostly indirect, to the seven Aməša Spəntas, the Holy Immortals; and the lesser divinities Vərəthraɣna, Mithra, Anāhitā, and Tīri are attested in Middle Iranian forms: Vahagn, Mihr, Anahit, and Tir. The Syrian god Ba'l Šamīn, Lord of Heaven, was worshipped alongside Aramazd as Baršamin. Vahagn, who bears the epithet *višapak'al*, 'dragon-reaper', appears to have combined features of the Indo-Iranian divinity attested in India as Indra *vritrahan*, 'killer of the (dragon) Vritra (i.e., Opposition)' and the local Urartean divinity Teišeba (Hurrian Tešup). The various temples were supported by estates; and those of Anahit were so extensive that the Greeks knew the province of Acilisene also as *Anaitikē khōrā*, 'the place of the Anahit (temple)'. The words for religious establishments were mainly Middle Iranian, as one might expect: that for a shrine was *mehean*, lit. 'place of Mithra' (cf. the modern Zoroastrian usage *dar-e Mihr*, 'gate/place of Mithra'); *bagin*, lit. 'of the god', probably was a shrine with a cult-image; and *atrušan* was a fire-temple, where the living icon of the Mazdeans blazed. Priests were called *k'urm*, though, an Aramaic term. An Aramaic inscription at Arebsun, near Nevšehir, describes the marriage of the Semitic god Bel to the Iranian *daēnā mazdayasnī*, the personified Good Religion of Mazdā-worship. Such syncretism was very much the usual pattern in Anatolia.

Reference has been made to the oral epic in which Artašēs marries Sat'enik. The same epic, as reported by Xorenac'i, refers also to the cursing by the king of his son Artawazd, who is subsequently captured by supernatural giants, the *k'ajk'*, while he is hunting on Mt. Ararat: they imprison him in the cleft of the mountain till the end of time. Dogs gnaw at his chains, and it was a custom for Armenian blacksmiths to strike their anvils thrice on the first day of the week, to strengthen the chains of Artawazd. Professor Nina Garsoian has suggested that a historical Artawazd who was taken captive by Mark Antony to Egypt, where he died in 35 BC, might have become in epic lore the occulted king. The legend finds an echo in the cursing of Little Mher by his father, David, in the Armenian Epic of Sasun, where Mher is confined till the end of time behind the Urartean Gate of God at Van. Epic theme has combined here with apocalyptic beliefs about the Zoroastrian *yazata*. One can reconstruct an entire, separate epic cycle about the Zariadrids to the west. Parts of it seem to have survived in Armenian balladry, and in the mediaeval Byzantine epic *Digenēs Akritēs*, whose locus is the Malatya region.

The most famous of the Artaxiad kings, though, was undoubtedly Tigran II the Great (95–56 BC), whose short-lived empire included Antioch; the Tykhē, or goddess of the fortune of that city, adorns the obverse of his tetradrachms, on which he styles himself *basileus basileōn*, 'king of kings'. Both written and oral epics about Tigran existed in early Christian Armenia, of which only fragments remain: it has not even been possible to identify with certainty the capital he founded near Amida (Turkish Diyarbekir), Tigranocerta (Tigranakert). Tigran forced thousands of Jews to migrate to Armenian cities: most of their descendants were exiled yet again, to Iran, by early Sasanian invaders in the fourth century AD, but some of the Jews of Armenia might have become the nucleus of the early Christian community there, as was the case elsewhere in Asia Minor. There is no indigenous Armenian Jewish community, however: Armenian and Christian identity quickly became inseparable, and the small Jewish communities of eastern Anatolia, most of whom lived close to the

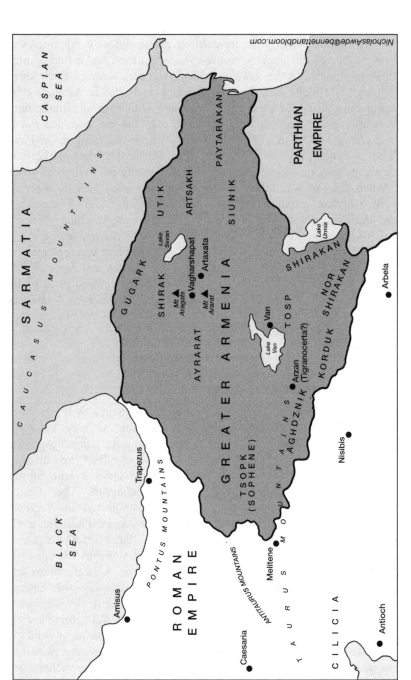

Figure 2.3 Armenia *circa* first century BC

older, established centres in Syria and northern Iraq, were Arabic- or Kurdish-speaking.

In the first century BC Armenia was a battleground for the Roman and Parthian Arsacid empires, with its cultural and political sympathies very much on the side of the latter. Armenia's alienation from Rome finds expression in Roman myth. In the *Aeneid* of Virgil, the hero receives a new shield whose design is a world map (as does Achilles in the *Iliad*); Aeneas's shiny new acquisition bears not the living, poignant cosmic map of Homer, but a self-conscious, propagandistic map of the Roman Empire, bounded not by the great stream of Ocean, but by the Araxes, which according to the historian Tacitus, 'suffers no bridges': Armenia is, irrevocably, part of the East. Plutarch expresses this same conviction in a vignette of barbarous splendour. When Crassus was killed by the Parthian general Surenas after the battle of Carrhae (modern Harran, just south of Urfa), a messenger brought the Roman's severed head to the banquet at Artaxata where the Armenian king was celebrating the marriage of his daughter to the son of the ruler of Parthia. A Greek actor named Jason, who had been entertaining the guests, seized the head and declaimed the speech of Agave in the *Bacchae* of Euripides as she holds up in triumph the severed head of her own son, Pentheus, who had denied the worship of the sensuous Asiatic god Dionysus. The import of the story is clear: the Oriental potentates might enjoy Greek culture, but they will never be part of the West – they are effeminate, cruel, luxurious.

The coming of Christianity to Armenia

Within a hundred years of the banquet at Artaxata, that is, by the mid-first century AD, Tiridates (Trdat), brother of the Parthian king Vologases (Valaxš, Armenian Vałarš), was on the Armenian throne. Christ's Apostles, tradition holds, had arrived shortly before, and the legend of their mission, deeply coloured by Artaxiad epic, was itself to serve as the literary template for the Apostolic legendry of Manichaeism. The Arsacid (Armenian Aršakuni) dynasty became firmly established in Armenia, despite constant Roman interference, both military and diplomatic, in the country's affairs; but in AD 226 Ardešīr, son of Pāpak, of the Sasanian house of Persia, overthrew the Arsacid Ardawān V. From the first, the Sasanians, who styled themselves successors to the Achaemenians and bearers of Iranian national renewal, sought to employ the militant Zoroastrian priestly hierarchy to impose a system of centralized rule and uniformity of cult. Such policies had been largely alien to Parthian society, and the Armenians, who in any case regarded the Sasanians as regicides and upstarts and felt bound to avenge Ardawān's blood, were now at war. Roman interests in the region prevented a decisive Sasanian victory; and the Persians were in any case as ready to woo as to fight the Armenians, knowing the way of life of the latter to be fundamentally similar to their own. The reasons for the conversion of Tiridates the Great of Armenia to Christianity in the early decades of the fourth century are not clear. Iran strongly opposed the move, and was on repeated occasions to attempt to force the Armenians to return to the Mazdean fold, most notably in 449–83, in the war chronicled by Ełišē *vardapet*, when Vardan Mamikonean was slain. If political considerations played a role, Rome at least would have had to approve, which would suggest a date of *c.* 325 or a little earlier during the reign of Constantine the Great, but Armenians traditionally hold the date of the Conversion to be 301, when they would have been entirely, rebelliously, splendidly, on their own.

St. Gregory the Illuminator baptized Tiridates: the father of the former was a nobleman, Anak Surēn Pahlaw, scion of one of the great Parthian families; and tradition thereby throws the weight of Arsacid prestige behind the act, which is itself safely enclosed in standard patterns of epic. At first, such Christian writings as there were in Armenia were in the Aramaic dialect of Edessa, Syriac, or, somewhat less frequently, in Greek; but at the end of the fourth century a restless, charismatic visionary named Maštoc' invented, for the first time, an alphabet for the Armenian language. The script was written, like Greek or Latin, in separate characters, from left to right, with the vertical strokes thick and the horizontal ones thin, and in all these respects the opposite of the majority of Eastern alphabets. The system of vowels derives, clearly, from Greek also, but many of the letters come from Aramaic prototypes, perhaps inspired in part by Manichaean experiments in the adaptation of the Aramaic alphabet to non-Semitic languages. With this invention, the establishment of schools for the training of priests, and the systematic translation of a vast corpus of Christian and classical literature into Armenian, the Christianization of Armenia, and its political orientation towards Christendom, became irrevocable. But the difficult position of the country, its relative remoteness from the West, and the proud sense of itself garnered over millennia of civilized development and the play of diverse cultural influences also ensured that, though Armenians might sometimes look to their co-religionists with hope, they were ultimately destined to stand alone.

Bibliography

Diakonoff, I.M., *The Pre-history of the Armenian People* (Delmar, New York: Caravan Books, 1983).

Garsoian, N., 'The Emergence of Armenia' and 'The Arsakuni Dynasty', chapters 3 and 4 of R.G. Hovannisian, ed., *The Armenian People*, vol. 1 (New York: St. Martin's, 1997).

Piotrovskii, K.B., *Urartu: The Kingdom of Van and Its Art*, translated by P.S. Gelling (London: Evelyn Adams and Mackay, 1967).

Russell, J.R., *Zoroastrianism in Armenia* (Cambridge, MA: Harvard Iranian Series 5, 1987).

—— 'On the Armeno-Iranian Roots of Mithraism', in J.R. Hinnells, ed., *Studies in Mithraism* (Rome: 'L'Erma' di Bretschneider, 1994).

—— 'The Formation of the Armenian Nation', chapter 2 of R.G. Hovannisian, ed., *The Armenian People*, vol. 1 (New York: St. Martin's, 1997).

——'Armenian and Iranian Studies', *Harvard Armenian Texts and Studies*, 9, Cambridge, MA, 2004.

3   Christianity to modernity

Boghos Levon Zekiyan[1]

Major historical events from the fourth to eighteenth centuries AD

The Arshakuni dynasty, the partition of Armenia and Byzantine and Sasanian dominion

The fourth century AD was a turbulent but formative period in Armenian history. Caught between the imperial powers of Rome (later Byzantium) and Sasanian Iran, the Arshakuni (Arsacid) dynasty and the frequently disunited and rebellious *nakharars* (nobility) sought to maximize their own advantage by balancing among more powerful adversaries. The adoption of Christianity brought Armenia into intermittent conflict with the Sasanians on religious grounds (see below), but it would be a mistake to see religion as the defining factor in political allegiances, and often Armenian kings and nobles sided with the Sasanians against Romans or Byzantines and each other. At times Armenia formed a buffer state between the two empires, at others it fell entirely under Iranian sway, and at others again it was partitioned between them. The 387 AD treaty between the emperors Theodosius and Shapur III partitioned Armenia – a pattern that was to be repeated in subsequent centuries – with the larger eastern part falling to Iran. In the subsequent decades the Arshakuni dynasty was allowed to die out, leaving Armenia as a mere province of the Byzantine and Sasanian empires (390 in Western Armenia; 428 in Eastern Armenia).

In the period following the end of the Arshakuni dynasty, the Armenian *nakharars* continued to rule at the local level, at least in the short term. In Eastern Armenia in the mid-fifth century the Sasanians abandoned their previous more or less *laissez-faire* approach to their Armenian provinces and began to govern in a more interventionist way, especially in religious policy, where they attempted to impose Mazdaism (Zoroastrianism) on the Armenians. This led to the rebellion known as the Vardanank Wars (c.

---

1   The first section of this chapter 'Major historical events from the fourth to eighteenth centuries AD' is by Edmund Herzig.

450–84), by the end of which, in spite of bloody defeats, the Armenians had succeeded in maintaining their faith and a degree of political autonomy. In the West during the reign of the Emperor Justinian (527–65) Armenia was fully incorporated and increasingly assimilated into the Byzantine Empire, producing strong pressure on both its political and its ecclesiastical autonomy.

From the mid-sixth century another period of war between the Byzantine and Sasanian empires led once again to extensive and damaging campaigning in Armenia, with Armenian nobles joining in on both sides. Especially destructive was the use of scorched earth tactics by Emperor Maurice (582–602), some of the Armenian deportees being resettled in Cyprus to found the Armenian colony there, while many others emigrated to other parts of the Byzantine Empire. During the decades of campaigning the advantage shifted between the two protagonists, but by 628 the Byzantines had gained the upper hand and won recognition of their control of the greater part of Armenia.

The Arab conquest and the Islamic Caliphate

In the mid-seventh century the Arab–Muslim conquest of the Sasanian Empire and most of the Byzantine territories in the Middle East radically altered Armenia's situation. The Arab conquest of Armenia was protracted, beginning with raids and the conquest of the capital Dvin in 640 and continuing until late in the eighth century, by which time most of Armenia had been incorporated into the Islamic Caliphate. For much of the time both of the major caliphal dynasties, the Umayyads (661–750) and Abbasids (750–*c*. 1000), allowed, deliberately or by default, a good deal of political autonomy and religious freedom to Armenia. While Christians were second-class citizens within the new Islamic jurisdiction, they enjoyed the right to follow their faith, and arguably the role of the Armenian Church as a representative of its congregation gained greater recognition than under any previous jurisdiction. In many ways Arab rule was less onerous than Byzantine, especially in this period when the Byzantines were determined to bring the Armenian Church into line with their own. The period of Arab rule witnessed several major Armenian rebellions and bloody wars, in which some of the great noble families – among them the Mamikonians – were irrevocably weakened, but it also saw the rise of other noble houses – most notably the Bagratunis (Bagratids) – and periods when Arabs and Armenians fought side by side against common enemies, such as the Khazar invaders from north of the Caucasus.

The Abbasid period also saw the beginnings of substantial migration into Armenia of settlers from other parts of the Caliph's empire. These incomers supplemented the Arab garrisons that had been established earlier and put down roots in the conquered territory, so that by the ninth century we find the existence of an established Arab nobility of emirs in Armenia, more or less equivalent to the Armenian *nakharars,* and like them ready to take advantage of any weakening of central authority to extend their own power and territory. This important development set the scene for the revitalization of local politics when the Abbasid Caliphate went into terminal decline following the death of the greatest caliph, Harun al-Rashid (786–809). Half a century later, however, Armenia bore the brunt of the last gasp of effective Abbasid rule when in 850–3 the country was ravaged by the armies of Caliph al-Mutawakkil, and many of the *nakharars* were obliged to convert to Islam. During this period complex and shifting alliances of local Christian and Muslim nobles battled one another and the imperial powers of Byzantium and Baghdad, demonstrating again that religion is a poor guide to political affiliation in this frontier land between Christendom and the lands of Islam.

The Bagratuni dynasty

Among the winners to emerge as the Abbasid Caliphate declined was the Bagratuni family, which succeeded in establishing itself as the royal household in both Armenia and southwest Georgia. In the mid-ninth century the Bagratunis, through a combination of conquests and marriage alliances, drew together a large part of Armenia. Bagratuni Armenia was never a solid and united political entity, rather it consisted of a network of alliances that periodically came unstuck as its component *nakharar* families, notably the Artsrunis and the Siunis and, later, scions of the Bagratuni house itself, reverted to the established pattern of exploiting opportunities to form other alliances. Moreover, the Bagratunis could not in the long term dislodge Arab emirs from a number of important Armenian territories and cities, including Dvin and Nakhichevan, and they faced periodic threats from Byzantium and local Muslim dynasties, particularly the Sajids of Azerbaijan.

The second half of the tenth century marks the high point of Bagratuni power, and the period of glory of their capital Ani. The dynasty's demise followed swiftly, when succession disputes and internal feuds coincided with a revival of Byzantine power to bring an end to Bagratuni power in Ani, Kars and other centres by 1065.

Cilician Armenia

Armenian settlement in Cilicia, like that in other parts of the Byzantine Empire, seems to have been partly voluntary and partly the result of deliberate policy, in this case the desire to repopulate the territory following its reconquest from the Arabs in the mid-tenth century. The population was swelled by immigration from Greater Armenia following the collapse of the Bagratuni kingdom. In this relatively contained (by surrounding mountain ranges and the sea) and remote territory, some Armenian noble families were able to create the only example in history of an independent Armenian

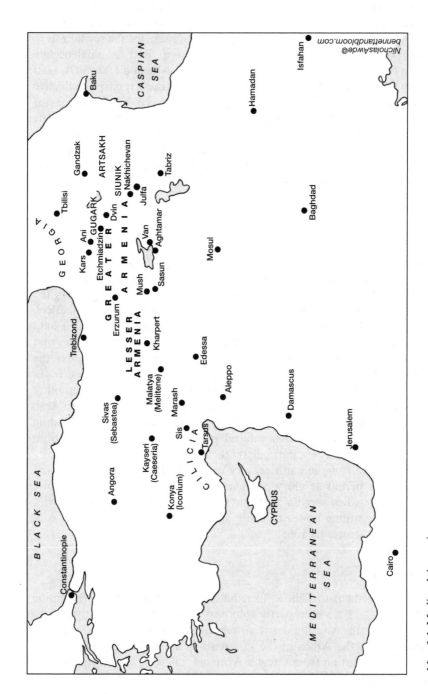

Map 3.1 Medieval Armenia

polity in diaspora. Two such noble families, the Rubenids and the Hetumids, dominate the history of Cilician Armenia. The former came into conflict early with their Byzantine overlords and threw off their suzerainty, taking advantage of the timely arrival of the Crusaders in the 1090s to consolidate their independence. The Hetumids, by contrast, for a long time remained loyal to the emperor in Byzantium, though they also achieved *de facto* independence.

The Hetumids and Rubenids were soon involved in the complex local politics of the period, with Byzantines, Franks (Crusaders), Arabs, Turks and Kurds vying for power and territory. In this ever-shifting and dynamic power play, immediate political circumstances rather than religion or ethnicity determined alliances, and there are instances of the Cilician Armenians fighting among themselves, forming marriage alliances with Muslim lords, and even converting to Islam. Yet in the main they retained a clear Armenian identity and provided the patronage for a flourishing Armenian culture (see below). So strong was the pull of Cilicia (and so dismal the situation in Greater Armenia) that for a century the seat of the Catholicos was located in Cilicia. In 1199 the Rubenid lord Levon was granted a crown by both the German and the Byzantine emperors, marking the emergence of Cilicia as a kingdom and its wider recognition in Europe. The Cilician kingdom was, in many respects, more like a feudal European kingdom than the *nakharar*-based polities of Greater Armenia, and its court culture bore a heavy impress from Western Europe, including the use of French and Latin alongside Armenian. The aristocracy and parts of the clergy also drew close to Roman Catholicism and expressed interest in reuniting the Armenian and Roman churches, though this trend does not seem to have penetrated to the popular level. The kingdom was remarkable also for its commercial importance, acting as an entrepôt between East and West, prefiguring the later explosion of Armenian commerce in the sixteenth and seventeenth centuries.

The Cilician Armenian Kingdom proved remarkably long-lived, thanks largely to the skilful alliance politics of its rulers. A good example of this is King Hetum's (1226–69) recognition of the power of the Mongols, persuading him to send his brother Smbat to their capital, Karakoram in Mongolia, to negotiate an alliance. In 1254 Hetum himself undertook the same journey to renew the alliance. In the long run, however, it was the rising power of the Mamluks in Egypt, rather than the Mongols' successors in Iran, that had to be reckoned with, and as the Mamluks and Mongols were bitter enemies, the Mongol alliance turned out to be a mixed blessing. The Cilician kingdom fell at last to the Mamluks in 1375.

The Seljuks, the Mongols and Emir Timur

The recovery of Byzantine power that had brought the Bagratuni dynasty to an end proved short lived. Just as Bagratuni Kars was falling to the

Byzantines, Ani was taken by the newly arrived Seljuk Turkish invaders. Within a few years the Byzantines were decisively defeated by the Seljuks in the battle of Manazkert (1071) and lost the bulk of their territories in Asia Minor, including Greater and Lesser Armenia. The Seljuk Empire soon fragmented, allowing a revival of Christian rule in Greater Armenia in the twelfth and early thirteenth centuries, this time under the suzerainty of the Georgian Bagrationis (a branch of the Bagratuni family). But the large-scale immigration of Turkish nomads into the Caucasus and Anatolia initiated in the Seljuk period continued through subsequent centuries, with new surges during the invasion of Chinggis Khan, whose armies reached Armenia in 1236, the subsequent intra-Mongol campaigning in the Caucasus between the armies of the Il-Khans (capital Tabriz) and the Golden Horde (occupying the steppes north of the Caucasus mountains), and the repeated and exceptionally brutal and destructive invasions of Emir Timur between 1386 and 1403. In the long run the combination of progressive Turkish (and Kurdish) immigration and Armenian decline, through massacre, famine and emigration, changed the demographic balance in a way that Arab immigration had never done. Increasingly, the remaining autonomous Armenian noble houses were restricted to remote mountainous regions such as Artsakh/Karabagh, Siunik/Zangezur, Gugark/Lori, Sasun and Mush. Elsewhere Armenian landowners were dispossessed in favour of the nobility of the ruling power of the day (a process which continued also into the fifteenth century under the Aq-Quyunlu Turkoman dynasty and into the sixteenth under the Safavids), while in many parts of Greater Armenia, in so far as it is possible to reconstruct the demographics of the period, Armenians ceased to constitute the majority of the population. Armenian emigration swelled the number of Armenians in the diaspora, in the Byzantine Empire, Cyprus and other centres on the Mediterranean and Black Sea coasts.

Ottomans, Safavids and the definitive partition of Armenia

Following the invasions of Timur, the Ottoman dynasty resumed its rise in Anatolia, Asia Minor and the Balkans, incorporating historic Lesser Armenia and the western parts of Greater Armenia. Ottoman rule consolidated Turkish power over large parts of Armenia, but produced a long period of relative political continuity and stability. In the East the establishment of a new dynasty in Iran, the Safavids, at the start of the sixteenth century similarly heralded a two-hundred-year period of relative political stability. Armenia, once more a battleground between two powerful empires, did not immediately benefit from this new, more stable political configuration. The first half of the sixteenth century witnessed successive campaigns through Armenia as the two empires vied for supremacy. Unlike in previous periods when Armenia had been a bone of contention between rival empires, by the sixteenth century there was no longer a significant Armenian political leadership capable of manoeuvring between the great powers of the day to try to secure its own advantage.

The 1555 Treaty of Amasya brought respite for nearly a quarter of a century, but fighting resumed in the 1570s and, with brief interludes, continued until 1618, the destruction of the military campaigns being augmented by a series of rebellions in the eastern provinces of the Ottoman Empire. The 1620s and 1630s saw fewer campaigns through Armenia, and the 1639 Treaty of Zuhab, which for the most part confirmed the frontier that had been agreed nearly one hundred years before at the Treaty of Amasya, ushered in a prolonged period of peace, extending until the collapse of the Safavid dynasty in the third decade of the eighteenth century. During this period of tranquillity there was a marked recovery of economic life in the cities and countryside of Armenia, and the many other cities of the region with significant Armenian populations.

The Ottoman–Safavid wars were extremely destructive and resulted in a further large-scale displacement of Armenians, partly through emigration to escape the insecurity and hardship of life in war-torn Armenia, and partly through deliberate relocation policies employed by both the Ottomans and Safavids. The most famous instance of this policy is the deportation of 1604–5 carried out by the Safavid Shah Abbas I 'The Great', which led to the founding of the Armenian colony of New Julfa in Isfahan, but this was only one in a long series. The Ottomans also removed Armenian artisans to their capital, while Abbas founded Armenian colonies in other parts of Iran. The New Julfa colony, however, is remarkable in that it became the centre of a new, commercial diaspora that saw satellite colonies established in many of the major trading cities of the Old World, from the Atlantic seaboard to the Philippines. New Julfa itself became a major centre of Armenian cultural as well as commercial life.

The partition of Armenia between the Ottomans and Safavids was the latest in a long series stretching back to the days of the Roman and Parthian empires but, unlike the many preceding and often short-lived partitions, this one proved to be decisive. The borders established by the Treaties of Amasya and Zuhab became, with minor adjustments, the permanent frontiers between the states that eventually became the Turkey and Iran of today, and also between Turkey and the Russian Empire (and its Soviet and post-Soviet successors).

'Between East and West'

The historic position of Armenia between Byzantium and Iran, with all of the social, political and cultural implications that position involved, especially at the time when Armenia adopted Christianity as the religion of the kingdom, is only one manifestation of a more general thematic thread running through Armenian history from its beginnings to the present day, a thematic thread that could be characterized as the question of Armenia 'between East and West'.

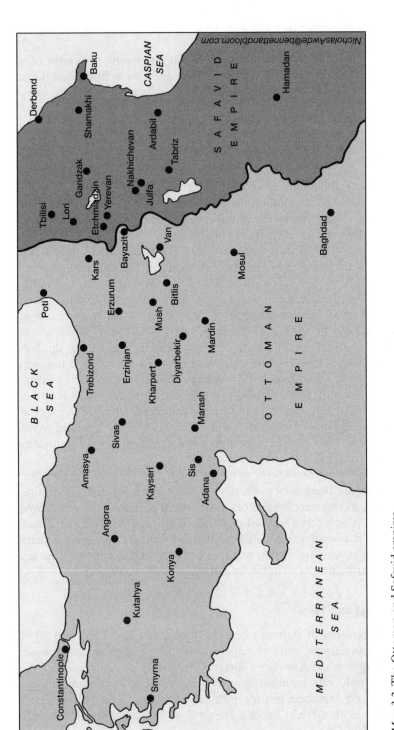

Map 3.2 The Ottoman and Safavid empires

NicholasAwde@bennettandbloom.com

What does 'between' mean in this context? Clearly it designates a function of bridging. But what is Armenia's specificity, if we can make the same statement or pose a similar question for other peoples and cultures, such as Arabs and Russians, or for cities like Bukhara, Istanbul and Isfahan? To say that anything is between two other entities means *first* that there is not a two-dimensional, but a three-dimensional relationship. *Second*, it means that among these three entities a meeting takes place, and for whatever is in between the other two entities the question is not simply one of a meeting with the other two; the crux is in its function as an intermediary. It accepts and transmits influences and conditionings from both. At the same time it may, in its turn, influence and condition them.

One of the most evident challenges for Armenia and the Armenians in their age-old function as a go-between is that they constantly had to adapt their function to assimilate and to transmit for the great diversity of peoples and cultures they encountered during their three-thousand-year history: Achaemenians and Greeks, Romans and Parthians, Byzantines and Sasanians, then Arabs, Seljuks, Franks, Mongols, Ottomans and Safavids, Russians and West Europeans, to mention only the main protagonists coming into contact with Armenia. To those we must add minor political actors such as, for instance, Georgia, and entities that were primarily ethnic or religious-confessional in the period when Armenians came into close contact with them, such as the Caucasian Albanians or the Syrian Christians.

In the dialectic between the Eastern and Western trends of Armenian identity, of the 'Armenian soul', the conversion of the Armenian kingdom to Christianity, at the beginning of the fourth century by the missionary work of St. Gregory the Illuminator (Surb Grigor Lusavorich), marks a turning point, however and in whatever terms it may be interpreted. In seeking to comprehend this momentous event, it is vital to avoid all sorts of unilateral, simplistic and polemical approaches in considering both the nature of the Christian religion and the mechanisms that led King Trdat (Tiridates) the Great to embrace Christianity. As far as Christianity itself is concerned or the conversion to it, it would be an oversimplification to consider these – as is frequently the case – as representing a Western option or a pro-West orientation for Armenia without further distinctions.

It is not possible here to go deeper into a discussion about whether notions like East and West can mean or symbolize anything, from a cultural, anthropological or philosophical viewpoint.[2] Here it is sufficient for our purpose to emphasize the following point: that not only does Christianity in general have deeply Oriental roots, but that Armenian Christianity in particular, especially in its earlier phases, derived a great deal from the Jerusalemite and proto-Syriac Christian traditions, which certainly represent the most prominently and genuinely Oriental faces of early Christianity. The

---

2   For a discussion of the subject, see B.L. Zekiyan, *La dialettica tra valore e contingenza. Dalla fenomenologia religiosa verso una rifondazione assiologica*, Istituto Italiano per gli Studi Filosofici (Naples: Edizioni 'La Città del Sole', 1998).

close relationship of the early Armenian liturgy to the Palestinian and Syriac has by now been definitively established. The same can be affirmed of some areas in early Armenian theology, such as the female function and representation of the Holy Ghost and the conception of the Church as *ukht* (covenant) by Eghishe.

But while all this may be true, one cannot ignore all those elements in the early Armenian Church which derive from a Western source, or demonstrate a pro-West tendency. It would be misleading to neglect the complexity and especially the multidimensional openness of Armenian culture; but it would also be an error to posit those dimensions as irreconcilable opposites. While it is clear that such an approach would lead us into a blind alley, it is much more difficult to precisely express the distinctiveness of the Armenian synthesis of 'Eastern' and 'Western' elements. What does it consist of? And does it make any original contribution to Christian thought, Christian spirituality and more generally to human culture, whether it be of a Western (i.e. Greek) or Hebrew or Arabic origin? This question defies a purely abstract discussion, but may be approached through a consideration of the most noteworthy and symbolic events in Armenian history.

Key moments in Armenian history from the fourth through to the eighteenth century

Conversion to Christianity

As noted above, the conversion to Christianity of the Armenian kingdom marks a turning point not only in Armenian history, but also and especially in the formation and consolidation of the Armenian identity. Among the various dates proposed by modern scholars for this event, from Mikayel Chamchian who indicates the year 304 to Poghos Ananian who puts it at 314 (while 302 is given by Maghakia Ormanian, 279 by Stephanos Malkhasiants, 219 by Nerses Akinian, 294 by Ervand Kasuni, 315 by Hakob Manandian, 305–6 by Marie-Louise Chaumont), Manandian's and Ananian's suggestion of 314/315 is perhaps the most credible, and has been accepted by Gérard Garitte and other authorities on Eastern Christianity. This relatively late date gives rise to concern among many Armenians, even among highly educated people, that it deprives the Armenians of the honour of being the heirs to the first Christian kingdom as of a whole nation in history, but this anxiety is unfounded. As a matter of fact, the earlier Christian kingdom of Edessa was rather a city-kingdom in the wake of the city-states of antiquity; moreover, Emperor Constantine's renowned 313 edict of Milan was in no way a recognition of Christianity as the religion of the Roman Empire – it merely granted freedom to the Christian cult. Moreover, as Archbishop Mesrop Ashjian has suggested, the traditional date of 301 for the establishment of Armenian Christianity retains its symbolic value since it can be considered, more or less, as the beginning of

St. Gregory the Illuminator's preaching in Armenia. Gregory the Illuminator became the first 'Catholicos' (a Greek word meaning 'general') of the Armenian Church, that is to say her primate or first archbishop (earlier sources give a number of equivalent terms: *Hayrapet, episkoposapet, kahanayapet,* etc.), a term which later came to be equated with Patriarch.

The Armenian alphabet

The next date to consider is that of the invention of the Armenian alphabet by St. Mesrop Mashtots with the blessing and collaboration of the Catholicos St. Sahak and King Vramshapuh. Among the various dates advanced (392–8 by Nikoghos Adontz, 392 by H. Manandian, 405 by Artashes Martirosyan, 406 by Ashot Abrahamian, 407 by Manouk Abeghian, 407–8 by Nerses Akinian, 413 by Galoust Ter-Mkrtchian), that of 404, proposed by Hrachia Adjarian, Norayr Bogharian, Poghos Ananian and Artashes Matevosian, seems to me to be the most probable. It is no exaggeration to characterize this invention as the most important and emblematic event in the life of the Armenian people.

The first great consequence of the creation of the alphabet was the profound rooting of the Christian faith in the Armenian spirit. So profound was this that only a few decades later, in 451, at the battle of Avarayr, under the leadership of the commander-in-chief St. Vardan Mamikonian and of the holy priest Ghevond (Leontius) Erets, the whole Armenian people did not hesitate to rise up as one against the Persian attempt to impose by force the Mazdean religion. It also started a strong, polyvalent and fecund process not simply of alphabetization, but also and primarily of acculturation. It gave birth to a great period in Armenian letters, a period whose splendour would accompany the Armenian people as a source of inspiration, light and support all through their history. Third – and this is, I believe, its most original and creative feature, one that explains the depth of impact of the previously mentioned effects – it gave the Armenian people not merely a self-awareness sufficient to distinguish them from the neighbouring nations, but also an 'ideology', in the wider cultural-anthropological sense of a vision of the world, or *Weltanschauung*. Thus the invention of the alphabet opened to the Armenian people a new path, a distinctive way of being, feeling, thinking as a nation, and in the given case as a Christian nation. 'Nation' in the given context has a peculiar meaning, different from the idea of 'nation' as developed in Western modernity in the frame of the nation-state ideology following the Enlightenment and the French Revolution.

Historians and thinkers of outstanding stature, such as Koriun, Eghishe (Elisaeus), Ghazar (Lazarus) of Parpi, Sebeos (Eusebius) and above all Movses (Moses) Khorenatsi, became the great interpreters of that invention, of its meaning and message in the life of the Armenians. Without going into the enduring controversies about the precise chronology of some of these, we can consider the period of the fifth through to the seventh century not only as a golden era in the Armenian culture, but also as the high point in the formation of the Armenian 'ideology', both as a nation and as a Christian nation. It is also in this golden age of Armenian culture that the foundations of other outstanding achievements in architecture, sculpture and miniature painting were laid.

The rejection of the Council of Chalcedon

An important moment in the definition of the Armenian confessional identity is the rejection of the Council of Chalcedon by the Armenian Church. I agree with those authors who locate this crucial decision in the mid-sixth century, and more exactly in the years of the '2nd Council of Dvin'.[3] This Council remains a turning point in the life of the Armenian Church, whatever its precise date. In fact, however the position of the Armenian Church in the first decade of the sixth century may be interpreted, there can be no doubt that consent and harmony with the Byzantine Church, with 'the blessed King of the Romans', was, for the Catholicos Babgen I of Othmus and the bishops gathered with him, a landmark in Church affairs, as clearly appears from Babgen's two surviving letters.[4]

The scene changes completely by the mid-sixth century when the rejection of Chalcedon is accompanied by a strongly anti-Byzantine attitude. Evidently something decisive had occurred in the meanwhile in Armeno-Byzantine relations. That change was the policy of the Emperor Justinian (527–65). It is not that earlier Byzantine emperors were in general very tender with Armenia and the Armenians, but Justinian introduced into a long-standing policy of ambiguity and distance towards the Armenians a radical new factor that threatened Armenia's traditional political structure, i.e. the *nakharar* system. This system went back to immemorial times and formed the backbone of Armenia's political cohesion, even more than its monarchy. Justinian's so-called 'reform' in effect turned that part of Armenia subject to his control into an ordinary Byzantine province. Not even the Sasanian Empire, the toughest Eastern antagonist of Armenia up to that time, had ever taken such a radical measure.

This new situation may not have been the only factor that can explain the Armenian volte-face towards Byzantium in the mid-sixth century, but it certainly helps to make sense of what actually went on. Of course, one cannot ignore the evolution of theological and purely religious and ecclesiological factors in such a grave decision as that of the Armenians to break

3   B.L. Zekiyan, 'Quelques observations critiques sur le "Corpus Elisaeanum"' [Some critical observations on the "Corpus Elisaeanum"], in R.F. Taft, ed., *The Armenian Christian Tradition,* Orientalia Christiana Analecta, 254 (Rome: Pontificio Istituto Orientale, 1997) pp. 71–123.

4   Archbishop Norayr Bogharian, *Book of Letters* (Tiflis, 1901), pp. 40–49; second edn (Jerusalem, 1994), pp. 147–62 (in Armenian).

with Byzantium. Rather than a single prime cause, it seems that a variety of factors, including both political and theological considerations, combined in a particular 'ecclesiastical policy' of rejection of the Council of Chalcedon. Moreover, we must not forget that the Council of Chalcedon was in no way a merely theological council. It took, in addition to its famous canon 28, some vitally important decisions for the ancient Church as far as the hierarchical order of the relationship between the greater sees of antiquity, or the Patriarchates, was concerned. It canonized the primacy of Constantinople over all the other more venerable sees of the East, including Alexandria, Antioch and Jerusalem. Thus Chalcedon upset the oldest common tradition, recognized by the earlier ecumenical councils. This point induced the Pope himself, Leo I the Great, to hesitate before approving the Council as a whole, and in any case canon 28 was never approved by any Pope, although it ended by imposing itself in practice thanks to the imperial splendour of the 'new Rome'. In the context of the Emperor Justinian's centralizing policies, acknowledging Byzantine primacy would have set the Armenian Church, which immediately bordered Byzantium, on an irreversible path towards absorption and assimilation.

As far as theological reasons are concerned, it would be misleading to ignore the complexity, even entanglement, of the theological situation, between Chalcedon and Justinian, on the borders of the empire, in the empire itself, and in all probability in Armenia too. An important point to be made here, with respect to theology, is that, while the Armenians after their final anti-Chalcedonian decision never agreed to discuss or negotiate with the Nestorians, they did so more than once with Byzantium. The reason was that they did not simply equate Chalcedon with Nestorianism, but they considered it as a temptation for, or an inclination to, Nestorianism. This emerges clearly later in the twelfth century during the negotiations for union between Catholicos St. Nerses IV Shnorhali and Emperor Manuel I Comnenus. St. Nerses explained in one of his letters that 'we were mentally ill for the scandal, as if you were partially inclined to Nestorius' opinion'.[5]

Arab dominion, and the Bagratuni kingdom

Important though they are, I will only briefly discuss two aspects from the subsequent centuries. The first relates to the period of Arab dominion (from around the mid-seventh to the eighth centuries), when the Arabs used the name 'Arminîya' for the whole of their large Caucasian administrative province, which included the greater part of historic Armenia, as well as Eastern Georgia and Caucasian Albania. This denomination is indicative of the importance of Armenia in the wider Caucasian area in this period.

---

5 '*Aegroti mente eramus ob scandalum, quasi vos ex parte ad Nestorii opinionem inclinati fuissetis*', S. Nersetis Clajensis, *Opera* [Works of St. Nerses of Kla], transl. by Josephus Cappelleti, vol. I (Venice, 1833), p. 232.

This may be taken as an example of the space occupied by Armenia in the mental maps of Armenians and others, a space that in any given period has often extended beyond the boundaries of the contemporary administrative-territorial entity 'Armenia'.

The second point relates to the Bagratuni period (804–1180) and especially to the Bagratuni kingdom (885–1045) in Northern Armenia, whose capital Ani, the legendary city of 'one thousand and one churches', is today in Turkey on the frontier with Armenia. As far as the Bagratuni kingdom is concerned, I want to stress the particular strain of political wisdom manifested by this dynasty. Though this kind of political wisdom also has many other manifestations throughout Armenian history, it is especially evident during the delicate period of Arab dominion and the subsequent reconstruction of a new national kingdom. The Bagratunis succeeded in following a policy of balance between the Arabs and Byzantium, at least until Byzantine megalomania, taking advantage of the weakening of the Arab Caliphate, put an end to the Armenian kingdom, but only by betrayal. The Bagratunis never formally claimed absolute independence, since this would have made the Caliphs suspect that they had ambitions to break with them completely. Evidence of this prudence can be found in the fact that the Bagratunis, like their contemporaries the Artzruni dynasty in Southern Armenia, did not leave any coinage of their own (or at least no such coinage has reached us). Arabic and Byzantine coins circulated in Armenia throughout the period.

The Cilician age

A similar wisdom is discernible in two of the greatest kings of the Cilician era in Armenian history (1080–1441 – the year in which the Catolicosate of all Armenians was transferred back to its original see of Vaghar-shapat/Etchmiadzin): Levon I the Magnificent (1198–1219, previously titled Levon II as a prince since 1187) and Hetum I (1226–69). Among the many achievements of the Cilician period, the most enduring are undoubtedly those of its exceptional miniature painters and above all of its two outstanding religious and literary figures, St. Nerses Shnorhali (see above) and Nerses of Lambron, whose ecumenism goes far beyond the usual limits of medieval Christianity, making them unique in Christian history. The fourteenth century put the seal on the displacement of the reference axis for the self-image of the Armenian Church from Byzantium to Rome. Until the end of the twelfth century the main referents for the consciousness of a distinct Armenian Church identity, in the midst of many vicissitudes through the centuries, and in the multiple dimensions of doctrinal orthodoxy as well as of liturgical and canonical specificity, had been Byzantine Orthodoxy and, especially, Byzantine Chalcedonism. After a transition period during the thirteenth century, from the fourteenth century onwards the main, often the sole, referent would be the Roman Church.

The Cilician age, especially the fourteenth century, is thus a decisive period for the later history of the Armenian Church and, especially, for the development of the various tendencies in the formation of Armenian ecclesiology. Not in the sense that those tendencies came to fruition during the Cilician period – that happened only much later – but in the sense that the premises which led to successive developments were already clearly delineated in this age.

The Armenian way to modernity

As I have tried to demonstrate in a recent work, modernity enters into Armenian society at a very early stage of its own development.[6] We can define as follows the main phases of Armenian modernity: *a)* an *initial period of gestation* that can be dated from the second decade of the sixteenth century to the 1620s, that is from the years of the first printed books in Armenian to the accession to the See of Etchmiadzin of Catholicos Movses I of Tathew (1628–33); *b)* the *great blossoming of Armenian capitalism*, that is from the 1630s to the end of that century, in other words until the symbolic date of the foundation in 1700 of the Mekhitarist Congregation in Constantinople (Konstantaniyya), the capital of the Ottoman Empire and, to some extent, already the 'capital' of the Armenian 'millet' (the term used for the Armenian community under Ottoman rule), since the Armenian Patriarch of the imperial city had a larger number of direct subjects under both his spiritual and his civil jurisdiction than the Catholicos himself at Etchmiadzin. The end date of this period is, arguably, too early, since Armenian capitalism continued to flourish for some fifty years more until the mid-eighteenth century, when its gradual decline started; *c)* the *humanistic period* stretching from the foundation of the Mekhitarist Order to nearly 1840, generally better known as the period of 'Rebirth' (*Veratznund*). This long period of about one-and-a-half centuries can be subdivided into various epochs which form two main ages of nearly seven decades each: (i) the first seven decades (1700–70) are predominantly characterized by efforts to shed light on and revitalize the religious and cultural heritage of the past; (ii) the following decades, even though they continue to cultivate the same interest in the past, are also increasingly concerned by the new intellectual atmosphere, the new ideals and the new vision of the world fermenting in Europe. This is, in fact, the period when the first expressions of modern political thought among Armenians can be identified, political thought that shares in the currents of the ongoing political processes and ideas in Europe and the New World. These first attempts took place, as we shall see, in India. Hence, in my

---

6   B.L. Zekiyan, *The Armenian Way to Modernity: Armenian Identity between Tradition and Innovation, Specificity and Universality*, Eurasiatica, 49 (Venice, 1998).

opinion, it is in the Armenian colony of India in the last three decades of the eighteenth century, under a strong British influence, that we have to look for the first expressions of Enlightenment thought, in the proper sense of the term, among Armenians; *d)* the *secularization period* from around the 1840s to the fatal date of 1915 (see chapter 5), better known as the age of 'Awakening' (*Zartonk*), which will be treated in detail in the next chapter.

Emerging features of Armenian thought and world view

Being 'on the frontier' and the vocation to martyrdom

Two basic features of Armenian Christianity help explain its distinctive development over the centuries: the first is its being a Church of the 'frontier', the second its vocation to martyrdom, both these characteristics being closely interconnected. The Armenian Church is a church of the frontier, not only because of her geographical and geopolitical situation, but also, and primarily, on account of her vital milieu. The Armenian Church lived in continuous, immediate and multifarious contact with a very large range of peoples, cultures, states and religions, which she encountered on her way through the centuries and into the farthest corners of the world to which various historical vicissitudes brought her congregation. As to martyrdom, it was applied in real life in the fullest sense of the term, as a testimony of word and of blood, and it acted both as a challenge to and as a result of that 'being on the frontier'. This equipped the Armenians with that keen sense of 'pragma' – not to be confounded with 'pragmatism' at all – of concreteness, of flexibility, even of compromise in dealing with their political, social and cultural environment.

The 'ancestral and native law'

The battle of Avarayr of 451 offers an eloquent paradigm of this: in front of the Sasanian King of Kings the Armenians declared themselves ready to continue to acknowledge Persian sovereignty and to serve the King, but only on condition that they be left free in their Christian worship. Christian worship is for them their identity, their dignity, their honour and their reason of life as a people, as a nation. General Vardan Mamikonean said on the night of the brink of war: 'He who thought that Christian faith was for us like clothes, will he now realize that he will not be able to remove it from us, like the colour of our skin' (Eghishe, chapter 5). The Armenians condensed this overarching conception of identity into a precise formula: 'our ancestral and native law', meaning in this context the basic principles and vision of the world regulating the moral existence and ethical behaviour of a human community. After thirty years of almost guerrilla resistance, in 485 the Armenians augmented, or rather emphasized in a new light, some further implications of that 'ancestral law' as equally inevitable, unbreakable. The *first* of these effectively reiterates the earlier declaration in a more juridical, legally clearer form: no one was to be forced to change religion. The *second* iterated that people were not to be judged on the basis of their social condition, but rather according to their actions; the *third* stated that no action based merely on hearsay was to be taken by the authorities against anyone.

Such a distinctive conception of 'national' identity – not, as we have already hinted, in the modern Western sense of the word 'nation' as linked to the nation-state – developed and maintained by Armenians over the centuries did not entail a confusion or a simplistic identification of the various factors and facets fusing to build that identity. An anthropologically deep and wide vision of what being a nation, and specifically a Christian nation, means led the Armenians to resolve this question in a way that is highly original in the framework of Mediterranean culture and gave the Armenians the secret of their determination and survival all through their troubled and tragic history. After a long period of gestation in the pre-Christian era, the man who laid the foundations of what I called above the 'Armenian ideology', which gave the Armenians a qualitatively new self-awareness, was Mesrop Mashtots with his great invention of the alphabet. Movses Khorenatsi, honoured as the 'father of Armenian historiography', has been its most ingenious interpreter. I shall try to sum up here the essence of this vision.

The 'incarnation of Christian faith' and a new vision of ethno-cultural identity

Mesrop's invention finds a congruent historical context in the fourth-century Christian Syriac area, where a particular interest blossoms in the use of the vernacular language in liturgy with a progressive consciousness of the 'sacred' character of the language as an instrument to bless and praise God. We can consider that as an initial theology of language, and at the same time as the starting point of Mesrop's own religious-national itinerary towards his invention and the full exploitation of its implications. Ethnic culture – one of whose main expressions is language – is seen in this context as the means of transposition and translation of Christian faith into human experience, to such an extent as to become a distinct and original incarnation of the same faith. This effort to achieve a global approach to religious faith as not disembodied from the ethno-cultural reality of a particular community explains the concern of Mesrop to teach and diffuse his alphabet also among the Armenians subject to the Byzantine Empire, whose knowledge of the Greek language spared them all the inconvenience arising from the need to translate the Scriptures and the liturgy from Greek or Syriac into Armenian, as happened in non-Byzantine Armenia.

Besides this new theological vision of ethno-cultural identity and the consequent 'incarnation' in it of the Christian faith, Mesrop's invention implied at once a profoundly new vision of ethnic/national identity even in its immanent and earthly dimensions. The ancestral tradition of the Armenians considers the alphabet – composed originally of thirty-six letters, though in the late Middle Age two additional letters were added – as the 'soldiers' or the 'bastion' of Armenian self-defence against assimilation or extinction, in other words as one of the main secrets of Armenian survival, which itself has something of a miraculous character. But to ascribe this 'miracle' only to the fact that in giving the alphabet Mesrop gave the Armenians some very clear sign or instrument to distinguish themselves from the neighbouring peoples – as is sometimes suggested – would be quite reductive and would not exhaust, I think, the deeper meaning and stronger influence of the alphabet's function in the life of the Armenian people. At a more profound level Mesrop invented a new vision of ethnic/national identity by detaching it from its connection with political power and displacing it radically on to a new plane, that of culture. Khorenatsi even goes so far as to introduce Mesrop in his history with the following words: 'Seeing that the Kingdom of Armenians had come to an end ... Mesrop ... '.[7] This certainly may be seen as an interpretation with the benefit of hindsight – while the 387 AD division of the Armenian kingdom between Byzantines and Sasanians may be said to have marked its effective demise, its actual extinction in Eastern Armenia occurred only in 428 with the deposition of the last Arshakuni king, Artashes IV – but is nevertheless a perceptive reading of events in that Mesrop's invention with all its 'ideological' implications supposed, no doubt, some ingenious and far-reaching intuition about the destiny of the Armenian people.

The leading idea in Mesrop's invention, its nerve centre, from an ethnocultural viewpoint, is the keen self-awareness that he inspired in the Armenian people, supported by a new and organic vision of language, culture, ethnic identity and related questions. The lack of such a developed 'national ideology' in this early Middle Age, between the fifth and seventh centuries, or in simpler terms the absence of a Mesrop Mashtots figure, may explain how and why the Syriac and Coptic populations, who already possessed a developed literary heritage, allowed themselves to be culturally arabized to a very large extent. It may also explain why the subsequent history of the two other Caucasian cultures – the Georgian and the Albanian – to develop their own alphabet, almost simultaneously with the Armenian in the first half of the fifth century, was so different from that of the Armenians. Georgian culture experienced its first great literary fluorescence only in the early seventh century, while Albanian culture never reached such an achievement, and indeed left behind a very sparse written legacy. The fact that, according to the Armenian tradition, Mesrop was also responsible for the formation of the Georgian and Caucasian Albanian

---

7   *Patmutiwn Hayots* [History of the Armenians], Book 3, para. 47.

alphabets is indicative of the role ascribed to him in establishing Armenian cultural ascendancy. While it will be difficult, if not impossible, to establish the veracity or otherwise of this tradition on the basis of philology and textual criticism, it is nevertheless difficult to understand and contextualize the fourth and fifth-century developments in Caucasian Christian history without recognizing Armenia's role as a model or pattern.

Movses Khorenatsi was, as noted above, the keenest and deepest interpreter of Mesrop's idea and ideals. He elaborated them, drawing on the Greek and Jewish traditions, into an original synthesis. Among many key ideas, borrowed from ancient Greece, that of *politeia* assumes a peculiar importance in his synthesis. From Jewish thought he borrowed the idea of *ethnos*, 'nation', but at the same time he detached it from its strictly religious content. In fact, he had to face the thorny problem of how to put together within the same concept of nation the old pre-Christian, pagan ancestors of the Armenians and their actual Christian reality. He resolved the problem by formulating an idea of nation whose unity is based mainly on its language, its culture, its common feelings and values, common struggles and hopes. I think it would not be misleading or exaggerated to say that, in the context of Mediterranean culture, Khorenatsi is the first to propose a secular concept of the nation, if we do not understand secular to denote 'ignoring religion', much less 'rejecting religion'.

Armenian ecumenicity

Being a Church with a congregation of relatively small demographic proportions, and being in quite frequent contact with greater Christian Churches, it was difficult for the Armenian Church, because of her very position, to pretend dominion over other Churches or to propose herself or her traditions as the only compatible ones with Christian doctrine. That doesn't mean of course that no Armenian apologist was struck by such an idea or temptation. It rather means that this was not the dominant or prevalent tendency in the Armenian Church. Apart from this general attitude, the Armenian Church also gave birth to some figures of an extraordinary ecumenical stature, whom we can consider quite rightly as forerunners of modern ecumenical theology at its very best. These two figures are the above-mentioned St. Nerses Shnorhali and St. Nerses of Lambron. It can be affirmed without exaggeration or hesitation that their thought offers a most valuable 'road map' for any search for Christian unity. Here I can but sketch very briefly the substance of that thought: *a)* that Christian unity is a divine goal, and that prayer is the basic means to reach it; *b)* that the only necessary thing for unity is communion in faith and charity. All differences of rites, traditions, canons are secondary. The same is true also as far as differences in the formulation of faith are concerned when they are compatible with a right interpretation; *c)* that a reciprocal predisposition to condescension will help to avoid an impasse in negotiations; *d)* that it is very important that both sides take great care not to create new lacerations within their own Churches while seeking for union; *e)* hence also that a very important factor to prepare for unity is to restore human psychology. The sad heritage of the past needs to be overcome by a delicate, patient, large-minded and far-seeing educational strategy; *f)* that it is very important that neither one of the partners tries to impose anything during the negotiations, because of its strength or splendour or whatever else in which it believes itself to be superior. Negotiations must offer the example of a true dialogue; *g)* that since Christian unity is a divine cause, it cannot have any other moti-vation than Christian charity, sustained by a sincere inner conviction. Any human motivation not rooted in the Gospel, such as political or other factors, represents a betrayal of faith and conscience.

Armenian modernity and Armenian Enlightenment

As suggested above, modernity in general as well as the European Enlightenment movement in particular entered into Armenian society at a very early stage of their own development. In any case, relative to its Western prototype Armenian modernity appears, on social and especially cultural grounds, to have had a slower rhythm of evolution and been rather limited in its early achievements. This limitation concerns above all the various fields in which modernity appears, and much less the quality of the specific phenomena. As to the slower rhythm of the Armenian course, we can, for instance, point to the relative delay of Armenian irredentism in comparison with similar movements in Europe, a delay which pushed the Armenian Question into a rather unfavourable historical context and arguably played a role in its unhappy consequences. A field, however, in which Armenians knew no limitations, but were even world leaders, was international trade and economics during the seventeenth century, a devel-opment which left noteworthy traces in subsequent periods.

Considering the main differences between the Armenian Enlightenment movement and its models, the different attitudes towards religion and the secularization process should be pointed out. It is not possible to identify deism or systematic anticlericalism as general trends of the Armenian Enlightenment. As a matter of fact, when Armenians are in close contact with Europe, they assimilate and espouse many of its achievements, they are enthusiasts for many of the novelties inspired by European modernity and the Enlightenment, but generally speaking they do not accept without crit-ical approval all the ideas and tendencies which may be involved in those movements, nor does their up-do-date interest lead to a slavish imitation of foreign models. On the contrary, there is often a happy marriage between Western forms, patterns, techniques, poetics, theories on the one hand, and a uniquely Armenian sensitivity on the other. European models are assimi-lated, so that we can even speak of an 'armenization' process of those models. Just as in the past, Armenians did not copy their models, they integrated and harmonized them in new and often brilliant syntheses. The printing press, capital power, mass and female emancipation, and secularization developed in the Armenian milieu without excessive conflicts or traumas. In simpler words, they could, for instance, secularize without a mass rejection of religious faith; they could pursue women's emancipation without the radical rejection of femininity, family and motherhood seen in some Western contexts. Their achievements were mostly natural, spontaneous passages, in line with the main trends of Armenian consciousness and culture as these had developed over the centuries in a continuous effort and tension towards that which was thought to be better or best, or simply to be different or new. These achievements were accomplished without any fear or complex about facing the new, but also by controlling the modern urge with a secular sense of fidelity to an ancestral heritage.

The Armenian diaspora

The problems posed to Armenian self-consciousness by its close contact with Western culture often implied and still imply today, apart from the more general question of the dialectics between change and continuity, innovation and identity, a more particular question linked directly with Armenian history. In fact, Armenian culture, art and forms of life have developed over the centuries not only in Armenia itself, but also in foreign lands. This peculiar situation shows, no doubt, in a clearer light the dialectics of identity and alienation that run through the whole cultural history of the Armenian people both in the homeland and in the diaspora. Those Armenians dispersed all over the world succeeded, even in the most difficult periods when their country was dominated by alien forces, in maintaining in their diasporan situation a vital cultural life, marked by a clear national character. This they were able to do by virtue of a singular understanding of their national identity, rooted in their 'ancestral' ideology, and of its relationship with the surrounding and dominating cultures. We can define this self-consciousness, from a philosophical point of view, as a 'multidimensional identity', and its relationship to the environment as a 'differentiated integration'. The king of the Armenian troubadour tradition, Sayat-Nova, and one of his most talented admirers in our time, Sergei Parajanov, can be regarded as models of this 'cosmopolitan' trend in Armenian culture in a happy synthesis with its Armenian stock. Such a tradition goes back to the significant artistic achievements of the Middle Ages and continues up to our time with a long series of artists, writers, merchants, people acting in every field of life, some of whom were of remarkable international importance, such as the Shehrimanian family of merchants in Italy, the first generation of the Balian family of architects in the Ottoman Empire, the painter Bogdan Sultanov in Russia, just to mention a few of those Armenians whose contribution had by the end of the eighteenth century been recognized in their non-Armenian host societies.

This has been the great challenge of the Armenian diaspora both in the past and today. It offers a model of dialectics between identity and transformation, a pattern of both a national and a cosmopolitan culture, whose roots are in the Armenian tradition of the homeland but which expresses itself within the milieu of a range of different host societies and cultures. It offers at the same time a message of great topical interest to peoples and societies everywhere concerned with problems of migration.

Inner conflicts and 'Armenian Messianism'

It can be argued that there have been only two grave inner conflicts within Armenian society to arise in connection with the process of modernization, although they are in different relationships with it. The first of these had at first an essentially religious nature, especially during the centuries-long formation process of the Armenian Catholic community, and the second had a more political-ideological nature. But the deeper reasons for the dynamics generating these conflicts were not precisely in the dialectics between modernity and tradition, change and continuity, but rather in a certain conception of identity, or rather in distortions or misinterpretations of identity on both sides, although in different ways.

Notwithstanding their high achievements in assimilating many positive lessons of Western modernity and Enlightenment, Armenians did not in one point understand the West at all. Armenians could not liberate themselves from a utopianism *vis-à-vis* Europe. I have called this utopia, in earlier works, 'Armenian Messianism' since it took the form of an almost 'Messianic' hope in a salvation that would come from the West. Armenians hoped against hope that 'Christian' Europe would save them or would, at least, not allow them to perish. They failed to comprehend that certainly since the Renaissance, but probably even before, 'Christian Europe' no longer existed in the field of politics. The Armenians, indeed, paid dearly for this misinterpretation of what could be expected from Europe. This failure of understanding belongs, however, to the developments of the nineteenth century, since it is evident that until at least the end of the eighteenth century Armenians maintained a more or less realistic understanding of their relationship with Europe. No doubt hope in Europe existed almost all the time, notwithstanding the tragic deceptions caused by the Crusaders. Otherwise the travel to Rome and to the European courts of the aged Catholicos of Etchmiadzin, Hakob IV of Jugha (Julfa) (1655–80), then in his eighties, travel during which he died in Constantinople, as well as the whole eighteenth century activity of Israyel Ori, and many similar phenomena, would remain without any reasonable explanation. But there was a big difference between their attitudes and those that would prevail in the second half of the next century. Up to this time no real action that might arouse suspicion in the dominant powers was undertaken, not even suggested, especially by the higher authorities of the Church, until they had some real basis for their hope, some seriously reliable engagement on behalf of their interlocutors. Things changed radically in the course of the nineteenth century. But the very survival of the Armenian people, after such an absolute catastrophe as the Genocide which closed the most fruitful period of Armenian modernity in terms of intellectual and social accomplishments, can be comprehended only with reference to the singular marriage in Armenian culture between modernity and tradition, change and identity, universality and specificity.

Conclusion

This survey of the most important moments and salient cultural characteristics of a long historical period of nearly fifteen centuries has suggested that this period played a basic, central role in forging Armenian identity, both in the sense of its 'ideological' grounding, as well as in developing its great capacity of adaptation, of remaining itself while responding to the numerous and diverse challenges of the Middle Ages and modernity. I am convinced that, however catastrophic the break caused by the Genocide may have been, the basic trends of Armenian identity established in the period considered in this chapter continued to inspire and provide an orientation for the post-Genocide generations both in the diaspora and in the reborn homeland.

Modernity has often been conceived as a destiny of tragedy. Armenians experienced this destiny to the full. But the Armenian adventure for survival contains something epic as well as tragic. Thus the most expressive creation of the Armenian soul, the masterpiece of Armenian literature, the *Book of Lamentation* of Saint Gregory of Narek (*circa* 951–1010), is both a tragedy and an epic. The last triumph in the work belongs to Hope, as it does also in the popular epic of David of Sasun. Taking root in pre-Christian ages and traditions, this work was elaborated and orally transmitted by innumerable generations down through the centuries considered in this chapter. The last hero of the poem, Mher the Younger, is swallowed up by a rock at the end of all his adventures. But twice a year, on the feast days of the Ascension and the Transfiguration, the rock opens and Mher comes out for a while before turning back again into the rock. He will not get out forever until the Earth will be renewed and a pure world will see the light. Tragic as its destiny has been, the story of Mher is a fitting parable for the continuing survival struggle of the Armenian people.

Bibliography

Nerses Shnorhali (St.), *General Epistle*, translation and introduction by Fr A. Aljalian (New Rochelle: St. Nersess Armenian Seminary Press, 1996).

Nersoyan, T., *Armenian Church Historical Studies: Matters of Doctrine and Administration*, ed. with an introduction by Revd N.V. Nersessian (New York: Caucasus World, 1996).

Sanjian, A.K., *The Armenian Communities in Syria under Ottoman Dominion* (Cambridge: Harvard University Press, 1965).

Sarkissian, K., *A Brief Introduction to Armenian Christian Literature* (London: The Faith Press,1960).

—— *The Council of Chalcedon and the Armenian Church*, second edn (New York: The Armenian Church Prelacy, 1972, first edn 1965).

Thomson, R.W., 'The Influence of Their Environment on the Armenians in Exile in the Eleventh Century', in *Thirteenth International Congress of Byzantine Studies – Oxford 1966. Supplementary Papers, Summaries* (Oxford: R. Mac Lehose & Co. Ltd. – The University Press Glasgow, 1966), pp. 138–49.

—— 'The Maccabees in Early Armenian Historiography', *Journal of Theological Studies*, n.s., vol. XXVI, 1975, part 2, pp. 329–41.

—— 'Architectural Symbolism in Classical Armenian Literature', *Journal of Theological Studies*, n.s., vol. XXX, 1979, part 1, pp. 102–14.

Zekiyan, B.L., *The Armenian Way to Modernity: Armenian Identity between Tradition and Innovation, Specificity and Universality*, Eurasiatica, 49 (Venice, 1998).

4 Into the modern age, 1800–1913

Aram Arkun

The nineteenth century, together with the early twentieth, formed a period of rapid and intense change for the Armenian people. Wars created new borders that divided up the ancient Armenian homeland, and migrations and massacres led to massive demographic changes. Changes in world trade, industrialization, state modernization, imperialism and the influence of ideas from the West led not only to changes in Armenian society and socio-economic status, but to a new formulation of the Armenian identity. Tsarist oppressions and Ottoman massacres at the end of the nineteenth century gave way to a series of revolutionary movements, and Armenians gained hope for the achievement of political liberty and security within radically transformed imperial societies. However, within a few years each of these movements was either repressed or changed in nature, with Armenians suffering persecution and even massacre in the process. More and more aware of their common national identity, and alienated from their imperial rulers despite distinct improvements in social status over the preceding century, by 1913 Armenians of the Ottoman, Persian and Russian empires ended up focusing on Ottoman Armenia. Despite past disappointments they saw little alternative but to seek Russian and European intervention to secure reforms for the Ottoman Armenians.

Wars: shifting borders and populations

The southward advance of the Russian Empire into the Caucasus at the expense of the Ottoman and Persian empires was the first major border change in the region since the seventeenth century. In turn, it led to mass transfers of population. By 1801 the Armenians living in Georgia had come under Russian rule. The territory thus acquired included part of the historical Armeno-Georgian marchlands, such as Lori, Pambak, Borchalu and Shamshadin districts. The Russo-Persian wars of 1804–13 and 1826–8 were concluded by the treaties of Golestan in 1813 and Torkmanchai in 1828. They gave Russia the historically Armenian territories of Karabagh and Zangezur, and Yerevan and Nakhichevan, respectively. The Russo-Turkish wars of 1806–12 and 1828–9 ending in the Treaties of Bucharest (1812) and

Adrianople (1829) led to Russian control of Akhalkalak (Akhalkalaki) and Akhaltskha (Akhaltsikhe). If the Crimean War of 1853–6 did not lead to any new transfers of territory, it did take place in part on historically Armenian territory. The Russo-Turkish war of 1877–8, however, gave Kars and Ardahan, (as well as Batumi) to the Russians.

An Ottoman–Persian war in 1820–2 merely added extra turmoil and destruction without any lasting changes being stipulated in the peace treaty of Erzerum of 1823. Ottoman–Persian border disputes continued on a small scale throughout the century, including over some historically Armenian districts like Kotur.

During each of the wars involving Russia, Armenians suffered as a result of pillaging and attacks by irregulars opposing the new northern power. Christian Armenians were often accused of sympathy for the Christian Russians, and, though in fact many preferred Ottoman or Persian rule, a massive wave of Armenians abandoned their homes and fled to Russian-controlled territory. As many as 45,000 from Persia and 100,000 from the Ottoman Empire left for Russian-controlled territory after the end of the 1826–8 Russo-Persian and 1828–9 Russo-Ottoman wars. Though immigration of Armenians was on a smaller scale after the Crimean War (1854–6), another twenty-five thousand left for the Russian Caucasus as a result of the Russo-Turkish war of 1877–8. As a result, by the end of the nineteenth century the province of Yerevan and several other areas had regained an Armenian majority for the first time in several hundred years. It should be noted that Armenians had already been a majority in some areas such as mountainous Karabagh before these wars. The new Armenian majorities would form the nucleus in the twentieth century of an independent Armenian state.

Naturally, the composition of the population in the remaining Ottoman and Persian Armenian districts also changed greatly. Though a substantial number of Muslims remained in the new Russian-controlled areas, such as the southern part of Yerevan province, many others emigrated. Since vast expanses of Persian and Ottoman territory were largely denuded of their Armenian population, many were resettled in these areas. Persian Azerbaijan received many Turkic immigrants from the Caucasus in areas formerly populated by Armenians. Later in the century small numbers of Armenians also emigrated to Persian Azerbaijan, fleeing the Ottoman Empire as a result of the Russo-Turkish war of 1877–8 and the massacres of the 1890s.

Muslims from the Russian Empire emigrated to the Ottoman Empire in large numbers after the wars in the mid- and late nineteenth centuries. Between 1854 and 1860 approximately 176,700 Nogai and Kuban Tatars settled in central and southern Anatolia, and between 1858 and 1866 roughly 470,000 Circassians are estimated to have migrated to various parts of the Ottoman Empire, including Armenian-populated areas. According to one Turkish scholar, between 1862 and 1870 as many as two million

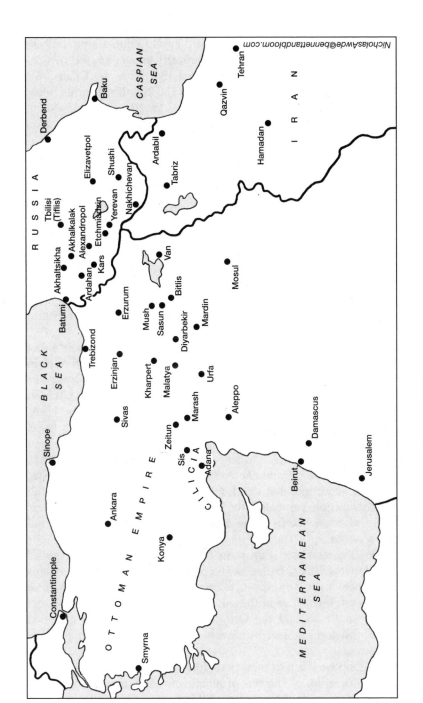

Map 4.1 Iran and the Russian and Ottoman empires *circa* 1880

Muslims left the Russian Caucasus for the Ottoman Empire. The 1877–8 Russo-Turkish war provided another stimulus to Muslim emigration, with at least 75,000 leaving Kars province alone for the Ottoman Empire. These voluntary and forced migrations had a significant impact on the demography of the region and on inter-communal dynamics. In Cilicia, for example, in addition to the Nogai Tatars from the North Caucasus, there was settlement of Muslims from Egypt, Crete, the Balkans and North Africa, mostly working as agricultural labourers in the burgeoning cotton production.

The settlements of Muslim immigrants in traditionally Armenian areas of the Ottoman Empire often worsened Muslim–Armenian relations, as the newcomers were embittered against Christians. Furthermore, they were not provided with sufficient resources by the Ottoman state, so that many ended up living a rather lawless life. Meanwhile, throughout the nineteenth century, Kurdish tribes moved north into traditionally Armenian-populated areas in order to fill a vacuum, as well as due to encouragement by the Ottoman government. By the latter part of the century the Ottoman government seems to have been deliberately attempting both to dilute centres of Armenian population and to pit various nationalities like the Kurds and Circassians against the Armenians in order to maintain control over distant border regions.

The majority of Armenians living in all three empires were villagers, but where Armenians lived outside their traditional homeland, it tended to be in the big cities. Throughout the century migration increased to cities like Constantinople (Istanbul), Smyrna, Tiflis, Batum, Baku, Tabriz and Tehran in the Middle East, and eventually further afield to Europe and the USA. Improved roads, security, communications and transport all made travel easier. Oppressive feudal landowners and, in the Ottoman Empire and Persia, harassment by nomadic tribes encouraged villagers to emigrate. Massacres in the Ottoman Empire accelerated the process. In the Caucasus, Yerevan and Alexandropol remained relative backwaters, lagging in all aspects of urbanization compared to Tiflis and Baku. The former areas benefited only relatively late from the development of the Russian imperial transportation system.

In all three empires cheap European textiles and manufactured goods weakened or destroyed local crafts, in the production of which Armenians played a prominent role. However, new opportunities opened up for those willing to act as intermediaries in the sale of European goods or translators for Europeans. In Persia and the Ottoman Empire, Armenians obtained special trade privileges through patents of protection from various European powers.

Attempts to impose Western models of freehold land ownership initially encouraged the migration of villagers of all religions and nationalities. Often those who had been tax farmers or leaseholders were given full ownership rights. In all three empires, the rich and powerful, including the Muslim elite, were better able to take advantage of the new land registration laws than the peasants, who for the most part were turned into mere tenants. This took place first in the Caucasus after the Russian conquest, with a form of Russian serfdom being created. Though the 1870 land reform freed the one-third of peasants living on the lands of landlords, it did not aid the majority of peasants, who worked state-owned lands. Only in 1912 were peasants allowed to begin redeeming their lands through payments over a fifty-six year period. A shortage of land was created in the Caucasus, while the demand for crops like cotton required greater concentrations of wealth for cultivation. In the Ottoman Empire an 1858 law and its 1867 amendment were important steps towards the creation of a capitalist economy. While landowners remained overwhelmingly Muslim, Armenians began to purchase land. In Persia similar developments in land tenure occurred only in the twentieth century.

Ottoman, Persian and Russian reforms

All three empires, Ottoman, Persian and Russian, faced major political and economic challenges from Western European states in the nineteenth century. In response, they all embarked on attempts to increase the power of the central government and state over its territories and population. Political and economic reforms were carried out at times as a result of, and at times in spite of, Western pressure. These reforms greatly affected the social status of the Armenians. First, these governments attempted to regain control over and implement regular empire-wide procedures and institutions in the territories in which Armenians lived. Then, on paper at least, as part of their reforms in the Ottoman and Persian case but simply as a result of the dominant Christian ideology in Russian society, they partially 'emancipated' the Armenians and some other non-Muslims in the sense that Napoleon emancipated the Jews: by removing various barriers to their equal participation in the dominant society. Initially, both the Ottoman and Persian empires used the Armenians to support and implement some of their general reform efforts, while the Russian conquest of the Caucasus led to major social changes there as the ruling Muslim elites were gradually removed from their positions and Armenians entered into state and military service.

Much of the Ottoman Empire, including the Armenian-populated provinces in Anatolia and Cilicia, was under the control of local feudal lords at the beginning of the nineteenth century. In fear of foreign intervention and consequent loss of territory and revenue, Sultan Mahmud II and his successor, Abdulmejid, strove to bring these areas back under the control of the central government through a series of military campaigns and new administrative measures. Many regions in the East were under Kurdish control, and the Ottoman central government encouraged Armenian support for their campaigns, promising an end to local violence and various obstacles to commerce. The Armenian Patriarchate of Constantinople issued appeals for Armenian assistance to the government, and indeed some Armenians served in the Ottoman armies as guides and volunteers. Others fought in the ranks of the Kurdish lords, but the Kurds in general were left mistrusting their former serfs. Central government control had been restored in much of the East by the 1850s, and in Cilicia by the 1860s. The Armenians began applying to Ottoman officials and courts for justice in cases of land usurpation, attacks, kidnapping and unlawful taxes.

In Persia the new Qajar dynasty worked to assert its control over the Iranian provinces, and, disturbed by the mass emigration of Armenians after the Russo-Persian wars, reassured them by granting various privileges to Armenian merchants and clergy. Armenians, under royal patronage, played important roles both as Muslim converts and as Christians in the Iranian government and army. Since only a small sliver of historical Armenia remained under Persian rule, Armenians could no longer pose a serious threat to the government in any way. On the contrary, their language skills and Western orientation were seen as useful in the modernization programmes of the government.

In the Russian territories the Tsarist government alternated between periods of rigid central control with Russification, and somewhat more liberal periods permitting local participation in administration and more gradual change. Armenians were soon disappointed with Russian rule, as the various newly conquered territories and their Armenian populations were divided administratively into separate provinces. Furthermore, many Muslim officials remained in power through the first half of the nineteenth century. This gradually changed, and Persian laws and administrative procedures were supplanted by Russian ones. In the 1860s and 1870s a uniform Russian judicial system and Russian legal procedures were introduced. The municipal law of 1870 granted urban communities the right to self-government, imposed property qualifications and limited non-Christian participation. This law, which began to be implemented in Transcaucasia (the South Caucasus) after a considerable delay, was favourable for the participation of rich Armenians in city governments such as those of Tiflis (Tbilisi), Yerevan, Batum (Batumi) and Baku. Yet by the end of the century the fact that barely one-third of the total Transcaucasian Armenian population lived in Yerevan province created growing dissatisfaction among Armenians.

More significant for the Armenians was the limited secularization taking place in the Muslim societies of the Ottoman and Persian empires, as well as the shift to a Christian-dominated Russian culture in newly annexed Transcaucasia. In the medieval Muslim empires of the Middle East, Christians and Jews were generally tolerated and, in exchange for a sort of tribute, the poll tax, they were protected from persecution and interference. Unlike Muslim subjects, however, they were required to remain unarmed and thus comparatively defenceless against attacks. Despite a certain amount of communal autonomy, Christians had an inferior status to

Muslims, with restrictions on their behaviour, dress and employment. Christian testimony carried less weight or was refused altogether in courts, and crimes committed against non-Muslims were punished less severely than those against Muslims. This protected second-class status established through religious ideology could easily be dehumanizing under certain conditions.

The Russian conquest of the Caucasus led to the lifting of the restrictions placed on Armenians and other Christians, though in time the Armenian Church came to face threats to its doctrinal and administrative autonomy from Russian Orthodoxy, the state-supported church of the empire.

Ottoman reformers, partly under European pressure and partly owing to their own desire to create a more competitive Ottoman state, gradually lifted many of the restrictions on Christians. These changes were part of the Tanzimat movement, which was partially based on Western nineteenth-century ideas of equality, citizenship, constitution and state, and led to the Imperial Reform Edicts of 1839, 1856 and 1875, and the abortive Ottoman constitution of 1876.

In 1839 the right of life, honour and property of all the sultan's subjects, irrespective of religion or nationality, was guaranteed. The tax system and the army were reformed to allow non-Muslims to serve in the army for the first time. The 1856 Reform Edict made more specific many of the general principles enunciated in 1839. It enshrined the prohibition of deprecatory designations based on religion, language or race, and a guarantee of equal access to government positions, education, justice, taxation and military service. It reaffirmed the traditional privileges of the administratively recognized, organized Ottoman religious communities, or *millet*s. The 1875 edict provided for reform of the courts, tax collection and the police, with measures to be taken for furthering freedom of religion and the effectiveness of the state bureaucracy. The abortive Ottoman constitution of 1876 included provisions establishing the equality of all subjects before the law, and equal access to public office based on merit. Measures for the improvement of tax collection were included, and freedom of religion was guaranteed.

These reforms even on paper could not have led to full equality because Islam was still recognized as the official state religion, and Islamic courts continued to operate alongside the new mixed court system. Even in the new, more secular courts the judges were still Muslim clerics by training, and the civil code incorporated many elements of Islamic law. The concept of Ottomanism, the common identity being promulgated for all the peoples of the Ottoman Empire, remained identified with Islam and Ottoman Turkish language and culture. Implementation of the many important new reforms also faced many obstacles. The reluctance of Armenians and other non-Muslims to enter Ottoman military service, combined with Muslim opposition, led to the generally accepted solution of converting the head tax into a military exemption tax, while theoretically upholding the principle of equal military access of the 1856 reform act. English pressure formally obtained the abolition in 1847 of the punishment of apostasy from Islam by death, but this did not end continued attempts at its enforcement through the early twentieth century, especially in the Armenian-populated provinces of Asia Minor. The tax and police systems remained corrupt, and full access to public office was never obtained. The further one moved from the capital of Constantinople, the less effective were these reforms.

Despite all this, the Tanzimat did have a very real impact. By the mid-nineteenth century, the old distinctions of dress and comportment required of Christians were beginning to be ignored. Armenians took the lead in introducing Western dress and customs to the empire. They played a prominent role in establishing the Ottoman theatre, photography and newspapers. They became closely associated with the reform movement, and from mid-century until 1876, when Abdulhamid became sultan, Armenians served as advisors to most grand vezirs and foreign ministers. They entered into local administration on a limited scale. Just as importantly, Armenians were not only given hope, but shown a way to work for change through the official Ottoman system. After a hiatus during the reign of Sultan Abdulhamid II (1876–1909), the restoration of the Ottoman constitution in 1908 by the Young Turks would restore that hope for equality through reforms in the empire.

In Persia efforts to improve the Armenians' status as non-Muslims owed much to the state's desire to keep a loyal and revenue-producing element in Persia which could help in modernization efforts, as well as to the pressure of foreign Christian powers like Russia and Great Britain, which often sought pretexts for intervention to increase their own influence. These efforts began in a piecemeal fashion after the great emigration of the Russo-Persian wars. The Persian crown prince placed the Armenians of northern Persia under the protection of the British minister in order to assure treatment equal to that of Shi'ite Muslims in criminal cases. The unwieldiness of the task for the British and Russian concern over English influence on Iranian Armenians halted this arrangement. Attempts to end religious discrimination in the Persian judicial system through reforms in the 1850s and the 1870s failed. Meanwhile, British, Russian and Christian missionary pressure in the 1850s allowed Armenians and Assyrians to be tried through a special system of courts run by the Iranian foreign ministry, though this and other initiatives achieved only limited success.

Russian pressure on the Iranian government led to the abolition of the special poll tax for Armenians most likely in the 1850s. In the same period attempts were made to create an Armenian corps in the state army, for which there were precedents in the past. Gradually restrictions on dress and comportment fell into disuse. Between the 1860s and 1880s the custom of beating Armenians who walked in the streets on rainy days (because this was believed to subject Muslims to the risk of ritual pollution) was ended in northern Persia following pressure from European diplomats and missionaries, as well as local Armenian efforts. In the 1890s Armenians won permission to mount conspicuous crosses on church buildings.

Armenians had less success in seeking the abolition of the death penalty for apostasy from Islam, so that even forcible conversion of kidnapped Armenian women was very difficult to reverse. A Shi'ite law entitling converts to possess the property of their relatives also continued to create difficulties. Armenians were still unable to hold certain high state posts, like judgeships, without conversion to Islam, and, at least informally among certain Persians, the idea of their being ritually unclean persisted. Nonetheless, Persian Armenians saw great improvements in their social status by the end of the nineteenth century, and some individuals, like Mirza Malkom Khan, played an important role in government service and the reform cause.

Imagined communities become culturally and administratively more real

A number of factors in the cultural, intellectual and administrative evolution of the Armenians led to a new understanding of the Armenian identity. Although scholars differ over exact definitions of the period, most accept the nineteenth and early twentieth centuries as the period of modern Armenian 'awakening', or *Zartonk*. Within each of the three empires, a standard written language, schooling, books and newspapers created a new type of unity. This was a result of Armenian activity, but Western influence as well as the intellectual and social changes in the three empires controlling the region created conditions that spurred on these developments. Catholic and Protestant missionaries from Europe and the US printed vernacular Armenian language books, established schools, and spread Western ideas as part of their efforts at converting the Armenians. Armenians themselves often went to Europe (including the German-run universities in the Russian Empire) to further their education in the nineteenth century, and seized upon useful ideas and parallel situations. The European economic and diplomatic presence in the Middle East also became more prevalent in this period.

After learning the art in Europe, Armenians became pioneers in printing in both the Ottoman and Persian states. Armenian-language presses spread through the century from the important diaspora cities of the Ottoman and Russian empires into the historically Armenian provinces, e.g. Shushi in Karabagh in 1835 and Van in 1857. Persian Armenians fell behind, as a gap of some two centuries separated their first seventeenth-century efforts at printing from the spread of new presses in the late nineteenth century.

As books became more widely available, the first bookstore for Western Armenians was founded in Constantinople in 1806. By the 1830s the eighteenth-century efforts of Armenians to produce dictionaries, lexicons and grammar books for classical Armenian had resulted in a set of good basic tools for schools. European techniques were adopted to teach larger numbers of Ottoman Armenians in the eighteenth century, and such schools mushroomed in number in the nineteenth. First they were established in Constantinople and western Asia Minor, but after mid-century the changed political circumstances, and European and American missionary competition, led to efforts to establish them in the provinces. A number of Armenian philanthropic organizations were established to assist in this process. Meanwhile, more advanced secondary schools began to spread in the larger cities. A similar process took place in the Russian Empire. In Persia, however, as with printing, the introduction of new educational methods proceeded more slowly. Despite the efforts of the 1830s, it was not really until mid-century that modern schools were created in Tabriz and New Julfa. Schools spread into the provinces by the end of the century. In all three states the schools were primarily under the aegis of the Armenian Church, but by mid-century were becoming agents of secularization due to the topics taught. Reading and learning were no longer a monopoly of the clergy.

By the middle of the nineteenth century Armenian newspapers were playing a vital role in standardizing a literary version of vernacular Eastern and Western Armenian for the first time, making reading more accessible to large numbers of Armenians. Literary Eastern Armenian was based on the dialect of the Yerevan region, and Western Armenian on the speech of Constantinople. Proponents of the now nearly archaic Classical Armenian fought a fierce but losing battle, as schools and administrative institutions switched to the new literary languages. The first Armenian newspaper had been published in distant Madras in 1794, followed by several European sites, but soon newspapers were being published in the inner diaspora of the Ottoman Empire, in Constantinople and Smyrna. Tiflis and other cities in the Russian Empire followed suit a bit later, while the Persian Armenian cities again lagged behind until the end of the nineteenth century. Alongside vernacular newspapers (and sometimes inside them), novels in the two written Armenian dialects began to be published around mid-century, and grammars and textbooks of Eastern and Western Armenian were prepared. By the 1860s Armenian newspapers dealt with a variety of topics, including the difficulties and oppressions of their compatriots.

Armenian theatre, a genre imported from Europe, served like the press and literature to inform Armenians about their historical past and recreate a common identity. National myths were formed. Yet during this period many Armenians remained within the spheres of Ottoman and Persian culture, contributing to many fields like music, art, theatre, literature, journalism and science.

Better communications and the elimination of local autonomous rulers helped bring Armenians closer in each of the three empires in the nineteenth century. Russian and Ottoman reforms also strengthened the Armenian Church as a unifying administrative framework for the Armenians of the two empires.

In 1815 the Tsarist government abolished the regional Catholicate of Albania, leaving the Catholicate of Etchmiadzin as the sole communal representative of the Armenians. An 1836 statute defined the Russian Armenians' religious and communal privileges, and regularized Armenian Church rules whether in the Caucasus, Moscow or the Crimea. It allowed a world Armenian ecclesiastical assembly to elect two candidates for Catholicos, or supreme head of the Church. The role of laymen, though limited, was institutionalized in these elections. Church synods and councils were established, and the formation of schools at parish and diocesan levels was encouraged. On the other hand, tight Russian state control over clerics and church property was confirmed.

The Ottoman Armenian community, termed a *millet*, was organized through the Armenian patriarchate of Constantinople. Throughout the nineteenth century its power over Armenians in the provinces increased, especially after the Ottoman reconquests, despite the existence of the regional Armenian Catholicates of Aghtamar (in the Van area) and Sis (in Cilicia), as well as the patriarchate of Jerusalem. At the same time, the patriarchate's administrative framework was expanded to allow the participation of greater numbers of Ottoman Armenian laymen. Constantinople formed the cultural, political and economic centre of the Ottoman Armenians, and its importance continued to increase throughout the century. In the first half of the century Armenian craftsmen, intellectuals and state bureaucrats of the capital attempted to participate in new cultural institutions such as schools and the press, as well as the patriarchate. With the support of the Ottoman state reform movement, they finally broke the stranglehold of the wealthy Armenian bankers, industrialists and notables. In 1863 the Ottoman government accepted a constitution for the community, which allowed for elected assemblies on the provincial and central levels and a decrease in clerical power. The voice of the wealthy was still given extra weight, along with the Armenians of Constantinople, compared to those of the provinces. The newly created elective Armenian National Assembly, though it did initially still focus on the concerns of Armenians in Constantinople, soon provided a forum for the problems of the Armenians throughout the empire, as the issue of provincial oppressions became more salient in the 1870s.

The Persian Armenians, like the Armenians in the Ottoman Empire, were allowed through their churches communal autonomous organization in the judicial and civil spheres. They were divided in the nineteenth century into the two dioceses of Azerbaijan (*Atrpatakan*) and Persia-India (though Indian and Far Eastern Armenian communities were included in the latter's jurisdiction, discussion of these communities falls outside the scope of this chapter). Regular councils with the participation of laymen were formed and assemblies held, but attempts to create diocesan constitutions were unsuccessful until the beginning of the twentieth century. Even then the Armenian Church was still divided into two dioceses, and so had no single representative body for all Iranian-Armenians. The smaller numbers of

Persian Armenians, their slower cultural development and the slower pace of Persian state reforms in this period are some of the reasons accounting for this time lag.

It should be noted that Western missionary influence, though spreading new ideas and technology to the Armenians in the three empires, also had a divisive effect. Conversion gradually led to the development of small separate Armenian Catholic and Protestant communities. In the Ottoman Empire these took formal administrative form as new *millets* in the first half of the nineteenth century; they ran all their communal affairs autonomously. Western states intervened through diplomacy to support missionaries of their own branch of Christianity and nationality together with 'their' communities of Armenian converts. This led to resentment and, on occasion, to a hostile reaction from the governments of each of the three empires.

The 'Armenian Question'

As Armenians began to communicate with each other through newspapers and books, learn about their past history and compare it with their present situation, and work together in common institutions, their horizons expanded beyond their immediate surroundings. The conditions of Armenians in the provinces, now more accessible due to imperial administrative reforms and better transport, began to elicit interest from the Armenians living in imperial diasporan centres like Constantinople, Tiflis or Tabriz. Cultural and educational associations turned their efforts to these areas. The Ottoman Armenian provinces, forming the greater part of historical Armenia, became a focus of attention for Armenians in all three empires by the 1870s. Ethnographic, literary, cultural and educational concerns were soon supplemented by economic and political ones. This was part of an evolution in Armenian political consciousness from purely cultural romanticism to a realism, still tinged with romanticism, that called for action.

In the newly subdued Ottoman eastern provinces local Armenians hoped that the central government would implement reforms in the 1860s. They appealed frequently for assistance against injustices perpetrated by feudal figures and corrupt local officials. The Ottoman government, having crushed Kurdish resistance by this point, no longer needed Armenian support, so it was not as responsive as before. Furthermore, it did not have sufficient means to maintain complete order in the East, so it continued to resort to a policy of pitting Kurds against Armenians in order to maintain control. The mediation of the religious heads of the Armenian community had no result, but greater attention began to be paid to this situation by the Armenians of Constantinople. Meanwhile, the 1862 battles of the Zeitun Armenians in Cilicia to maintain their local autonomy and tax privileges inspired Armenians in Constantinople, Moscow, Paris, Tiflis and even as far afield as

Indonesia to organize and raise money in support of Zeitun, the 'Armenian Montenegro'. Eastern and Western Armenian poets wrote nationalistic works praising the heroes of Zeitun.

The Armenian National Assembly, the community's central governing body in Constantinople, was inspired by the hopes of the Tanzimat movement. It sent two formal reports in February 1872 and September 1876 to the government asking for relief for the Armenian-populated provinces from abuses of taxation, the corruption of officials, non-acceptance of non-Muslim testimony in courts and oppression by semi-nomadic tribes. The latter imposed tributes on the Armenians and encroached on the lands of Armenian peasants, even taking over entire villages. The reports pointed out that many of the Tanzimat reforms were not being carried out in the provinces. As far as the Kurds and other semi-nomadic tribes were concerned, the Armenians asked either for them to be disarmed or for the Armenians to be provided with the means to defend themselves. Aside from the acceptance of Christian testimony in court, the National Assembly suggested that criminal and commercial cases no longer be tried by Muslim religious courts but by the civil courts. These reports received no response. This was partly due to the Ottoman policy of wooing the Kurds, as well as to bad timing. The great Ottoman reformer Ali Pasha died in 1871, and the reform movement had begun to lose its vigour.

By the 1870s, seeing little response from the government, small Ottoman Armenian political groupings in the provinces formed for self-defence purposes against armed Kurdish, Turkish and Circassian bands and feudal notables. In the Caucasus several secret societies worked to send arms and aid to these Ottoman Armenian groups. The Caucasian Armenians were more radical and went beyond self-defence to advocate the liberation of Armenia from Ottoman rule. Many were influenced by Russian populism, but substituted the Armenian homeland (*erkir*), most of which was within the borders of the Ottoman Empire, for the Russian countryside that Russian populists were idealizing.

The 1877–8 Russo-Turkish war proved to be an important turning point for Armenian political development, as well as the commencement of a period of greater international diplomatic involvement in what became known as the 'Armenian Question'. When the question of Ottoman reform was placed on the table of international diplomacy by various European powers during uprisings and fighting in the Balkans prior to Russia's entry into the war, Armenians hoped that the Ottoman Armenian provinces would benefit from the general Ottoman reforms. The patriarch for the first time contacted a representative of a foreign government, that of Great Britain, to express this desire. The Ottoman government approved of this, as it would show the Europeans the awkwardness of special reforms for the Balkan peoples only. In any case, the West Europeans were interested in forcing reform only in so far as it would impede Russia from altering the European balance of power at the expense of the Ottomans, and the latter quickly cut short an international conference on these topics by proclaiming a constitution in December 1876.

During the war, though the Armenian patriarchate in Constantinople and conservative Armenian elements supported the Ottoman forces, a large number of Ottoman Armenians hoped for a Russian victory to liberate the Ottoman Armenian provinces. The fact that Kurdish and other irregular Ottoman forces took advantage of the war to pillage and massacre in a number of locations in the eastern provinces strengthened this sentiment. By early 1878 the news of Russian successes led even the patriarchate to apply to the Russians for local autonomy in the Armenian-populated provinces. Patriarch Nerses Varzhapetian was encouraged by the Ottoman government to apply for autonomy under Ottoman rule, as this could become an obstacle to Russian control of this region. The improbability of its acceptance could also create a rift between the Armenians and the European powers. Indeed, English support of the Ottomans led ultimately to a watered-down clause, Article LXI of the Treaty of Berlin, which placed the responsibility for supervising Ottoman reforms in the Armenian-populated provinces upon the European powers collectively, as opposed to the Russians alone. As the European powers could seldom speak with a unified voice, this practically eliminated any real possibility of reforms, let alone autonomy. As part of the settlement, English military officers were appointed after the war as consular officers in many of the chief cities of Ottoman Armenia and Kurdistan in order to assist the Ottomans in enacting reforms and bringing cases of corruption and oppression to the knowledge of the government. By the early 1880s it was clear that a combination of Ottoman foot-dragging and European disunity would block effective reform. Nevertheless, Armenians would repeatedly attempt in the future to persuade the various European signatories to enact the reforms of Article LXI.

Ottoman Armenians in the 1880s faced a period of repression, with heavy censorship and no hope of democratic reform. The bureaucracy of the central government was expanded, with the telegraph, advances in European weaponry and other modern technologies assisting in increasing the sultan's power and reach. Yet this was an empire on the defensive, rapidly losing territories to the West. Pan-Islamic doctrine supported, partly as a reaction, by the sultan alienated his non-Muslim subjects. Often local Christians, identified as advocates of Western culture as well as reforms based on Western principles, were reviled for changes already introduced in the Ottoman Empire. At times they were threatened with massacre upon news of defeats inflicted by European powers in distant parts of the Ottoman Empire.

In order to defend themselves against all this and the by now traditional provincial oppressions – and ultimately to achieve Armenian self-rule – the Armenians organized themselves into political parties. First came the Armenakans in 1885, followed in 1887 by the Hnchakians and then in 1890 by what became known as the Armenian Revolutionary Federation (ARF), or Dashnaktsutiun. All three parties engaged in revolutionary activities against the Ottoman Empire. They formed branches in the three empires ruling over historic Armenian territories, as well as in many other countries with Armenian diaspora colonies. The Armenakans were the only party to be born in Ottoman Armenia, in Van, with the other two parties established by Russian Armenians in Geneva and Tiflis, respectively. All three believed in achieving the right to Armenian self-rule, but only the Hnchakian party initially demanded outright independence. The two later parties added socialist ideology, filtered through various Russian revolutionary movements, to nationalist goals.

The political parties attempted to supplant the traditional clerical leadership and institutions of the Armenians, and to unite Armenians of different Christian denominations, or those living under different governments, through their goals and ideologies. Their members often taught in schools in order to recruit youth and instil in them a new nationalistic attitude. They distributed party literature and newspapers, and formed small guerrilla bands to attack those they considered Armenian traitors, local feudal and tribal oppressors, usurers and corrupt government officials. They were a small minority of the total Armenian population, but were to have an influence much greater than their numbers would indicate.

Paradoxically, these parties advocating self-reliance for the Armenians hoped to force the European powers to intervene, as they had in Greece, Serbia and Bulgaria in the past. Their actions led the already repressive Ottoman government under Sultan Abdulhamid II to arm Kurdish irregular forces and acquiesce in injustices against Armenians. The sultan seemed to fear, according to some high officials like the imperial secretary, that the Armenians were increasing in number and gaining control of Ottoman lands. He recognized as quickly as the revolutionaries that reforms backed by outside powers could lead to autonomy, which in turn could bring independence and loss of more Ottoman territory. Yet Ottoman repression of political party activities often attracted more recruits, especially when government officials falsely accused rich Armenians of revolutionary activity for purposes of extortion.

The Hnchakians organized a demonstration in Constantinople in 1890 but failed to get either the Ottoman government or the European powers to act. It did focus attention on provincial conditions. They then became very active in Sivas and Ankara provinces, Sasun and Cilicia. In parts of these regions in the 1890s they actually took over the role of local government among Armenians, forbidding recourse to government courts. Although their plan was to foment a general uprising of Ottoman Armenians, which would lead to European intervention and reforms as a first step towards independence, their activities in the three above-mentioned areas reached their zenith at different times.

In Sivas, Ankara and Diyarbekir provinces they posted placards in January 1893 calling for Muslims to overthrow the Ottoman government.

Mass arrests and torture, some executions of revolutionaries, and rumours of forthcoming massacres of Armenians or Muslims led to a tense situation that periodically exploded into mob violence in the next few years.

Hnchakian agents were sent to mountainous Sasun in 1891, where conflict was already brewing. Local Kurdish tribes were attempting to regain their feudal supremacy and tribute from Armenians lost during the mid-century Ottoman reconquest of the region. The party encouraged the Armenian mountaineers to refuse to pay both government taxes and tribal tribute. This was interpreted as rebellion by government forces, and escalating clashes culminated in the defeat of the Armenians by government forces allied with local Kurds. The fighting degenerated into indiscriminate massacres of men, women and children, with several thousand killed in all.

Though no immediate European intervention occurred, international pressure led to the presentation of a modest reform plan to the sultan in May 1895. The Hnchakian party organized a demonstration in Constantinople on 30 September in order to speed an Ottoman response to this plan and to protest against the Sasun massacres. Fighting broke out, and in the next few days widespread attacks on Armenians throughout the Ottoman capital led to several hundred deaths.

Even more serious was a wave of massacres of Armenians which rapidly spread throughout the Armenian-populated provinces in the East in the autumn of 1895, continuing intermittently until early 1897. In most cities and villages it was a combination of tribal Kurds, lower-class urban Turks, and émigré Muslims from the Caucasus and the Balkans that attacked the Armenians, with soldiers and policemen at best passive observers and at worst sometimes initiating or actively participating in the massacres and plunder that ensued. Frequently, the massacres started on the call of a bugle, and ended upon the same signal in a very orderly fashion. In some instances, courageous Muslim civilians, and even some officials and officers, were able to prevent deaths. As many as one hundred thousand Armenians were forcibly converted to Islam.

One of the few places where the Hnchakians had some success in protecting Armenians through force of arms and diplomacy was mountainous Zeitun in Cilicia. The party had sent agents to Cilicia as early as the autumn of 1892 to organize a rebellion, as dissatisfaction existed with taxes and the behaviour of Ottoman soldiery in the area. Though other Armenian-populated areas declined to act, the martial Zeitun Armenians, convinced by the Hnchakians that Ottoman troops were preparing massacres in Cilicia, and that European intervention assuring reforms was imminent, took the initiative in the autumn of 1895. They defeated government and local Muslim forces in October, and resisted until European diplomats mediated an armistice in January 1896.

The Armenian Revolutionary Federation, aside from participating in some self-defence actions, organized its own protest in August 1896 against the widespread massacres. It too hoped to spur European involvement in the implementation of reforms. A small group of members occupied the Ottoman Bank in Constantinople, but immediately armed bands began hunting down Armenians throughout the city. In a few days some 5,000–6,000 were killed in what appeared to be a prearranged massacre.

The Armenian political parties deliberately stirred up trouble in this period, but ultimately the government of the land bore responsibility for assuring public order. The argument can certainly be made, as it has by revisionist scholars of the Russian pogroms of the late nineteenth and early twentieth centuries, that what became known as the Hamidian massacres of 1894–7 may have been permitted but not organized by the central government, even if officials and factions in the government encouraged or even participated in massacres at local level. But even if this argument is accepted, the government is not absolved of its responsibility for failing to take measures to stop the massacres and protect its subjects. As the English diplomat Fitzmaurice pointed out during his visit to Urfa after the massacres, the government should have foreseen the disastrous results of sending instructions to that province, after the 1895 Constantinople demonstration, to sternly quell Armenian disturbances. The instructions stressed that if the Armenians resisted, they should be taught a terrible lesson.

The thesis that the massacres were organized from the centre is supported by a good deal of mostly circumstantial evidence, but awaits further research for decisive confirmation. Eyewitnesses noted in a number of instances that the central government kept in close contact with local authorities during massacres in which the local authorities were implicated. There is some evidence implicating high-ranking imperial officials in the organization of massacres, some in multiple instances. Many of the perpetrators of the killings were soon rewarded by the government, unlike those who attempted to aid the Armenians. The fact that generally Armenians were carefully chosen targets, while other Christians like Greeks, Europeans and even the Syrian Orthodox were protected; the similarity in methods of organization of the attacks; and the occurrence of most attacks in regions where reforms were requested for the Armenians, all amount to circumstantial evidence in favour of centrally organized massacres. It is also noteworthy that, in most cases, government officials or troops were able to stop the massacres without serious difficulty, when that was felt necessary.

The 1894–6 massacres had a strong economic impact because many of the Armenians killed were shopkeepers, artisans, traders and businessmen. Shops and homes were plundered and burnt. Plunder was often a more important objective than murder for the local perpetrators. In the villages Kurds, many of whom became sedentary or semi-sedentary for the first time, occupied vacated land. Much of the remaining peasantry fell into debt to Kurds and the government, as they had difficulty under the circumstances in paying new taxes. The sultan encouraged many of these economic changes, weakening the Armenians' economic status. For example, soon after the 1896 massacres he issued an edict depriving all Armenians who had left the Ottoman Empire of the right to own real estate if they did not return within six weeks. Few returned, of course.

Politically, the massacres increased the Ottoman hold on the Armenian-populated provinces. This was the real goal of the central government. Not only were as many as 200,000 Armenians killed, but between 60,000 and 100,000 emigrated. Forced conversion to Islam was widespread; an incomplete early estimate was that altogether 642 villages converted. Reversion to Christianity was difficult as apostasy from Islam was traditionally punishable by death. Many women were raped, then forcibly married to Muslims. Women who escaped or were saved often had difficulty in finding Armenian husbands to accept them in marriage. The demographic balance was thus significantly altered, making the Armenians a pronounced minority in many regions. Court-martials after the massacres, with some minor exceptions, punished Armenian revolutionaries and not the perpetrators of the massacres, despite the fact that comparatively few Muslims were killed in these events. The Armenians remained politically and even culturally cowed for some time, while European demands for reform largely remained a dead letter.

Difficult times for the Eastern Armenians

Russian and Persian Armenians did not face the terrible massacres of the Ottoman Armenians, but they too faced difficulties at the end of the nineteenth century.

Despite their generally improving social and economic conditions, Iranian Armenians were the target of a number of riots at the end of the nineteenth century and the beginning of the twentieth in the northern parts of Persian. Persia at this time was under ever-increasing economic and political pressure from the Russians in the north, and the English in the south. Many Armenians were involved as economic agents for these powers, and were seen as representatives of the alien Western and Christian culture that seemed to be threatening traditional Muslim Persian ways. The Armenians thus seem to have been taken as symbols of foreign exploitation and modernization, who were easier to attack than the Europeans. Furthermore, an influx of Armenian refugees from the Hamidian massacres, together with Ottoman pressure on Persia due to the use of Persian bases by Armenian revolutionary parties, created opportunities for misunderstandings. Fortunately, however, many elements in Persian society, including the Qajar shahs and the state, and even some religious leaders, appreciated the Armenians' positive role in Persia. Typically, riots would begin with minor quarrels between individuals, which then escalated; usually the mobs were quelled by government forces or by local Persians before matters had gone beyond pillaging. This is in marked contrast to the Ottoman handling of local riots, which often degenerated into serious bloodshed.

Russian Armenians also entered a difficult period after 1881. Tsarist policy regarding Armenians changed in line with a general turn towards conservatism and Russification. All Armenian schools after the first two grades were to use only the Russian language, and various other restrictions were imposed. The schools were completely shut down by 1885, and only a massive protest succeeded in reopening them the next year. An 1889 regulation prohibited the teaching of Armenian history. Again, in 1896 the parochial schools were closed down, with their properties to be used to finance state schools. Many Armenians were imprisoned or exiled at this time as a result of their agitation against the Hamidian massacres. By 1900 Armenian benevolent societies were no longer permitted to publish books, finance writers, or open or even subsidize libraries. The press and arts were subject to strict censorship, especially of anything resembling nationalism. No Armenians were appointed into the Russian civil service after 1896. By the beginning of the twentieth century the civil administration in Transcaucasia was manned almost exclusively by Russians though in 1877 Armenians had held 22 per cent of these posts.

Things came to a head in 1903, with Tsar Nicholas II's decree confiscating Armenian Church property. This led to mass protests, a boycott of Russian schools, and assassination attempts against Russian officials. Armenian nationalist sentiment was actually stimulated by the repressive Russian measures. The nationalist Armenian political parties for the first time shifted their focus and became widely involved in operations against the Russian authorities.

Meanwhile, a wave of strikes and turmoil throughout the Russian Empire intensified following defeat in the 1904–5 Russo-Japanese War, and turned into the first Russian Revolution in 1905. Demands for a broadening of the political franchise, economic improvements for workers, and land reform for peasants combined with calls to end the war. Things soon took a different turn in much of the Caucasus. Intercommunal violence broke out between Armenians and Caucasian Muslims with an attack on Armenians in Baku in February. Many felt the Tsarist government, weakened by war, was trying to divide the two peoples in order to divert them from participation in revolutionary activities. The Armenians' prominent role as capitalists and as labourers in Baku, a cosmopolitan city surrounded by land populated by Muslim Azerbaijanis, created resentment, while economic clashes between Muslim pastoralists and Armenian farmers added to the tension. With the advances that the Armenians had made in socioeconomic status in the Russian Empire, as well as their access to military training and weaponry (in contrast to the Armenians of the Ottoman and Persian empires), the Russian Armenians were not defenceless victims. They inflicted as much damage as they received, and so, though there are some cases of local massacres or pogroms, the period of fighting between 1905 and 1907 is often called the Armeno-Tatar war. Three to ten thousand were killed on both sides, along with extensive property damage. The Armenian nationalist political parties continued to gain influence among Armenians, as they played an important role in organizing the Armenians' fighting efforts. Some

Ottoman Armenian partisan fighters in exile participated too. The relatively new Caucasian sphere of action engendered serious disputes within these parties as to the relative amount of effort that should be devoted to revolutionary action in Russian as opposed to Ottoman territory.

The difficulties of controlling the Russian revolutionary movement, combined with the fear of increasingly radical Armenian nationalism, led to a temporarily more conciliatory Russian policy towards the traditional Armenian institutions. Church properties were restored, and Armenian schools allowed to reopen by the autumn of 1905. The October Manifesto made the empire into a constitutional monarchy. As security was re-established in the Caucasus, Armenian liberals and the bourgeoisie regained confidence in their future under Russian protection. However, the Tsarist government under Prime Minister Stolypin soon began to repress its opponents and to limit the political rights won during the revolution throughout the empire; conservatism and Russian chauvinism gained strength from 1906 to the outbreak of the First World War. Representation was reduced for the Caucasus in the Russian State Duma or assembly. Armenian political organizations were repressed, and hundreds of Armenian leaders and activists were arrested in the next few years.

Hope springs eternal

Although the first Russian Revolution failed to bring about lasting change, it did help to inspire constitutional movements in Persia from 1905 to 1911, and from 1908 in the Ottoman Empire. Both movements built on the earlier reform efforts of the nineteenth century and sought to revive weakened states and strengthen central governments while tempering monarchical caprice through constitutional representation and increasing the political rights of citizens. Armenians supported these efforts in the hope that their own living conditions and social status would consequently improve. Some members of the Armenian Revolutionary Federation, the Hnchakian party, and other Armenian socialists actually participated in all three revolutions. The repression in Russia led many to join the Persian movement, and shortly afterwards the Ottoman one. The Persian and Ottoman constitutional movements helped mobilize Armenians politically to greater levels than before, and broke through some of the restrictions remaining on their participation in society at large. Ultimately, however, these movements faltered and Armenians suffered the consequences.

Despite initial suspicion and even fear on the part of conservative elements in Persian Armenian society, individual Armenians supported the constitutional movement in Persia from the beginning. Monarchist pillaging of Armenian villages, Ottoman incursions into Persian Azerbaijan and concurrent Kurdish attacks, the rapid success of the neighbouring Ottoman constitutionalists, socialist ideology, and the potential benefits for Armenians in a true democracy led by autumn 1908 to the organizational involvement of the Armenian Revolutionary Federation, the Hnchakian party, and Armenian social democrats.

These groups played an important role in the Tabriz uprising, and several times were the core of dwindling forces supporting the constitutionalist Sattar and Baghr Khans. Armenian fighting forces helped gain control of various parts of Persian Azerbaijan for the constitutionalists in late 1908 and 1909. Though Russian troops occupied Tabriz, the rebellion spread to other regions of northern Iran. Armenians contributed to the capture of cities in Gilan province, and Eprem Khan Dawtian, an Armenian Revolutionary Federation member, took the initiative in organizing the expedition which captured the capital of Tehran in July 1909. Afterwards, as head of city police and then gendarmerie, he instituted various reforms and put down a number of anti-constitutionalist rebellions until his death in a campaign in May 1912. Meanwhile, Armenians in Tabriz again fought in favour of the constitution until Russian troops crushed resistance in 1911. The occupation of much of the country by British and Russian troops and the dissolution of the Persian parliament at the end of December 1911 is usually taken to mark the end of the revolution.

The Armenians in this period, intellectually as well as militarily and administratively, joined Persian movements at many levels. They helped found two Persian political parties: Armenian social democrats were prominent in the formation of the Democratic Party of Iran in 1909, while Hnchakians assisted in the founding of an early Persian social democratic party in Gilan in 1910. Despite their participation on various levels in Persian society and government, they did not realize full equality even at the peak of the revolutionary period. Some religious bias remained in personal relations with Muslim comrades. Legally, Islam was enshrined as the official law of the realm and the rank of minister or judge was restricted to Muslims. Correspondingly, the recognition of the distinct communal rights of Armenians through their Church administration was confirmed, along with the provision for the separate election of Armenian representation in the Persian parliament.

With the occupation of much of northern Persia and the waning of the constitutional movement, Armenian supporters of the movement were persecuted or exiled, and Armenian participation in Persian politics declined. Instead, Persian Armenians were again to direct their attention to the fate of their fellow Armenians in the neighbouring empires.

The Young Turk constitutional restoration in the Ottoman Empire in July 1908 brought to the fore some of the same issues that the Persian Armenians faced in their struggle to achieve full political emancipation. The renewal of the Ottomanist ideology of the Tanzimat reform period, with all Ottoman citizens to enjoy equal rights regardless of religion or ethnicity in a constitutional regime, was attractive to a people newly recovering from massacre and repression based on religious and national identity. The Armenian political parties, now numbering four with the addition of the Constitutional

Democrats and the Reformed Hnchakians, ended revolutionary activity directed against the government and entered the parliamentary elections. The Armenian Revolutionary Federation, the strongest Armenian party, had already allied itself with the Committee of Union and Progress (CUP), the strongest of the Young Turk organizations. In the long run, the CUP wanted to eliminate distinct religious-national bodies like the Armenian *millet* that served as intermediaries to the Ottoman government and create new citizens with an Ottoman culture and parliamentary representation. The Armenian Revolutionary Federation cooperated in the hope that this new system would provide equality and freedom to Armenians, and, more self-interestedly, would allow it as a political party to grow stronger by creating a new secularized Ottoman Armenian administrative structure in place of the dominance of the Church and the conservative Armenian establishment. Contradictory understandings of what being Ottoman would entail and the question of administrative decentralization for the Armenian-populated provinces were left unresolved.

From the start, Muslim opponents of the constitution were agitating throughout the empire, with many claiming it to be contrary to Islamic law. By the autumn of 1908 and through the spring of 1909 instability flared up in the Armenian-populated provinces, including Cilicia, as many Kurdish tribes, local notables and government officials, often with close ties to the Palace and fearing loss of power and status, fought against the new regime. As in the reforms of the prior period, many Muslims felt that Armenians would be the main beneficiaries of the changes of the new regime. As in the Hamidian period, there was also a fear that the Ottoman Empire's control over its territories as a whole was weakened by a constitution.

When, in April 1909, an abortive counter-coup was attempted against the constitutional regime in Constantinople, massacres broke out in Cilicia. Starting in the city of Adana, the massacres quickly spread throughout the rest of Cilicia, where incidents continued until as late as the end of May. Usually they lasted two or three days, but in some areas where Armenians were able, due to numbers or topographic advantage, to defend themselves, sieges lasted several weeks. Over 200 villages were destroyed, and at least 20,000 Armenians and as many as 2,000 Muslims were killed throughout Cilicia. Rape, forced conversion to Islam and property damage were extensive.

The return of Armenian exiles to Cilicia after the constitutional restoration, the influx of seasonal Armenian agricultural labourers to the area, along with the settlement of embittered Muslim refugees from the Balkans, and the exacerbation of famine conditions in 1908–9 had already created tensions between Armenians and Muslims. Armenians were identified with the constitution and modern, Western ways, which many Muslims disliked, while Armenian commercial success was resented. Furthermore, the ending of many informal restrictions on Armenian public behaviour made some Muslims fear that the Armenians would be the beneficiaries of the new regime at their expense. Rumours began to spread of Armenian intentions to create their own kingdom.

Hostility to Ottoman societal changes led to attacks on Armenians as well as on Young Turk constitutionalists in the eastern Ottoman provinces during the counter-coup attempt in Constantinople. Pro-constitutionalist military officers as well as some civil officials prevented real massacres there for the most part. In Cilicia, by contrast, local officials and the military were supporters of Abdulhamid, and local factionalism led some Young Turks to side with them. As a result, there was no official response to the massacres, which the reactionaries hoped would discredit the new regime in the eyes of the Europeans.

As was often the case with the Hamidian massacres, a quarrel, on this occasion in Adana, between an Armenian and a Turk served as the immediate pretext for mob violence involving massacre, pillaging and rape. Migrant Kurdish, Turkoman, Circassian and other Muslim workers attacked their Armenian competitors of the same economic class, but Muslim notables and storekeepers were the ones to benefit most economically. Soldiers and police participated in the massacres.

The disinclination or inability of the victorious constitutional Ottoman government to punish those responsible for the 1909 massacres had important repercussions. It discredited Ottomanism in the eyes of the Armenians and even led to suspicions that the Young Turks may have had some involvement in the massacres. Just as importantly, the lack of punishment of perpetrators in 1909, as well as after the Hamidian massacres, would encourage the perpetration by local elements of such actions again to gain wealth, land and power.

Many Armenians, including the leaders of the Armenian Revolutionary Federation, felt there was no choice but to support the Committee of Union and Progress even after the Cilician massacres, as the alternative would be a dangerous reactionary movement. Yet attempts to resolve perennially important Armenian issues like land reform, provincial corruption and discrimination, and increasing Kurdish violence were constantly stalled through the various shifts in parliamentary government that took place over the next few years. Cabinet changes and various international crises were not satisfactory excuses for Armenians increasingly upset with the lack of governmental remedy despite their repeated petitions and protests. On the ideological level, also, there was a growing alienation between the Young Turks, whose conception of Ottomanism increasingly laid emphasis on Turkism and Islam, and the Armenians, who wished to see Ottomanism as a multinational coalition. All of these factors helped undermine Armenian belief in a true Ottoman equality. Moreover, the administrative decentralization that Armenians desired was opposed by the Committee of Union and Progress. When, by the end of 1912, the weakening of the Ottoman Empire in the Balkan wars and changes in international politics led Russia to raise the question of Armenian reforms through diplomatic channels, Ottoman

Armenians already felt the need for outside, international guarantees. They reverted to purely Armenian nationalism, but were demographically dispersed and powerless to achieve anything alone. Their actions would be countered by an authoritarian Ottoman regime soon installed by the Committee of Union and Progress to bolster the faltering empire.

In the course of the nineteenth century Armenians partially overcame their tripartite imperial division through the unifying force of schools, common publications, national ideology, and new international organizations. They strove in each empire to create conditions of greater freedom and equality, and participated in various reform movements. During the periods of greatest repression they relied on their own forces for self-defence. Even then, perhaps inspired by examples stretching back in Armenian history to the Crusades and earlier, and by the more recent Balkan nationalist movements, they still ended up seeking outside help from Western Europe and Russia. The results would not be good.

Bibliography

Allen, W.E.D., and Muratoff, P., *Caucasian Battlefields: A History of the Wars on the Turco-Caucasian Border, 1828–1921* (Cambridge: Cambridge University Press, 1953).

Berberian, H., *Armenians and the Iranian Constitutional Revolution of 1905–1911: 'The Love for Freedom Has No Fatherland'* (Boulder, CO: Westview Press, 2001).

Bournoutian, G.A., ed. and trans., *Russia and the Armenians of Transcaucasia 1797–1889: A Documentary Record* (Costa Mesa, CA: Mazda, 1998).

Chaqueri, C., ed., *The Armenians of Iran: The Paradoxical Role of a Minority in a Dominant Culture* (Cambridge, MA: Harvard University Press, 1998).

Etmekjian, J., *The French Influence on the Western Armenian Renaissance 1843–1915* (New York: Twayne Publishers, 1964).

Gregorian, V., 'The Impact of Russia on the Armenians and Armenia', in W.S. Vucinich, ed., *Russia and Asia: Essays on the Influence of Russia on the Asian Peoples* (Stanford: Hoover Institution Press, 1972).

Hovannisian, R.G., ed., *The Armenian People*, vol. 2, chapters 4–7 (New York: St. Martin's, 1997).

Krikorian, M.K., *Armenians in the Service of the Ottoman Empire, 1860–1908* (London: Routledge and Kegan Paul, 1978).

Lynch, H.F.B., *Armenia: Travels and Studies*, 2 vols, reprint edition (New York: International Book Centre, 1990).

Nalbandian, L., *The Armenian Revolutionary Movement: The Development of Armenian Political Parties through the Nineteenth Century* (Berkeley: University of California Press, 1963).

Suny, R.G., *Looking toward Ararat: Armenia in Modern History* (Bloomington and Indianapolis: University of Indiana Press, 1993).

Walker, C.J., *Armenia: The Survival of a Nation*, revised second edition (London: Routledge, 1990).

5 Genocide and independence, 1914–21

Richard G. Hovannisian

The brief time span from 1914 to 1921 was a decisive turning point, perhaps the most significant millennial moment, for the Armenian people. At the beginning of the period, Armenians lived everywhere from Constantinople to Baku, with most of them still inhabiting their traditional homelands, known as the Armenian Plateau, stretching from the Antitaurus mountain range and Euphrates River eastward to the Karabagh highlands. By the period's end, however, Armenians had been swept clean from the shores of the Bosporus and the Black Sea all the way to the borders of Persia and the eastern slopes of Mount Ararat. Within those seven years this people would experience genocide, seek resurrection as a united, independent republic, and manage to salvage only the eastern reaches of their ancient homeland as a small landlocked and dependent Soviet state.

Russian (Eastern) Armenians and Turkish (Western) Armenians

At the turn of the twentieth century, the Armenians were experiencing a cultural and political revival. Education had become widespread, even for girls, and Armenian intellectuals who had studied in Europe returned home to forge a modern identity for their people. With their homeland divided between the Ottoman and Russian empires, the Armenians were affected by different social, economic, cultural, and political currents, spoke in different dialects, and had different lifestyles. Yet within these contradistinctions they developed a sense of belonging to a common nationality with a common destiny. Russian Armenian intellectuals writing in St. Petersburg, Moscow, and Tiflis (Tbilisi) made their subject and their cause the Turkish Armenian peasant's struggle to protect his family, goods, and property. The Armenian cultural renaissance was followed by political ferment and demands for change. Armenian activists were engaged both in the underground opposi- tional movements in the Russian Empire and in the reform and resistance movements in the Ottoman Empire.

Through the course of the nineteenth century the proportion of Armenians in the Transcaucasian (South Caucasus) region of the Russian

Empire, grew steadily, so that by 1914 they constituted more than 20 per cent of the total population in the area as a whole, and within the province of Yerevan they made up nearly 70 per cent. Of the two million Armenians in the Russian Empire, more than 85 per cent lived in Transcaucasia, but there they were dispersed into every province. In some ways, this demographic dimension worked in their favour, for they had reliable contacts and associates wherever they went. Armenians played a leading role in the economic, professional and administrative life of areas outside the Armenian Plateau, such as Tiflis and Baku. In fact, there were more Armenians living in Tiflis than in any other city of the empire. For so long as Transcaucasia constituted a single unit within the Russian Empire, Armenians were at ease no matter where they lived or travelled in the region. It was of no great concern that the eastern sector of the Armenian Plateau, which centred around Yerevan and became known as Russian (Eastern) Armenia, was kept undeveloped and agrarian by the imperial economic planners, since Armenian capital found other lucrative outlets in Batum, Tiflis, Elizavetpol (Ganja, Gandzak), Shemakha, Baku, Petrovsk, and elsewhere. The advantage that Armenians seemed to enjoy because of their broad dispersal was to cripple them once Transcaucasia splintered into separate states in 1918, leaving most Armenians of the Russian Empire beyond the borders of the Armenian Republic and reducing them abruptly to the status of second-class citizens in the Republics of Georgia and Azerbaijan.

In 1912 there was widespread Armenian resentment towards the government of Tsar Nicholas II, because of its antagonistic policies, including the confiscation of Armenian Church properties in 1903–5, the stoking of Armenian–Tatar (Azerbaijani) hostilities in 1905–7, and the arrest and imprisonment of hundreds of Armenian political and intellectual leaders during the Stolypin repression of 1906–11 (see chapter 4). But suddenly in 1912 Tsar Nicholas professed affection for his Armenian subjects and quickly wooed even former political opponents and exiles by voicing renewed Russian concern over the plight of the Armenian population in the Ottoman Empire. Between 1912 and 1914 imperial Russia championed Armenian efforts to secure administrative, social, and economic reforms in the Armenian provinces of the Ottoman Empire and in February 1914 was a signatory to a compromise reform plan that held out great hope for the Ottoman Armenians. By the summer of 1914 Tsar Nicholas had been successful in winning back Armenian loyalty and even advancing a plan to organize a number of Armenian volunteer detachments in the Caucasus to assist the regular imperial armies in case of war with the Ottoman Empire. There was not long to wait. The Turkish bombardment of Russia's Black Sea naval installations in October 1914, pursuant to a secret treaty with Germany, served as a highly effective declaration of war. The commencement of hostilities was viewed with general optimism by Russian Armenian leaders, who believed that the moment of liberation of the homeland (*erkir*) in Turkish (Western) Armenia had arrived.

The religious and political leaders of the more than two million Armenians in the Ottoman Empire did not share this enthusiasm. They were terrified by the prospect of a war that would range the Ottoman and Russian empires on opposing sides and make the Armenian Plateau a major field of battle. The Ottoman Armenians had seen their bright hopes of 1908, inspired by the Young Turk revolution and the overthrow of Sultan Abdulhamid's bloody regime, quickly dissipate as massacres engulfed the region of Cilicia in 1909 and the ideology of the Young Turks bent increasingly towards Turkish nationalism and Islamism. The radical wing of the Young Turk movement seized power in a coup d'état in 1913, heightening apprehensions, even though the leading Armenian political party, the Armenian Revolutionary Federation or Dashnaktsutiun, continued to profess support for the ideals of the Young Turk revolution.

The Young Turk rulers of the Ottoman Empire, suffering from a number of international and domestic setbacks between 1908 and the first Balkan War in 1912, were vexed further by Russia's sponsorship of the Armenian reform measure. The sense of grave danger gripping the Young Turk leadership exacerbated suspicion and distrust of the Christian minority elements, especially the Armenians, who straddled both sides of the Russo-Turkish border. The Armenians constituted a major stumbling block in the vision of reshaping the empire by turning back to Asia and uniting the lands of 'Turan' (the homeland of the Turkish peoples), lyricized and mythologized by Young Turk ideologue Zia Gökalp. Multinational Ottomanism was to give way to monolithic 'Turkism', if necessary through concerted violence. In her pioneering study *Accounting for Genocide,* Helen Fein has concluded: 'The victims of twentieth century premeditated genocide – the Jews, the Gypsies, the Armenians – were murdered in order to fulfill the state's design for a new order ... . War was used ... to transform the nation to correspond to the ruling elite's formula by eliminating the groups conceived of as alien, enemies by definition'.[1]

The Armenian Genocide

Beginning in 1912, various schemes for dealing with the Armenian problem were considered in the inner circles of the Young Turk party, but it is not clear at what point the general objective to achieve a homogeneous Turkic society was transformed into the decision to annihilate the Armenian population through deportations and massacres. If one accepts the view that insecurity and adversity stimulate potential perpetrators to mass violence, then this would relate to the terrible Turkish defeat in the first major encounter with the Russian armies in December 1914–January 1915 in the blizzard-swept mountain passes around Sarikamish. Minister of War Enver

---

1   Helen Fein, *Accounting for Genocide* (New York: The Free Press, 1979), pp. 29–30.

Pasha launched that offensive in the dead of winter, but was decisively defeated, with most of his 90,000-man army being killed, frozen, taken prisoner or dispersed. This fiasco left the eastern Ottoman provinces open to Russian advances. The sense of crisis was heightened a few months later in April with the ill-fated Allied descent at Gallipoli, aimed at capturing Constantinople (Istanbul).

Whether or not these factors contributed to the ultimate decision, the genocidal process began in the spring of 1915, and its fury continued unabated for months. It is inconceivable that such a widespread operation, methodically following the same pattern over an expanse of several hundred kilometres, could have been conceived and put in motion within a few days or weeks. Clearly, the plan was already in place on the night of 23/24 April when Armenian intellectual and political figures in Constantinople were arrested, then dispatched to the interior provinces and murdered. Ironically, some of those first victims had been on close personal terms with the Young Turk elite, including Enver Pasha, Minister of the Interior Talat Pasha, and Minister of Marine Jemal Pasha, the so-called Young Turk Triumvirate.

The removal of the Armenian leaders left the Armenian population entirely unprepared for what was to follow. Throughout their history the Armenians had suffered invasion, captivity, and massacre, but the times of adversity, no matter how long and oppressive, had come and gone, and the survivors had rebuilt and perpetuated the national existence. In recent times the Armenians had been subjected to terrible persecutions and massacres in 1894–6 and once again in 1909, but these, too, had passed and the living had turned to personal and collective reconstruction. Hence, it was incomprehensible to any Armenian in 1915 that what was to occur in the next few months was to be a radical departure from previous tribulations, both quantitatively and qualitatively – so much so that the chain of Armenian history in the region would be for ever broken.

Under the cover of a world war the full force of the state was applied in an internal war against one segment of the population. In city after city and province after province the pattern was the same: arrest, imprisonment, torture, and execution of teachers, priests, and intellectuals; separation of the adult males from the rest of the population and their mass killing at river crossings, mountain passes, and remote valleys within a short distance of their homes; death marches of the remaining population under the blistering summer sun to unknown destinations – the barren deserts of inner Syria and Iraq, symbolized by the name Deir ez-Zor, a vast open-air death camp in the Syrian steppeland that was the final destination for many of the deportees. The caravans of wretched deportees were attacked and molested all along the way. Thousands, perhaps hundreds of thousands, of women and children were abducted and forced to convert and take on new identities. While there was widespread public participation in the persecution of the Armenians and the expropriation of their goods, a number of officials and many individual Turks tried to protect or harbour their neighbours but to little avail. By 1916 virtually the entire Armenian population of Anatolia and the Armenian Plateau had been eliminated in one way or another. The rationalization of the government then and of deniers now is that the Armenians were removed from a dangerous war zone for their own safety and because they constituted a security risk, but the argument is exposed by the fact that the zone of deportation included the entire expanse of the empire from the coastal shores to the most distant and remote valleys. Not even the small Armenian communities in the Anatolian Turkish heartlands were spared.

In a few places the Armenians attempted to resist: Shabin-Karahisar, Gemerek, Urfa, Musa Dagh, Van – but in most instances these acts of desperation ended in the death of the defenders. Only at the village cluster of Musa Dagh were the Armenians saved because of their proximity to the Mediterranean Sea and the chance passing of a French vessel, and at Van where the month-long resistance was rewarded with deliverance by the Russian army and Armenian volunteers from Transcaucasia. But the exhilaration of the Armenians of Van province was short-lived for they were soon forced to withdraw with the Russian army into Transcaucasia, where they became homeless refugees suffering exposure, epidemic, and starvation. The arrival of thousands of pitiful, panic-stricken refugees from Van, Alashkert, and other border regions quickly sobered the Russian Armenians, who had viewed the outbreak of war as the golden opportunity to free their Turkish Armenian brethren. Even then the full impact of the Armenian Genocide was not comprehended, nor could it be for decades to come, if at all.

The Turkish wartime denials and rationalizations were roundly refuted by statesmen and humanitarians of many nations. Not Armenian treachery, wrote the German Johannes Lepsius, but the exclusivist nationalism and ideologically motivated expansionist objectives of the Young Turks lay at the root of the tragedy. United States Ambassador Henry Morgenthau summarized the reports of numerous American diplomatic and missionary personnel in the Ottoman Empire when he wrote: 'I am confident that the whole history of the human race contains no such horrible episode as this. The great massacres and persecutions of the past seem almost insignificant when compared to the sufferings of the Armenian race in 1915.'[2] Following the First World War, American General James G. Harbord led a mission of investigation through Anatolia and the Armenian Plateau, reporting: 'Mutilation, violation, torture and death have left their haunting memories in a hundred beautiful Armenian valleys, and the traveler in that region is seldom free from the evidence of the most colossal crime of all the ages.'[3] And even the first post-war Turkish prime minister admitted that the crimes

---

2　Henry Morgenthau, *Ambassador Morgenthau's Story* (Garden City, NY: Doubleday Page, 1918), pp. 321–2.

3　US Congress, *Conditions in the Near East: Report of the American Military Mission to Armenia*, prepared by General James G. Harbord, 66th Congress, 2nd session, Senate Document 266 (Washington, DC: Government Printing Office, 1920), p. 7.

of the Young Turk dictators had been such 'as to make the conscience of mankind shudder with horror for ever'.[4] A Turkish military court martial tried and sentenced to death in absentia Enver, Talat, Jemal, and two other notorious organizers of the Genocide, but no attempt was made to carry out the sentence and within a few months the proceedings were suspended because of domestic and international developments. Thousands of the perpetrators were neither tried nor even removed from office.

The Armenian psyche has been so traumatized that the Genocide haunts the entire nation and colours how it views itself and its neighbours. There is not only the enormously painful sense of victimization of an entire generation but even more the loss of beloved patrimonial lands of three millennia. The legacy of the loss of forebears and of homeland weighs upon succeeding generations. This may help to explain why for most Armenians the conflict in Mountainous Karabagh and the flight of the Armenians of Baku, Ganja, and elsewhere in Azerbaijan during the disintegration of the Soviet Union were simply a continuation of what had begun in 1915. Time collapsed as 1988–90 became an immediate sequel to 1915 and the Azerbaijani was no longer a Caucasian neighbour but rather the ruthless traditional Turkish perpetrator. The lasting impact of the Genocide cannot be overstated, especially as there was no recompense or restitution for the victims and no real punishment for the perpetrators. Until the issue is addressed by the international community it is likely that the trauma will cause a constant sense of isolation and insecurity and stand as a major obstacle to normalcy even as the Armenians move deeper into a new century.

Establishment of the Republic of Armenia

The Armenian Genocide of 1915 was followed in 1916 by a Russian offensive that led to the occupation of the eastern half of Turkish Armenia, including most of the provinces of Van, Bitlis, and Erzerum, together with the coastal province of Trebizond (Trabzon). Once more, Armenian visions of a liberated, autonomous homeland under Russian auspices soared, but again bitter disappointment and disillusionment followed upon such unfounded hopes. As soon as the imperial armies had reached their objectives, the Russian government disbanded the Armenian volunteer regiments that had participated in the campaign, prevented Armenian refugees from returning to their homes in the newly conquered Turkish Armenian provinces, and imposed strict censorship and other restrictions on the Armenians in the Caucasus.

The logic of these moves became clear only after the Bolshevik revolution in 1917, when the new Soviet government made public a collection of

---

4   US Department of State, *Papers Relating to the Foreign Relations of the United States, 1919: The Paris Peace Conference*, vol. 4 (Washington, DC: Government Printing Office, 1943), p. 509.

documents showing that the former tsarist regime had entered into a number of secret wartime agreements with its Entente allies, Great Britain and France, on the partition of the Ottoman Empire. While the other Entente powers were to gain direct or indirect control over almost all of the Arab provinces, Cilicia, and the western half of Turkish Armenia, Russia would take possession of Constantinople and the eastern half of Turkish Armenia, that is the sector that the imperial armies occupied in 1916. Once in control of that area, there was no longer any reason to cater to the Armenians or allow their separate military detachments to exist. On the contrary, plans were made to move more reliable Cossack settlers to the new borders in the heart of the Armenian Plateau.

It is not surprising, therefore, that the Armenians, together with the other peoples of Transcaucasia, hailed the February/March Revolution in 1917 which forced Tsar Nicholas to abdicate and brought to an end the three-hundred-year reign of the Romanov dynasty. Great hopes were pinned on the Provisional Government, among whose first acts was the replacement of the Viceroy for the Caucasus, Grand Duke Nicholas, with a special committee (ozacom) that included Russian, Armenian, Georgian, and Muslim members. Thousands of Armenian refugees now streamed back to their towns and villages to begin the process of rebuilding, and many Armenian officials were appointed to help administer these territories. The Armenians soon became alarmed, however, as the Russian soldiers abandoned the front and, affected by the Bolshevik slogan 'peace without annexations and indemnities', dropped or sold their weapons and hastened homewards in quest of the promised 'land, peace, and bread'. The danger posed by the abandonment of the front prompted Armenian leaders to seek and win the consent of the Provisional Government in St. Petersburg to transfer to the Caucasus theatre Armenian soldiers serving in the regular armed forces on the German and Austrian fronts. That movement had only just started, however, when the Bolshevik revolution engulfed the empire in civil war and left many of the Armenian soldiers stranded along the railway leading to Baku and from Baku to Tiflis and Kars.

Taking advantage of the opportunity provided by the first Russian revolution in 1917, the Armenians of the empire held a national congress in Tiflis in October to devise a strategy regarding the war effort, the relief and repatriation of refugees, local autonomy and the administrative structure in Transcaucasia, and many other issues. The more than 200 delegates from all over the former Romanov realm selected a fifteen-member permanent executive committee, known as the Armenian National Council, which was headed by Avetis Aharonian, a noted writer and activist belonging to the Dashnaktsutiun. To ensure the participation of Armenian Socialist Revolutionaries, Social Democrats, Constitutional Democrats (Zhoghovrdakan party), and non-partisans, the Dashnaktsutiun consented to hold only six of the fifteen seats even though it had dominated Armenian political life since the turn of the century. It was the Armenian National Council that was destined several months later to declare the formation of the Republic of Armenia.

The Bolshevik revolution in November 1917 was denounced throughout Transcaucasia, except in Baku, the single proletarian centre of the region, where a few months later a local soviet would take control. In Tiflis, representatives of the leading Armenian, Georgian, and Muslim political parties immediately organized a caretaker administration known as the Transcaucasian Commissariat pending the liquidation of the 'Bolshevik adventure' and the restoration of 'Russian democracy'. Although by its own definition the Commissariat was not an independent government, it was soon forced to take actions usually reserved for sovereign states. Together with a regional legislative body, the Seim, the Commissariat had to face the threat of a renewed Turkish military offensive. In an effort to avert such a calamity, first a truce was concluded with the Turkish command and then the Seim made its ultimate concession to the Ottoman Empire at the expense of the Armenians by offering to restore the pre-war boundaries and return all occupied territories in Turkish Armenia in exchange for the unhindered repatriation of all refugees and the granting of local Armenian autonomy.

Even before the Transcaucasian delegation was able to present this package to the Turkish side at Trebizond, the Ottoman armies had resumed the offensive, driving the Armenian defenders out of Erzinjan and Erzerum and approaching the pre-war Russo-Turkish frontier from the Black Sea coast down to Van. But the Young Turk leaders were not content with the reoccupation of Turkish Armenia, for through the Treaty of Brest-Litovsk (3 March 1918) between Germany and its allies, on the one hand, and Soviet Russia, on the other, the Ottoman Empire had also won the right to take control of Batum and its Ajarian hinterland and the Russian Armenian districts of Kars and Ardahan, all of which had belonged to Russia since the war of 1877–8. Georgian resolve to defend Batum was short-lived, as the Turkish army rolled into the area with no difficulty. By April of 1918 Turkish divisions had pushed the Armenian defenders back to the pre-war borders, again driving thousands of newly returned Armenians back into the Caucasus or northern Persia. Now the Turkish conditions for peace included not only acceptance of all the conditions of the Treaty of Brest-Litovsk but also a declaration of Transcaucasian independence in order to allow Turkey to deal directly with the region. The Armenians tried desperately to avoid such a declaration and to take whatever protection might still be afforded by claiming to be a part of the 'Russian democracy'. In the end they were met with the ultimatum of their Georgian and Muslim counterparts either to join in separating from Russia or else to continue the struggle against the Turkish armies alone. There was no real choice, and on 22 April 1918, the Seim declared the independence of the Transcaucasian Federative Republic with the Georgian Menshevik A.I. Chkhenkeli as its president.

Among Chkhenkeli's first acts, even before his cabinet had been confirmed by the Seim, was to order the Armenian army corps at Kars to surrender the great fortress to the Turks. This was necessary, he insisted, so that negotiations for peace could resume. The loss of Kars brought the Turkish armies to the Arpachai (Akhurian) River and the heart of Russian Armenia. When in May the interrupted negotiations resumed, now at Batum, the Turkish side was no longer satisfied with the borders as determined by the Treaty of Brest-Litovsk but now demanded additional compensation: the heavily Armenian-populated southern counties of Tiflis province (Akhalkalak and Akhaltskha) and the western half of the province of Yerevan, including the entire plain of Ararat and the railway leading from both Kars and Tiflis through Aleksandropol (Leninakan, Gyumri) to the Persian frontier at Julfa. The Armenian members of the Transcaucasian delegation were frantic and protested bitterly that the Ottoman delegation was violating the treaty its own government and Germany had concluded with Soviet Russia, but such pleading was to no avail. The Turkish command did not await the outcome of the diplomatic exchanges at Batum before moving into the province of Yerevan and occupying Aleksandropol as well as the railway all the way to the environs of Sardarabad, the gateway to the Holy See of Etchmiadzin and the city of Yerevan itself.

Turkish ambitions extended to territories far beyond the limits set at Brest-Litovsk, especially Baku and the North Caucasus. This conflicted with the interests and strategies of Germany, the senior partner in the Central Alliance. Germany was then engaged in negotiations with the Council of People's Commissars (Sovnarkom) of Russia about securing a share of the vast oil resources in Baku, and insisted that the Turkish army concentrate on the threat posed by the Allied forces in the Balkans and in Palestine. Moreover, the Georgian regions of western Transcaucasia held mineral deposits valuable to German industry and the war effort. Failed German attempts to hold the Turks to the Brest-Litovsk boundaries culminated in the decision to protect at least the strategic Georgian territories, even if this meant abandoning the Armenians to their fate. Hence, as negotiations between the Turkish and Transcaucasian delegations in Batum reached an impasse, secret German–Georgian exchanges resulted in an accord by which Georgia was to withdraw from the Transcaucasian Federation, declare its independence, and place itself immediately under German protection to avoid further Turkish encroachments.

This strategy was enacted on 26 May 1918, when the Georgian Menshevik faction of the Seim announced that it could no longer participate in a regional federation, which had proved to be illusory. Casting blame on the Muslim factions for their collaboration with the enemy and expressing sorrow for the plight of the Armenians, Menshevik veteran I.G. Tsereteli declared that Georgia had no choice but to fend for itself. The Transcaucasian Federative Republic was then voted out of existence. That same day the expanded Georgian National Council declared the independence of the

Republic of Georgia, among whose first acts was to sign the treaty placing the country under the protection of the German Empire. The Muslim National Council decided the next day to declare the independence of a new entity, the Republic of Azerbaijan, encompassing 'eastern and southern Transcaucasia', an act that was proclaimed on 28 May.

The collapse of the Transcaucasian Federation and the declarations of Georgian and Azerbaijani independence placed Armenian leaders in a quandary. The Turkish armies were still advancing towards Yerevan, and the collective Armenian financial, professional, and intellectual strength lay in the newly declared Republics of Georgia and Azerbaijan, not in the minor provincial capital of Yerevan. Still, with no choice but to follow suit, the Armenian National Council issued a declaration on 30 May 1918 (retroactive to 28 May) that it was assuming control of the Armenian provinces in Transcaucasia. So insecure was the Armenian position that the National Council could neither define the territories under its jurisdiction nor venture to use the terms 'independence' or 'republic'. That would happen only after a last-ditch defensive effort at Bash-Abaran (Aparan), Karakilisa (Vanadzor), and Sardarabad had halted the Turkish advance. On 4 June an Armenian delegation in Batum signed, in the name of the Republic of Armenia, a treaty of peace and friendship with the Ottoman Empire.

The Treaty of Batum was suffocating. It left to the Armenians a few thousand square kilometres of barren land while requiring the small state to demobilize and comply with many humiliating and debilitating conditions for peace. In the summer of 1918 the Armenian National Council reluctantly transferred from Tiflis to Yerevan to take over the leadership of the republic from the popular dictator Aram Manukian and the renowned military commander Dro (Drastamat Kanayan). It then began the daunting process of establishing a national administrative machinery in an isolated and landlocked state abounding with suffering and misery. This was not the autonomy or even independence about which Armenian intellectuals had dreamed and for which a generation of youth had been sacrificed. Yet, as it happened, it was here that the Armenian people was destined to continue its national existence and that the Republic of Armenia would give way to Soviet Armenia, which in turn would yield in the final decade of the twentieth century to a new independent Republic of Armenia.

The Republic of Armenia

The short history of the Republic of Armenia, 1918–1920/21, evolved on several separate but interlinked planes: domestic, regional, and international. The leaders of the republic, many holding public office for the first time, had to face virtually insurmountable obstacles to creating the mechanisms of effective government, establishing the rule of law, rebuilding the shattered economic and agrarian infrastructure, caring for more than 300,000 embittered and impatient refugees, and dealing with the hostility

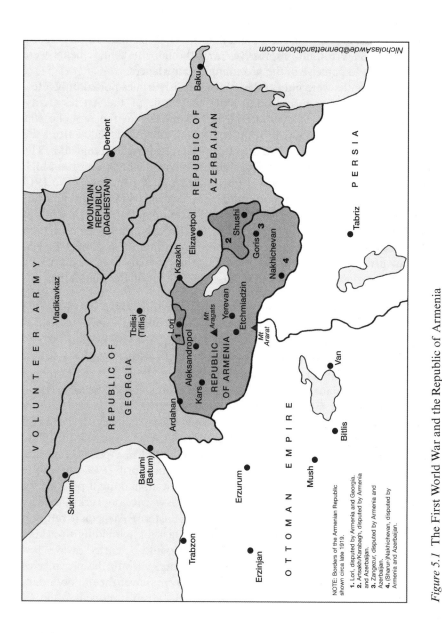

VOLUNTEER ARMY

Sukhumi

Batumi
(Batum)

REPUBLIC OF
GEORGIA

Vladikavkaz

Tbilisi
(Tiflis)

MOUNTAIN
REPUBLIC
(DAGHESTAN)

Derbent

Baku

REPUBLIC OF
AZERBAIJAN

Elizavetpol

Kazakh

Lori

1

Aleksandropol

Kars

Ardahan

Mt
Aragats ▲

REPUBLIC
OF ARMENIA

Yerevan

Etchmiadzin

Mt
Ararat

2

Shushi

Goris **3**

Nakhichevan

4

P E R S I A

Tabriz

Van

Bitlis

Mush

Erzurum

O T T O M A N   E M P I R E

Erzinjan

Trabzon

NOTE: Borders of the Armenian Republic
shown circa late 1919.

1. Lori, disputed by Armenia and Georgia.
2. Artsakh/Karabagh, disputed by Armenia
and Azerbaijan.
3. Zangezur, disputed by Armenia and
Azerbaijan.
4. (Sharur-)Nakhichevan, disputed by
Armenia and Azerbaijan.

Figure 5.1 The First World War and the Republic of Armenia

and open rebellion of several Muslim-populated districts. Issues such as relations between church and state and between party and government, land distribution, minority rights, education, and fiscal policies all demanded serious attention. And these were only the domestic challenges. Considering the gravity of the situation, the strides that the republic made in responding to these issues were quite impressive, even though the achievements were rather difficult to perceive in the prevailing circumstances.

The first months were unbearable. With Turkish armies poised only a few kilometres from Yerevan and controlling the whole of the Araxes (Aras) river valley and plain of Ararat, the little land left to the republic was crammed with refugees and in total economic collapse. Isolated from the outside world, the country had no means of receiving external aid. The economic dislocation was staggering. Industrial income had never been high in Russian Armenia, but in 1918–19 it totalled only 8 per cent of the 1914 pre-war level. The overall agricultural decline exceeded 80 per cent, and this was paralleled by the losses of livestock and farm implements. Thousands of animals had been slaughtered for food by the Turkish armies of occupation and thousands more were driven towards Kars when those armies had to withdraw after the war. Most of the remaining animals were devoured by the refugees or else succumbed to disease. The plight of the population was pitiful.

Only in the spring of 1919 did the first life-sustaining shipments of American surplus wheat reach Batum and, with the assistance of British railway guards, get transported to Yerevan. By that time more than 150,000 people, almost 20 per cent of the population, had perished. Spring renewed hope once again. Under the terms of the Mudros Armistice, the Ottoman Empire had capitulated to the Allied powers at the end of October 1918, and a few days later Germany, too, surrendered. British forces came ashore at Batum and Baku and occupied the Transcaucasian railway. The Turkish armies were compelled to withdraw from most of Transcaucasia, including the occupied portions of the provinces of Baku, Elizavetpol (Ganja and Karabagh), Tiflis, Batum, and Yerevan. Then, in April 1919, they were ordered to pull back from Kars and Ardahan as well, making it possible for the Armenian Republic to fill out towards the pre-war Russo-Turkish border and to triple in size. Thousands of Russian (Eastern) Armenian refugees streamed homewards to begin the formidable task of rebuilding in a land that had been stripped bare of everything that could be carted away. Now the Turkish (Western) Armenian refugees also pressed into the province of Kars in anticipation of the day when they could cross over the old boundary and return to their native districts, which they fervently hoped would be incorporated into a united Armenian state.

Although the independent Armenian state did not last long enough to resolve many of its domestic problems, dedicated individuals of all political parties laboured tirelessly to lay plans for a progressive democratic republic. Under the premiership first of Hovhannes Kachaznuni and then of Alexandre Khatisian, Armenian specialists, arriving from all parts of the former Russian Empire and from as far away as the United States, took the first steps to reorganize the judicial system to include branches for civil, criminal, and administrative law, appellate courts, a supreme court, and the jury system; to introduce a national currency, a sound budgetary system, and a progressive income tax; to create an educational system based on universal, secular, compulsory elementary education, advanced technical training, adult literacy courses, and the establishment of Armenia's first university – a vision realized with great fanfare in January 1920; to implement advanced social legislation, including equality of the sexes and the granting of women's suffrage, enacted in the first national parliamentary elections in June 1919, when women not only voted but three of whom were elected to membership of the legislature; and to study the soil and mineral resources of the country and the means to develop its communication, transportation, and irrigation systems. Amid ruin and turmoil a generation of specialists born and educated outside the narrow bounds of the existing republic sought to ensure a bright and permanent future in a restored Armenian state that would gather in the divided historic homelands.

The most vexing domestic issues, aside from the refugee problem, were inter-party and intra-party conflicts and the refusal of most Muslim-populated districts to recognize the jurisdiction of the Yerevan government. Armenian political life, especially in the Caucasus, had long been dominated by the Armenian Revolutionary Federation – the Dashnaktsutiun. Providing a broad umbrella for many shades of nationalist and socialist thought, the party had focused on the emancipation of Western Armenia and defence of the Armenian peasant against internal and external exploiters. In the Russian Empire the Dashnaktsutiun had led the battle against tsarist discriminatory policies and had gained widespread influence within the Armenian labour force and peasantry. The party was not, however, structured or intended to act as a government, a function to which it was beckoned in 1918 with the unexpected creation of an amorphous 'republic' in the national backwater around Yerevan.

Although the Dashnaktsutiun understood the importance of united action with the less popular Armenian political elements, its leaders sometimes assumed an overbearing attitude and, unlike moderate comrades such as premiers Kachaznuni and Khatisian, ridiculed and intimidated the opposition groups. A coalition government formed at the end of 1918 fell apart in the following June, and national elections held that month only reinforced the dominance of the party. The shell of a parliamentary democracy had been created, but time would be needed to fill that shell with practical experience. Still, although the Dashnaktsutiun would hold almost all cabinet positions until the waning days of the republic under Prime Minister Simon Vratzian, civil servants of all political persuasions and non-partisans continued to staff the state ministries.

Intra-party discord was perhaps greater than that between the dominant and minor parties. The Dashnaktsutiun had to adjust to this bewildering phenomenon of Armenian independence. So long as the emancipation struggle had consumed the party's energies, the broad differences between its conservative nationalist and its socialist internationalist elements had been of no great consequence. As the leader of an independent state, however, the party was called upon to determine policies relating to social, economic, and religious issues, all of which pulled elements within the party in opposing directions. The Western Armenian comrades in particular had little understanding or sympathy for socialism and for the anti-clerical and seemingly Marxist bent of many of their Eastern Armenian comrades. But it was on the issue of party–state relations and the problem of Muslim insurgency that the most severe intra-party strain developed. The governmental wing of the party, represented by Kachaznuni and Khatisian, believed in a gradual, patient approach to change and gaining the trust and fidelity of the republic's minority elements. They emphasized that this was not an 'Armenian Republic' but rather the 'Republic of Armenia', where all inhabitants should enjoy equal rights regardless of race or religion. But the fact that the southern portion of Yerevan province (Sharur-Nakhichevan) and much of Kars province refused to acknowledge the Armenian government and frequently interrupted the flow of rail traffic strengthened the position of the hard-liners, who insisted that these were extraordinary times requiring revolutionary measures to preserve the fragile infant state. Repressive measures should be used if required, for in the view of militants such as Ruben Ter-Minasian, who became Minister of War in 1920, the Turkic elements understood not the persuasion of words but the language of fire. What was more, democratic ideals were all well and good, but they would be hollow indeed if the republic collapsed. Hence, there should be firm party control over the government, which should serve at the pleasure of and submit to all directives of the party's central organ, the Bureau. A world party congress in the autumn of 1919 sided, on balance, with the moderate faction by establishing an indirect chain of command between the cabinet and the Bureau and by forbidding comrades from serving at the same time in both the cabinet and the Bureau. The prohibition was nonetheless sidestepped in May 1920 because of the sovietization of Azerbaijan, an abortive Bolshevik uprising, and renewed Muslim insurgency.

Relations with the Armenian diaspora were shaped by regional and political factors. The diaspora was made up overwhelmingly of Western Armenians, some of whom had emigrated from the Ottoman Empire years before the First World War either for economic reasons or in the aftermath of the massacres of 1894–6 and 1909. Then there was the post-1915 refugee population, most of which was concentrated in the Arab provinces that came under French or British control by the end of the war. It was natural, therefore, that the diaspora should think of the Armenian homeland as being centred in the Ottoman Armenian provinces, on the great plateau in the provinces of Van, Bitlis, Erzerum, Kharpert (Mamuret-ul-Aziz), Tigranakert (Diyarbekir), and the region of Lesser Armenia west of the Euphrates River, now the province of Sivas, historic Sebastia. Many Armenians even considered the Mediterranean coastal region of Cilicia, where an Armenian state had existed from the eleventh to the fourteenth centuries, to be part of the national patrimony. But few Western Armenians could envisage the Russian Armenian provinces or the city of Yerevan as being the focal point of Armenian national aspirations. There was even some concern among Western Armenian leaders that the formation of a small Armenian state in the Caucasus might prompt the Allied peacemakers to reduce the Ottoman territories to be awarded to the Armenians. It was possible, therefore, to celebrate the existence of the 'Araratian' Republic, but this 'little brother' should not be regarded as the natural child and heir of the emancipation struggle of the Western Armenians.

The strong Armenian regional loyalties were not the only cause of discord. Among the Western Armenians, the Dashnaktsutiun did not enjoy the near monopoly of power that it possessed in the Caucasus. Although most Armenians were non-partisans, there were a great many sympathizers and supporters of the Social Democrat Hnchakian party, founded in 1887, and the constitutional democratic Ramkavar party, which had been formed in 1908 by the merger of several pre-existing groups. The Ramkavar intellectuals were also linked with the Armenian General Benevolent Union, which like the party had been organized in Egypt with the active support of Boghos Nubar Pasha, son of a former Armenian prime minister of that country. Since 1912 Nubar had become the foremost spokesman of the Western Armenians and, after the end of the war in 1918, he was to champion the Armenian cause in the Paris peace negotiations. He and his supporters did not welcome the arrival of a separate delegation headed by Avetis Aharonian to represent the Armenian Republic. The adherents of the Dashnaktsutiun in the diaspora were not insignificant, and their newspapers were unwavering in their loyalty to the Armenian Republic, but just beneath the surface many Western Armenian members of the Dashnaktsutiun shared some of the reservations and doubts of their political opponents. Still, by 1920 the tensions had eased greatly, in part because all Armenian political leaders came to understand that the entire Armenian case was in extreme jeopardy and that any remaining hope of a united, independent Armenia had to be built around the Yerevan government, which had been granted de facto recognition by the major Allied powers and the United States of America. But the heritage of alienation between homeland and diaspora was to grow even more intense when what was left of the Armenian state was transformed into a Soviet Republic. Nor would the strong sense of separation and difference be erased with the collapse of the Soviet Union and the emergence of a new Armenian Republic in 1991. Professions of unity and solidarity notwithstanding, underlying mutual suspicions and distrust have not disappeared.

Regional issues

The break-up of Transcaucasia into three separate states created enormous problems that would take years to sort out and settle. The demographic patch-work of the region would leave hundreds of thousands of Armenians and Azerbaijanis outside the boundaries of their titular republics no matter how the borders were ultimately drawn. Armenians were the most widely dispersed, with more living outside than inside the Armenian Republic. The issue of minority rights, including a definition of 'national cultural autonomy', was often discussed and debated but never resolved during the existence of the three independent states, which despite their sharp differences did recognize one another and establish diplomatic relations. For the Armenians it was espe-cially painful to see the prominent place and status attained by the communities in Tiflis, Baku, and other cities eroded by social and economic legislation in the Republics of Georgia and Azerbaijan, and sometimes through outright confiscation and usurpation. On the other hand, the spectre of Armenian rule created a deep sense of danger among the Muslim popula-tion in the provinces of Yerevan and Kars. But the Muslims were supplied with money, weapons, and officers by both Azerbaijan and the retreating Ottoman armies, allowing them to defy the Yerevan government for months on end.

The perilous status of ethno-religious minorities, however serious, was less of an issue than the entangled border disputes. In the contest with Georgia over control of the southern counties of Tiflis province, the Armenians staked historic, ethnographic, and geographic claims to Lori and Akhalkalak (Javakhk). These districts formed a part of the northern perimeter of the Armenian Plateau and were inhabited overwhelmingly by Armenians. The dispute spilled over into the adjacent counties of Ardahan and Olti when the Turks evacuated the province of Kars in the spring of 1919. Georgian kingdoms had extended into all these areas at one time or another, and if the Armenians were now a majority in certain districts, this, said the Georgians, was because of the haven Georgia had long accorded Armenians fleeing from Turkish persecutions.

The dispute led to a brief armed conflict in Lori in December 1918, deeply embarrassing the two peoples who had lived in peace through the centuries. The British military authorities finally arranged a truce, whereby the southern portion of Lori remained under Armenian occupation, while the northern sector was made into a neutral zone. Georgian leaders had effective ways of reminding the Armenian government that the lifeline to Yerevan from the port of Batum passed through Tiflis and that the half-million Armenians remaining in Georgia were vulnerable. Armenia was still deeply resentful of having been abandoned by the Georgians and was now equally resentful of Georgia's ability to interrupt the flow of rail traffic almost at will. Still, it was fortunate that the scope of Armenian–Georgian disagreements could be defined and relatively localized. With both govern-ments realizing that the survival of one republic was essential for the well-being of the other, the two sides began in 1919 to put forth compromise proposals to settle their disputes. Subsequently, in 1921, the Lori neutral zone became a part of Soviet Armenia, while Georgia held on to Akhalkalak and Akhaltskha. In the long run, neither side was to have Ardahan and Olti.

Hostility between Armenians and Azerbaijanis was deep-seated and widespread. Racial, religious, and cultural differences were only the backdrop to the bitter territorial feuds. Azerbaijan claimed all of the provinces of Baku and Elizavetpol, much of Tiflis province, most of Yerevan province, and all of Kars and Batum. This would have left an Armenia surrounded entirely by Azerbaijani territory and limited to the small area between Yerevan city and the western shore of Lake Sevan. Armenia, on the other hand, advanced historic, economic, cultural, and strategic claims to the whole of Yerevan province and the western, highland sector of Elizavetpol province, from Kazakh to Mountainous Karabagh and Zangezur.

Armenian–Azerbaijani relations were characterized throughout the entire period by repeated clashes along the still-undefined borders and even deep within the two republics. Just as the Muslim-populated districts to the south of Yerevan defied the Armenian government, the Armenians of Karabagh and Zangezur rejected Azerbaijani jurisdiction and declared themselves integral parts of the Armenian Republic. The British command at Baku came to accept the Azerbaijani rationale and practical arguments for provisional jurisdiction in Karabagh and Zangezur and sanctioned the appointment of Dr. Khosrov Bek Sultanov as temporary governor general. Zangezur successfully withstood both Azerbaijani and British pressure, but the attempts of the Karabagh Armenians to do likewise resulted in bloodshed and the razing of several Armenian villages in June 1919. The Yerevan government could afford little assistance to the isolated Karabagh Armenians, who in August finally yielded to provisional and conditional Azerbaijani jurisdiction. Violations of the conditions of the agreement led to an abortive Armenian rebellion in March 1920. In retribution, the Azerbaijani forces burned the city of Shushi, hanged its bishop, and massacred many of its inhabitants. After Armenia was sovietized at the end of 1920, Azerbaijan, which had already become Soviet, briefly offered Mountainous Karabagh and other disputed territories to Armenia, but the gesture of Soviet fraternalism was soon withdrawn. Then, in 1923, a part but not all of the highland was formed into the autonomous region (*oblast*) of Nagornyi Karabakh within Soviet Azerbaijan. Armenian resentment smouldered down through the decades until in 1988 it erupted into a renewed bloody contest for Mountainous Karabagh.

The international scene

From the outset, the republic's leaders adopted a pro-Western political orientation. It was upon the West that the realization of Armenian aspirations to a united, independent state depended. Arriving at a *modus vivendi* with the defeated Turkish government seemed out of the question, for not only were the Armenians unwilling to deal with the state that had carried out the Genocide, the effects of which were daily manifest on the streets of Yerevan, but also the victorious Allied powers had proclaimed from the outset that the Armenian lands in the Ottoman Empire were to be liberated from Turkish rule. And with the emergence of the Turkish resistance movement under Mustafa Kemal (Ataturk), there was even less likelihood of bilateral relations, for that movement was predicated on maintaining the territorial integrity of the non-Arab regions of the empire and on preventing the formation of an Armenian state in the eastern provinces. Nor did the Armenian government enter into serious negotiations with the Soviet government in Moscow. Ideologically, the Dashnaktsutiun was an avowed political opponent of Bolshevism, and practically Bolshevik power appeared far removed, with the vast plains that separate the Caucasus from central Russia under the control of the White Armies fighting to crush the 'Reds' and put an end to the 'Bolshevik adventure'. Of all its close and immediate neighbours, Armenia maintained cordial relations only with Persia, although most Iranians were linked by their Shi'ite Muslim faith to the Azerbaijanis. But the friendship of the Persian government was of little real help, as the railway from Yerevan to Tabriz and on to Tehran was controlled throughout most of this period by Muslim insurgents in Sharur-Nakhichevan. In the end, it was the West that held the key to the attainment of Armenian national aspirations.

When the heads of all major Allied countries gathered in Paris in January 1919 to impose a peace settlement on Germany, the Ottoman Empire, and the other defeated countries, the Armenians were euphoric in anticipation of the enactment of the wartime pledges of the Western leaders regarding the punishment of war criminals and the guarantee of a secure national future for the Armenian people. And, indeed, among its first acts the Paris Peace Conference declared that 'because of the historical misgovernment by the Turks of subject peoples and the terrible massacres of Armenians and others in recent years, the Allied and Associated Powers are agreed that Armenia, Syria, Mesopotamia, Palestine and Arabia must be completely severed from the Turkish Empire'. These states could be recognized provisionally as independent nations 'subject to the rendering of administrative advice and assistance by a mandatory power'.[5]

When the Peace Conference invited Boghos Nubar Pasha and Avetis Aharonian in February to present Armenia's claims, they made their case for an Armenian state extending from Transcaucasia and the Black Sea to Cilicia and the Mediterranean Sea. Subsequently ridiculed as being totally

---

5   US Department of State, *Papers Relating to the Foreign Relations of the United States, 1919: The Paris Peace Conference*, vol. 3 (Washington, DC: Government Printing Office, 1943), pp. 795–6.

unrealistic, the Armenian claims nonetheless closely paralleled the maps that had been sketched in the privacy of the British Foreign Office and the United States Department of State. The French had their own plans for Cilicia and were not enthusiastic about Armenian pretensions there, but Prime Minister Georges Clemenceau ultimately assented to the region's inclusion in Armenia if the United States was prepared to assume a protective mandate for the new country. Despite the professed sympathy of the Allied powers, Armenia was not given a seat at the peace conference or the financial and military support that it sought. The Western Armenian territories remained under Turkish control and the refugee population was unable to return home. Allied spokesmen advised patience, as many of these issues would be resolved once a peace settlement had been imposed on Turkey and the boundaries of Armenia had been determined. The extent of those boundaries depended on whether a mandatory power could be found for Armenia. President Woodrow Wilson favoured a mandate for Armenia, yet he decided to hold the issue in abeyance until he could get the Senate to ratify the peace treaty with Germany, inclusive of the Covenant of the League of Nations.

When the Treaty of Versailles between the Allied powers and Germany was signed on 28 June 1919, Wilson had still not put the mandate question to the Senate. The Allied heads of state dispersed without having settled either the Armenian Question or the larger Eastern Question. This postponement was a major setback for the Armenians and gave impetus to the Turkish resistance movement led by General Mustafa Kemal. Still, nothing was very clear in mid-1919, and the Armenians could take solace in the sharp rebuke that the Allies handed the official Turkish delegation when it had pleaded for clemency. In their reply the Allied leaders condemned Turkey for the perpetration of massacres 'whose calculated atrocity equals or exceeds anything in recorded history'. As for leaving alien races under Turkish rule, 'the experiment has been tried too long and too often for there to be the least doubt of its results'.[6]

Delay of the Turkish peace treaty turned out to be much longer than anyone had expected. The United States had already begun its retreat into 'splendid isolation', as the Senate twice refused to ratify the German peace treaty, which anticipated American participation in the League of Nations. In the bitter rivalry between President Wilson and the Republican leadership, even many senators sympathetic to the Armenians voted to reject Wilson's belated request for authorization to assume a mandate for Armenia. The United States in effect withdrew from the peace process.

It was not until 1920 that the European Allies, who had been quarrelling among themselves over the spoils of war, took up the matter of the Turkish

---

6 British Foreign Office, *Documents on British Foreign Policy, 1919–1939*, 1st series, vol. 4, ed. W.L. Woodward and Rohan Butler (London: HMSO, 1952), pp. 645–6.

settlement in earnest. The beginning of these deliberations in February coincided with the receipt of alarming reports that the Armenians of Cilicia were again being massacred. Following the war, some 150,000 Armenians had returned to the cities and villages of Cilicia, which was placed under French supervision. But this was the region that the Turkish nationalist movement chose for its first test of strength. The battle for the city of Marash culminated on 10 February 1920 with the withdrawal of the French garrison, the flight of most of the Armenian inhabitants into a raging blizzard that claimed thousands of lives, and the massacre or captivity of those unable to escape. The struggle for Cilicia would continue until 1922, when the Armenians were forced to abandon the Taurus and Amanus mountains and the great alluvial plain of Adana and pass into permanent exile.

The problems in Cilicia reinforced the view of the Allied leaders that the new Armenian state should be relatively compact, so that not only Cilicia but also the western half of the Turkish Armenian provinces had to be excluded. In their half-hearted attempts to determine Armenia's boundaries without having to commit armed forces to implement their decision, the European Allies, prompted by British Prime Minister David Lloyd George, struck upon a clever way out of the dilemma. They invited President Wilson to draw the final boundaries between Armenia and Turkey within the limits of the eastern provinces of Van, Bitlis, Erzerum, and Trebizond. The manoeuvre was intended to coax the United States to shoulder some share in the Armenian settlement and to shift the responsibility for any future unfortunate developments to the American president. Wilson took the bait and agreed to appoint a commission to define the boundaries. Thus, the European Powers were able to announce that they had fulfilled their solemn pledges to the Armenian people.

By the Treaty of Sèvres of 10 August 1920 the Turkish government committed itself to accept the boundary that President Wilson would draw within the four provinces, recognized Armenia as a sovereign, independent state, and pledged to assist in the repatriation and restoration of survivors, in the rescue of Armenian women and children held captive in Muslim households, and in the prosecution of the perpetrators of the Armenian massacres. Avetis Aharonian, as the plenipotentiary of the Republic of Armenia, was a signatory to the treaty, and both he and Boghos Nubar signed an additional protocol guaranteeing minority rights. As a party to the treaty, Armenia received formal diplomatic recognition from all other signatory states. Moreover, by that time the republic had opened diplomatic missions in a score of countries from Argentina to Ethiopia and Japan. As a hopeful precursor of what might follow, the assimilated Armenian communities of Central and Eastern Europe demonstrated a stirring of renewed national consciousness and sent deputations to Yerevan to explore the possibility of return to the homeland after centuries in the diaspora. If Armenia could endure as an independent state, a reversal of the centuries-long tides of exodus could bring back hundreds of thousands of Armenians.

It was not until November 1920 that President Wilson submitted his decision on the Armenian boundaries. 'Wilsonian Armenia' encompassed most of the provinces of Van, Bitlis, and Erzerum, and, as an outlet to the sea, the city and port of Trebizond and their hinterland. A viable, united Armenian state had been created, but only on paper. For the Armenians it was both sad and ironic that Wilson's decision was announced at the very time that the Republic of Armenia was waging a losing struggle for survival.

Partition and sovietization of the Republic

While the Allied Powers completed the Turkish treaty without making any provision for the military enforcement of its terms, Mustafa Kemal and other Turkish resistance leaders sought Soviet support in the struggle against their common adversaries. Soviet leaders, in their turn, recognized the potential role that Turkish influence could play in stirring the Muslim colonial world against the Western powers. The first contacts were made by fugitive Young Turk leaders such as Enver and Jemal. Thereafter, Kemal sent his own delegation to Moscow to press for the elimination of the Caucasian barrier between Turkey and the Bolsheviks. Already Turkish elements in Baku had been instrumental in persuading the government of independent Azerbaijan not to resist the Red Army, which had finally overwhelmed the White Armies and arrived at the flanks of the Caucasus Mountains. The attempts of Foreign Affairs Commissar Grigorii Chicherin to gain some territorial concessions in favour of Armenia were emphatically rejected by the Turkish representatives, and in this they ultimately received the concurrence of Stalin and apparently of Lenin himself. In a draft Soviet–Turkish treaty initialled on 24 August 1920, the two sides pledged themselves to make every effort to open an unobstructed avenue between the two countries for the free flow of men and material, to establish diplomatic and economic relations, and to reject any international act not accepted by the other side. Soviet Russia accorded both financial and military aid to the Turkish 'revolutionary' movement. It was only after receipt of the text of the treaty and the first instalment of Soviet gold that Kemal gave the orders to his commander of the eastern front, General Kâzim Karabekir, to invade the Armenian Republic.

After the sovietization of Azerbaijan, the Armenian government, too, dispatched a delegation to Moscow to seek a *modus vivendi* with the impending victors in the Russian civil war. Chicherin and his assistant Lev Karakhan stated that Soviet Russia was prepared to recognize the independence and inviolability of the Armenian Republic. They seemed sympathetic to Armenia's claims to the disputed territories of Karabagh, Zangezur, and Nakhichevan, and even suggested the possibility of a moderate border rectification with Turkey, but they also insisted on the unhindered transit of men, goods, and supplies over Armenia to Anatolia. Although the principles of a treaty were agreed upon by the beginning of summer, the negotiations were suddenly suspended, probably because the Turkish delegation was then already *en route* to Moscow.

Then, in September 1920, the Turkish army invaded Armenia and within two months Armenia lay prostrate in defeat. The crushing terms imposed on Armenia by the Treaty of Aleksandropol on 2/3 December 1920 cast the republic back to where it had begun – confined to a part of the province of Yerevan and the Sevan basin. All of Kars province and from Yerevan province the southern area of Sharur-Nakhichevan and the county of Surmalu, including Mount Ararat, were lost. The remaining terms effectively made Armenia a vassal of Turkey. But this treaty, signed with great reluctance by Alexandre Khatisian, was rendered illegal by the fact that the Armenian government had already given way to a Soviet administration. The transfer of power on 2 December had taken place without bloodshed under the terms of a treaty negotiated between the cabinet of Simon Vratzian and the Soviet plenipotentiary Boris Legran. Armenia was declared a Soviet Socialist Republic, and for its part Soviet Russia pledged to take immediate steps to furnish the requisite military force to consolidate and defend the state and to restore the boundaries as they had existed prior to the Turkish invasion – signifying the recovery of all the recently lost territories. Neither the Armenian army command nor members of political parties were to be persecuted for any previous anti-Soviet activities. In view of the prevailing circumstances, the possibility of preserving at least the Caucasian Armenian Republic in the form of a Soviet satellite state was more than might have been expected. Khatisian's heavy responsibility of signing the Aleksandropol treaty with the Turks late that night was intended simply to avert a further Turkish advance, pending the advance of the Red Army into Armenia.

Within a week the Military Revolutionary Committee (Revkom) of Armenia and the first echelons of the Red Army had arrived in Yerevan. Among the initial acts of the Revkom, dominated by young, vindictive Bolsheviks, was the repudiation of the Armenian–Soviet treaty signed by Legran. Hundreds of former government officials and non-Bolshevik political leaders were imprisoned, the army officer corps was exiled, and a harsh regime of retribution and requisition was imposed. These repressive policies led to a rebellion in February 1921, driving the Revkom out of the capital and surrounding districts. Not until Georgia had been sovietized in March were sufficient Red Army reinforcements brought in to suppress the revolt. In April thousands of insurgents and civilians withdrew into Zangezur, where the battle continued under the command of Garegin Nzhdeh until the summer, when a reorganized government of Soviet Armenia issued an amnesty, with assurances that Zangezur would be included in Armenia, not Azerbaijan. Many of the partisans and political leaders of the independent Republic of Armenia then crossed the Araxes River into Persia (Iran) and exile.

As it turned out, Soviet Russia sacrificed the Armenian Question to cement the Turkish alliance. By the Treaty of Moscow of March 1921 Kemal's government of the Grand National Assembly in Ankara dropped its claims to the port of Batum in return for Russian abandonment of efforts to retrieve some of the lost Armenian territory, especially the Surmalu district with Mount Ararat. What was more, the treaty provided that Sharur-Nakhichevan and even the southern sector of Yerevan district would not be attached to Soviet Armenia but rather would be constituted as an autonomous region of Soviet Azerbaijan. Whatever qualms Chicherin and Karakhan may still have had paled before the decisive support the Turkish delegation received from Stalin. As stipulated by the Treaty of Moscow, almost identical terms were included in the Treaty of Kars of October 1921 between Turkey and the three Soviet republics of Transcaucasia. Described by Bagrat Borian, a prominent Soviet historian later purged by Stalin, as one of the most oppressive and ignominious treaties in the annals of history, that document clamped the lid on the Armenian Question and locked Soviet Armenia within its narrow space of less than 30,000 square kilometres. The European powers put their own seal on the Armenian Question two years later by renegotiating the Treaty of Sèvres. The Turkish victory in the resultant Lausanne treaties was so complete that neither the word 'Armenia' nor 'Armenian' was allowed to appear anywhere in the texts. It was a bitter irony for the Armenians that, of the several defeated Central Powers in the First World War, Turkey alone expanded beyond its pre-war boundaries – and this only on the Armenian front.

The interlude of Armenian independence had ended. Born of desperation and hopelessness, the Armenian Republic lacked the resources to solve its enormous domestic and international problems. Yet within a few months it had become the fulcrum of national aspirations for revival, unification, and perpetuity. Limitations and shortcomings aside, the rudiments of government were created and organic development began. The failure to achieve permanent independence left a worldwide Armenian dispersion with unrequited grief, frustration, and resentment. Nonetheless, the legacy of the Armenian Republic was not lost. Armenian government and statehood had been recovered for the first time in centuries, if only on a small part of the historic territories. The colossal Armenian sacrifices had not been entirely in vain, for the core of the Republic of Armenia continued as the Armenian Soviet Socialist Republic, where a part of the nation would strive to etch a place in the sun.

Bibliography

Bournoutian, G.A., *A Concise History of the Armenian People: From Ancient Time to Present* (Costa Mesa: Mazda, 2003).

Crimes against Humanity and Civilization: The Genocide of the Armenians (Brookline, MA: Facing History and Ourselves Foundation, 2004).

Dadrian, V.N., *The History of the Armenian Genocide: Ethnic Conflict from the Balkans to Anatolia to the Caucasus* (Providence: Berghahn 1995).

Hovannisian, R.G., *Armenia on the Road to Independence* (Berkeley and Los Angeles: University of California Press, 1967).

—— *The Republic of Armenia,* 4 vols (Berkeley and Los Angeles: University of California Press, 1971–96).

—— ed., *The Armenian People from Ancient to Modern Times*, vol. 2, chapters 8–10 (New York: St. Martin's, 1997).

—— ed., *Remembrance and Denial: The Case of the Armenian Genocide* (Detroit: Wayne State University Press, 1999).

Kazemzadeh, F., *The Struggle for Transcaucasia, 1917–21* (New York and Oxford: Philosophical Library, 1951).

Suny, R.G., *Looking toward Ararat: Armenia in Modern History* (Bloomington and Indianapolis: University of Indiana Press, 1993).

Walker, C.J., *Armenia: The Survival of a Nation*, revised second edition (London: Routledge, 1990).

6   Soviet Armenia, 1921–91

Ronald Grigor Suny

The first independent Armenian Republic collapsed late in 1920, the victim of dual threats: from the advancing forces of Soviet Russia and the Turkish nationalists in Anatolia. With Western Armenia in the hands of the triumphant Kemalists, only Eastern Armenia, that small portion of historic Armenia that had been under Persian rule until 1828 and then part of the Russian Empire until 1917, remained under the control of Armenians at the end of the Russian Civil War (1918–21). When General Dro (Drastamat Kanayan), the plenipotentiary of the government of independent Armenia, and Otto Silin, the representative of Soviet Russia, proclaimed Armenia an 'independent socialist republic' on 2 December 1920, the country was at the nadir of its modern history. Armenians had been driven out of the Turkish-held parts of the Armenian plateau in the genocidal massacres and deportations of 1915. The population of Russian Armenia had also fallen precipitously since the outbreak of the First World War because of warfare, migration and disease. By 1920 only 720,000 lived in Eastern Armenia, a decline of 30 per cent. Moreover, almost half of that population was made up of refugees. Many of the social and political institutions that Armenians in the Caucasus and the Ottoman Empire had built up over centuries had been destroyed. The Armenian middle class, the once privileged elite of Tiflis and Baku, was now suspect in the eyes of the new Soviet governments in Georgia and Azerbaijan. Their unenviable choice was either to accommodate themselves to the alien socialist order or to emigrate to the West. In the seven years of war, genocide, revolution and civil war (1914–21) Armenian society had in many ways been 'demodernized', thrown back to its pre-capitalist agrarian economy and more traditional peasant-based society.

Soviet rule

The first tasks of the new Soviet government in Yerevan were to feed the 'starving Armenians', rebuild the economy, and establish the new political order. They quickly established a political monopoly over the country, eliminating other political parties. A secret police organization modelled on the Russian Cheka was set up within days, and all governmental institutions of the old republic were abolished. The old Russian imperial law code, which had been used in the independent republic, was replaced by the legal statutes of the Soviet Russian republic. And most onerous of all, the economic policy later known as War Communism – nationalization of banks and industries, confiscation of foodstuffs, severe restrictions on the market – was imposed on Armenia. The rapidity and harshness of the Communists' initial policies created great dissatisfaction with the Soviet government. It failed to take effective measures to alleviate the food and fuel shortages that were caused in part by Menshevik Georgia's blockade of Armenia. Red Army men moved into villages and seized grain from the peasants to feed soldiers and townspeople. The hope that the Red Army would drive out the Turks proved illusory. Bolshevik Russia viewed the Turkish nationalists as allies against Western imperialism and was reluctant to challenge them in Armenia.

When the Red Army marched out of Armenia to overthrow the Mensheviks in Georgia in February 1921, nationalist party leaders organized a revolt, which lasted a few months. Having subdued Georgia, the Red Army returned to Armenia, overcame the resistance of the nationalists, and retook the capital, Yerevan. The rebellion had a sobering effect on the Communists. Moscow replaced the Armenian Communist revolutionary committee with a new government headed by Aleksandr Miasnikian (1886–1925), a man trained in the law but with a long period of service fighting on the western front during the Russian Civil War. He was commissioned by Vladimir Lenin, the chairman of the Soviet government in Moscow, to carry out a more moderate policy towards the Caucasus. In a letter to his Caucasian comrades Lenin pointed out that the Soviet republics in Transcaucasia were more backward, 'more peasant than Russia', and that socialist policies had to be implemented very slowly. He called on the party to exercise 'greater gentleness, caution, concessions in dealing with the petty bourgeoisie, the intelligentsia, and especially the peasantry'. Lenin was suspicious that many Communists were not sensitive to local and ethnic peculiarities, that their 'internationalism' and calls for unity with Soviet Russia were really disguised forms of Russian nationalism. 'Scratch a Communist', he once said, 'and you will find a Great Russian chauvinist!' A degree of autonomy for the smaller nationalities was necessary, he believed, in order to win them over to the Soviet cause.

This second Soviet Armenian government to come to Yerevan introduced the more moderate economic programme known as NEP (the New Economic Policy), which denationalized much of the economy and gave the peasants the right to control their own grain surpluses. Lenin called this new policy a tactical retreat to state capitalism. Rather than fully nationalizing the economy and eliminating the market, NEP decreed that only the 'commanding heights' of the economy – large-scale enterprises, railroads and banks – were to be nationalized. In Armenia the peasant economy was gradually restored, while at the same time the Communists tightened their exclusive political control over state and society. Great efforts were made to convince people that the Soviet system was superior to capitalism, that Soviet democracy was a higher form of democracy, and that history was on the side of socialism. Though Armenia lost its actual sovereignty, the Communists promoted Armenian culture and education. The Soviet government encouraged Armenian intellectuals to return to Armenia by subsidizing a national culture, schools in the national language, the new university in Yerevan, a conservatory, and a national film studio. In many ways the tiny territory of the new republic became ever more 'Armenian'.

But once Armenia came under the control of the Communists, the territorial and political interests of Caucasian Armenians were subordinated to those of the Soviets. Because of Lenin's support for the anti-imperialist struggles of the Muslim East, Soviet Armenia soon gave up its claims to Turkish Armenia in the 1921 Treaties of Kars and Moscow. Defeated and displaced by the Bolsheviks, the Armenian Revolutionary Federation (Dashnaktsutiun), now the major diaspora political party, opposed these 'anti-national' policies and adopted a vehement hostility towards the new regime. In the view of supporters of Soviet Armenia, the new republic provided a degree of physical security that Armenians had seldom known in their long past. Armenia was part of the largest country in the world, a great power that could easily prevent incursions from Turkey or Iran. But in the view of the opponents of Soviet Armenia, the state was a fraudulent homeland, which did not represent the national aspirations of Armenians. The Soviet government would not push the Armenian cause and attempt to retrieve lost lands in Turkey. Indeed, the Soviets had granted the neighbouring Republic of Soviet Azerbaijan the Armenian-populated region of Mountainous Karabagh. Only a minority of Armenians living outside the Soviet Union recognized Soviet Armenia, and for decades many diaspora Armenians spoke as if no Armenian state existed.

Soviet Armenia was a haven for Armenian refugees from around the world and for Armenian migrants from other parts of the USSR. The pull towards Armenia, even in its Soviet incarnation, and the fear of *odaratsum* (denationalization) proved irresistible for many. When the Soviet government invited repatriation, 28,000 refugees, mostly from Greece, Iraq and Istanbul, some from France and the USA, settled in Soviet Armenia in the first decade. The Norwegian explorer and humanitarian Fridtjof Nansen, as League of Nations' High Commissioner for Refugees, worked assiduously to convince the League to finance the repatriation of Armenians to Soviet Armenia. 'There is, in fact,' he argued, 'in this little republic a national home for the Armenians at last, and I ask the members of the Assembly whether they sincerely and earnestly believe that any other national home can be hoped for. I believe I know the answer which their consciences will give, and I appeal to the Assembly to approve this one effort to carry out all

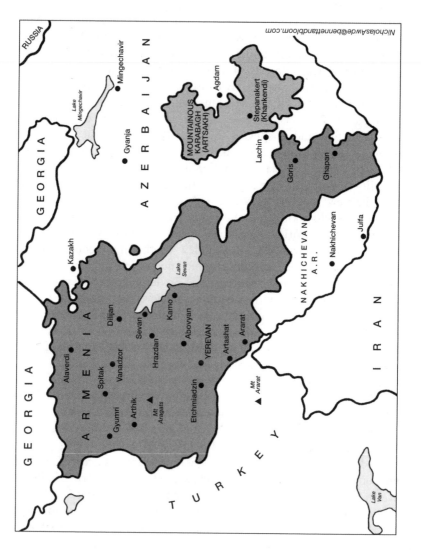

Figure 6.1 Soviet and post-Soviet Armenia and Mountainous Karabagh

the promises which have been made in the past concerning a national home for the Armenian nation'.[1] Ultimately the loan was not given, but from 1929 to 1937 16,000 more refugees arrived in Armenia, mostly from Europe and financed by the Soviet government.

The Stalin years

The gradual restoration of the economy under NEP ended in 1928 with the adoption of a new programme of rapid industrialization and the forced collectivization of agriculture. The period from 1928 through the early 1930s is known as the 'Stalin Revolution', for Joseph Stalin, the unchallenged dictator of the Soviet Union, both initiated and directed this monumental state-driven social transformation. Collectivization was a profoundly revolutionary change for the majority of the Armenian population. Once and for all, it ended independent private farming. Peasants lost control over their own household economy and became producers for the state procurement agencies. The Communist Party increased its political hold over the peasants and created the instruments with which it could extract by force and heavy taxation the grain needed for cities and workers. Village headmen, who had been the traditional leaders of rural society, were now treated as kulaks and exiled from their homes. Peasants became a second-class social group in Soviet society – not included in the social security system, underpaid for their produce and labour, and regarded as a backward element. After 1932, when internal passports were issued for urban dwellers in the USSR, peasants were not given the precious documents and therefore could not freely leave their collective farms. Yet they thwarted the law, and thousands of villagers left the countryside and migrated to the towns, where they made up the greater part of the expanding industrial labour force. Those who remained in the villages suffered enormously, though eventually the state allowed them the right to cultivate small household plots and to sell some of their output at collective farm markets.

In brief, collectivization was a war of the state against the peasantry, and its effects reached far beyond agriculture. The mass migrations from the countryside eventually turned Armenia from a country of villages into a country of towns and cities. Instead of producing primarily agricultural goods, Armenia became an industrial economy. But its economy was closely tied to the rest of the Soviet economy. Supplies of raw materials and of energy came from outside the republic, and what was produced, in turn, was sold outside of Armenia. Many products were only partially produced in Armenia and finished elsewhere. The modest prosperity Armenians achieved in the Soviet period, particularly after the death of Stalin in 1953,

---

1 K. Davis, *The Soviets at Geneva: The U.S.S.R. at the League of Nations, 1919–1933* (Chambéry: Réunies, 1934), p. 41.

was highly dependent on the Armenian Republic's connections with the rest of the USSR.

Stalinism, which lasted from roughly 1928 until 1953, not only fundamentally changed Armenia but also established the rigid authoritarian political system and state-run economy that lasted until the Gorbachev reforms of the late 1980s. During the years of Stalin's life the state used violence not only against the peasants but also, in the Great Purges of 1937–9, against other ordinary citizens, army officers, Communist Party officials, and intellectuals. The popular young Communist leader Aghasi Khanjian died in mysterious circumstances in 1936, and his followers were condemned as political deviants. His successor, Haik Amatuni, was executed, and thousands of high officials were either killed or imprisoned. The writers Aksel Bakunts and Vahan Totovents and the poet Eghishe Charents perished. Any work that was suspected of nationalism was attacked and could condemn its author to prison. The Armenian Church was ruthlessly disciplined and made subordinate to the Soviet authorities. This led to disaffection among diaspora Church members, and a schism eventually divided the international Armenian Church. Some churches recognized the direct and exclusive authority of the Holy See of Etchmiadzin, which lay in Soviet Armenia, while others rejected any but formal association with the Catholicos at Etchmiadzin and gave their loyalty to a rival see at Antelias in Lebanon.

By the outbreak of the Second World War all the essential features of Stalinism were in place: the state-run command economy, one-party rule enforced by arbitrary and massive terror, state control of the media and culture, and the propagation of an official Soviet patriotism. Though thousands suffered from the ruthless application of state power, other thousands enthusiastically participated in the building of Stalin's variant of socialism. When the Germans invaded the USSR in 1941, tens of thousands of Armenians fought and died in the defence of the Soviet Union. During the Second World War the Soviet state and the Armenian Church made an uneasy peace. In its desperate struggle for survival the Soviet government quickly made a number of concessions to the Armenian Church, which became the major link between Soviet Armenia and the diaspora. Within a month of the German invasion of the USSR, the Supreme Religious Council of the Etchmiadzin Catholicate issued an appeal for unity with the Church and the homeland. There was no other haven for the Armenians, proclaimed the supreme body of the Church, and to aid the Soviet Union is to aid the fatherland.

In late 1942 some of the closed churches in Armenia were reopened, and exiled clergy returned from Siberia. In April 1943 a Council of Ecclesiastical Affairs was created, and a seminary and printing press were allowed in Etchmiadzin. A year later Gevork Cherekjian, who had been the acting head of the Church since the violent death of the last Catholicos in 1938, was received by Stalin in the Kremlin.

The interests of the Church, the Armenian diaspora and the Soviet government almost completely coincided in the brief interlude between the end of the Second World War and the onslaught of the Cold War. The Church supported, indeed encouraged, Soviet efforts to 'repatriate' diaspora Armenians to the Soviet republic. Tens of thousands migrated to Armenia, only to find an impoverished country with no political freedom. Some of them were exiled from their new homeland to prison camps in Siberia. At the same time, Stalin made claims to historic Armenian lands across the border in Turkey. Shortly after the Yalta Conference, the Soviet government initiated a campaign to encourage Armenian settlement in the Armenian Republic and to recover Armenian irredenta in eastern Turkey. On 7 June 1945 Foreign Minister Molotov told the Turkish ambassador to Moscow that the USSR demanded a revision of the Soviet–Turkish border in the region of Kars and Ardahan. Stalin's policy reversed Lenin's agreement with Turkey to give up any Armenian claims against the new Kemalist state and removed one of the most serious impediments to the Soviet Armenian state's defence of Armenian national interests. This change in policy occurred almost simultaneously with the gathering of lay and clerical delegates to the congress in Etchmiadzin to elect a new Catholicos (16–25 June). After his unanimous election, Gevork VI sent a letter to Stalin supporting the repatriation of diaspora Armenians and the return of Armenian lands in Turkey. But the advent of the Cold War and Turkey's integration into the United States-led Western alliance made any border change impossible.

'The Thaw'

With the death of Stalin life became easier in the USSR. The worst aspects of political terror ended, and though the monopoly of Communist Party power remained, there was a significantly greater degree of social and cultural freedom in the years that Nikita Khrushchev ruled the Soviet Union (1953–64). This was a period of reform, sometimes known as 'the Thaw', and material and social life improved for the Armenians. Visitors from abroad became more common in Yerevan, and many Soviet Armenians moved from communal to private apartments. While the standards of living lagged far behind the most developed countries in the West, Armenians were able to meet their needs and many of their desires through the semi-legal 'second economy'. Almost everyone knew someone who could get something outside of the official government stores, which were often marked by empty shelves. Consumer taste improved, and people began to discriminate in their preferences, seeking out foreign-made goods whenever possible. The early revolutionary élan of the 1920s and 1930s had long since been replaced by a more mundane materialism. In the 1950s and 1960s, however, many people still believed in the system and its promises to improve the lives of the Soviet people. That optimism began to fade in the mid-1970s, and the long stolid years of Leonid Brezhnev's rule (1964–82) eroded much of the remaining enthusiasm for the Soviet system. Along with new interest in the ordinary material amenities of normal life, Armenians comforted themselves with a renewed interest in their own history and culture, and nationalism became a unifying sentiment among both intellectuals and ordinary folk.

In the Khrushchev and Brezhnev years the Armenian Communist leaders managed to wrest a degree of autonomy from the central Soviet leaders. High-ranking officials stayed in power for many years, enriched themselves at state expense, and permitted a low level of local nationalism to develop. While a quiet official commemoration of the fiftieth anniversary of the Armenian Genocide (24 April 1965) took place in the Yerevan Opera House, thousands of Armenians demonstrated without permission in the streets of the capital. They called on Moscow to recover Western Armenian lands in Turkey for Armenia. Even the revered Catholicos of All Armenians, Vazgen I, had difficulty trying to calm the crowds. The Kremlin reacted by removing the head of the Armenian Communist Party. Eventually, however, the pressure from popular nationalism was rewarded with the building of an official monument to the Genocide on the hill of Tsitsernakaberd in Yerevan.

Armenian nationalism had its roots in the long textual tradition that Armenian clerics and scholars had elaborated ever since the invention of the Armenian alphabet in the fifth century. In the late eighteenth and through the nineteenth centuries a coherent sense of Armenians as a nation with a distinct and distinguished history was spread by patriots, teachers, writers, and revolutionaries. Though the Soviet regime was ostensibly antinationalist, in fact Soviet nationality policies contributed to a powerful feeling of territorial nationalism. Soviet Armenians were better educated, and knew their history, language and culture more thoroughly than most of their predecessors. Once the heavy hand of Stalin's terror was replaced by the greater tolerance of the late 1950s and 1960s, the pent-up demand for greater national and personal expression exploded in the form of a new nationalism.

The achievements of Soviet Armenian culture were respected both within the USSR and throughout the world. Most famous was the composer Aram Khachaturian, composer of the ballet *Gayane* from which the popular composition 'The Sabre Dance' originated. The painter Martiros Saryan and the filmmaker Sergei Parajanov also enjoyed international reputations. Within the republic an officially sanctioned canon of Armenian art was developed. Certain authors, artists and musicians, like the ethnomusicologist Gomitas (Komitas) or the poet Avetik Isahakian, received state recognition and were taught in schools, while others, like the musician Grigor Suni or poet Vahan Tekeyan, fell out of favour and were deliberately forgotten. Armenians also excelled in science, and large numbers of Armenians with higher education emigrated from the republic to other parts of the Soviet Union.

The end of Soviet rule

Brezhnev died in November 1982 and was succeeded briefly by the former head of the KGB Yuri Andropov (1982–4) and the moribund Konstantin Chernenko (1984–5). Clearly the system, like its leaders, was creaking with age. The Soviet leaders then made a bold move and appointed the youthful Mikhail Gorbachev to the top party position in March 1985. Within a few years the conservative party regime was shaken to its foundations. Gorbachev boldly began a programme of restructuring the Soviet economic and political system (*perestroika*), expanding enormously the bounds of free expression (*glasnost*), and decentralizing political control and increasing democratic participation (*demokratizatsiya*). For the non-Russian peoples he promised greater autonomy and more respect for national cultures and languages, but he opposed any moves towards separation from the Soviet Union.

In Armenia three concerns combined to stimulate a broad-based national movement by 1988. The transformation of Armenia into an industrial-urban country had brought in its wake severe ecological problems, most importantly the threat from a nuclear plant at Metsamor, not far from the capital, Yerevan. Secondly, many Armenians were angered by the pervasive corruption and arrogance of the local Communist regime. Thirdly and most immediately, they were concerned about the fate of Mountainous Karabagh (*Lernayin Gharabagh* in Armenian, *Nagornyi Karabakh* in Russian) an Armenian-populated enclave that lay in the neighbouring Republic of Azerbaijan. This was undoubtedly the single most volatile issue among Armenians (a detailed account is given in chapter 8).

Mountainous Karabagh had been formed as an autonomous region within Azerbaijan shortly after the establishment of Soviet power. In the 1920s 94.4 per cent of its 131,500 people were Armenian and only 5.6 per cent were Azerbaijani, but by 1979 the Armenian proportion had declined to just under 76 per cent while that of the Azerbaijanis had increased to nearly 24 per cent. Armenians were fearful that their demographic decline would eventually match that of the Nakhichevan, also historically Armenian and also placed under Azerbaijani administration, where the initial Armenian minority of 15 per cent had fallen to 1.4 per cent by 1979. Karabagh Armenians blamed the Azerbaijani authorities for an assortment of cultural and economic discontents, and open friction occurred from the 1960s onwards. By 1988 this had developed into clashes, demonstrations and calls for unification with Armenia proper – demands that provoked Azerbaijanis in Sumgait, an industrial town on the Caspian, to go on a rampage that killed at least 31 people.

The rioting and killings in Sumgait made the peaceful transfer of Mountainous Karabagh to Armenia impossible. Through the next year, while Moscow hesitated to take decisive action, Armenians increasingly grew disillusioned with Gorbachev and the programme of *perestroika*, and Azerbaijanis organized into a powerful anti-Armenian nationalist move-ment. The popular Armenian movement, led by the Karabagh committee in

Yerevan and the Krunk (Crane) committee in Stepanakert, continued to grow until its leaders were effectively the most popular and influential political forces among the Armenians.

On 7 December 1988 a massive earthquake devastated northern Armenia, killing at least 25,000 people and rendering hundreds of thousands homeless. World attention focused for several weeks on Armenia, and aid poured in from many countries. Gorbachev flew to Armenia to survey the damage, but he was given a hostile reception because of his Karabagh policies. Even as the country lay crippled by the earthquake, the Communist Party decided to arrest the Karabagh committee members and place the region under the direct administration of Moscow. The attempt by the Communist Party to rule Armenia without the popular representatives of the national movement only worsened the political crisis. In March 1989 many voters boycotted the general elections. Massive demonstrations started up again in early May demanding the release of the members of the Karabagh committee, and in the elections to the Congress of People's Deputies in May Armenians chose people identified with the Karabagh cause. Finally, on the last day of May the Karabagh committee members were released to the cheers of demonstrators who greeted their arrival in Yerevan. Already emerging as the most important of the movement's leaders, the philologist Levon Ter Petrosian made it clear that the committee had a broader vision than merely the solution of the Karabagh question. Ultimately determined to bring full democracy and independence to Armenia, the trajectory of the movement led to a head-on collision with the Communist Party.

On 1 December 1989 the Armenian Supreme Soviet defied Moscow and declared Mountainous Karabagh a part of Armenia. By this time Gorbachev's strategy to reform the political structure while preserving a renewed Communist Party had led to a deep polarization of Soviet politics. His policies had failed to revive the stagnating Soviet economy and instead threatened the unity of the Soviet Union. His extraordinary foreign policy successes were generally acknowledged, but inside the USSR he was faced by ever more frequent and ever more threatening crises. In Transcaucasia, as in the rest of the disintegrating Soviet Union, the cycle of economic decline and radicalized politics fed on each other. Both the incomplete political reform, in part democratic, in part preserving the old structures, and the national revolts had negative effects on the economy. In January 1990, pressured by the Pan-Armenian National Movement (ANM; in Armenian *Hayots Hamazgayin Sharzhum* or HHSh), the Armenian Supreme Soviet revised the republic's constitution and gave itself the power to validate USSR laws. Central state authority withered, and the writ of the Kremlin could only be enforced by police and soldiers.

Ethnically the most homogeneous of Soviet republics, Armenia was perhaps the most unfortunate economically – with nearly a quarter of the population homeless, victims of both political and natural earthquakes.

Armenia had a population of about three million. The population of its neighbour Azerbaijan numbered around seven million, and of Georgia five-and-a-half million. The fewer than sixteen million inhabitants of Transcaucasia represented just under 6 per cent of the total Soviet population. The Republic of Armenia was home to only 1.1 per cent of the Soviet population, produced only 0.9 per cent of the USSR's national material product (NMP), retained 1.4 per cent of the state budget revenue, delivered 63.7 per cent of its NMP to other republics, and exported 1.4 per cent abroad. It was highly integrated into the Soviet economy. Its exports flowed almost entirely to other parts of the Union, and its imports came from its sister republics. Along with Estonia and Tajikistan, Armenia had the highest level of imports of any Soviet republic. Forty per cent of all enterprises in Armenia were devoted to defence and were in particular trouble after the collapse of the Soviet defence procurement system in 1991.

After more than two years of the Karabagh conflict, Armenians had moved from being one of the most loyal Soviet nations to a complete loss of confidence in Moscow. What had begun as a peaceful constitutional movement for Armenian rights in Karabagh had, by the spring of 1990, degenerated into vicious pogroms in Azerbaijan, the evacuation of the Armenian community of Baku, and a guerrilla war between two nations in the southern Soviet Union. With the Communist Party in rapid decline and the popular nationalist forces far from united, a vacuum of power could be felt in Armenia. In the elections of the spring and summer of 1990 non-Communists won a parliamentary majority. After several rounds of voting, the newly elected Armenian parliament chose Levon Ter Petrosian instead of the Communist chief as its chairman. With the HHSh in power and the Communists in opposition, Armenia began a rapid transition from Soviet-style government to an independent democratic state. The Armenian national movement leaders argued that Armenians must abandon their reliance on a 'third force', rethink their traditional hostility towards and fear of the Turks, and be prepared to create their own independent state by themselves now that the opportunity had arisen. The HHSh was prepared to deal more directly and forthrightly with the Turks and believed that the question of Armenian lands in Turkey had to be deferred until the issue of full sovereignty and independence was resolved.

On 23 August 1990 Armenia formally declared its intention to become a sovereign and independent state, with Karabagh an integral part of the new Republic of Armenia. The Armenian nation was defined broadly to include not only those on the territory of the republic, but the worldwide diaspora as well. And the government set out to redefine Armenian national interests, recognizing but laying aside for the moment the painful question of the Armenian Genocide and seeking improved relations with Turkey and Iran. In Armenia the new government attempted to extend democratic rule while reducing Communist Party power in enterprises, institutes and the military. Late in October the Supreme Soviet passed a law on privatization of the economy. Ter Petrosian was wary about Gorbachev's efforts to renew the Soviet federation through the signing of a new union treaty, and the Armenian parliament, led by the HHSh, refused to participate in the referendum on the union treaty. At the beginning of March 1991 the Armenian Supreme Soviet announced its intention to secede from the Soviet Union. When in May 1991 Soviet paratroopers landed at Yerevan airport to protect Soviet defence installations in Armenia, without notifying the Armenian government, Ter Petrosian told his people that the Soviet Union had declared war on Armenia.

On the morning of 19 August the world awoke to hear the stunning news that a self-proclaimed 'Emergency Committee' had overthrown Gorbachev and taken control of the Soviet government. For three tense days the forces loyal to Russian president Boris Yeltsin and the democratic movement withstood the threats from the conservative leaders of the army, KGB, and the party. In his Crimean isolation Gorbachev refused to give in to the coup organizers, and after a strained stalemate the army and police refused to obey the plotters. The coup collapsed, and with it the last hopes of a new union treaty.

While Azerbaijan's Communist boss had welcomed the coup, and Georgia's nationalist president vacillated, Ter Petrosian resolutely opposed the plotters. He believed that Gorbachev's personal blunders, indecisiveness and concessions to the conservatives were to blame for the coup. Armenian leaders hoped that a more powerful Russia under Yeltsin would provide the economic and political support that the central government under Gorbachev had denied them. At the same time, there was an awareness that some kind of relationship, particularly in the realm of economics, was essential between Armenia and whatever remained of the Soviet Union.

Within the first two months of the failed coup, Armenians went to the polls twice: the first time on 20 September to reaffirm the commitment to independence; the second on 16 October to elect Levon Ter Petrosian as president of the republic. Receiving 83 per cent of the votes cast, Ter Petrosian now had a popular mandate to realize his vision of Armenian independence and self-sufficiency. On 8 December the leaders of the three Slavic republics – Russia, Ukraine and Belarus – announced that the USSR had ceased to exist and that a commonwealth had been set up by the three republics, which other republics were invited to join. An economic declaration linked the three republics in a common currency system and a joint economic programme. In Yerevan Ter Petrosian offered full support for the initiative and signalled Armenia's intention to join the new Commonwealth of Independent States. On 25 December 1991 the Soviet Union ceased to exist.

The Soviet achievement

For all its faults Soviet-style Communism had changed Armenia fundamentally in its seventy-year rule. The small territory that made up the only existing Armenian state was now demographically more Armenian than it had been in the last several centuries. Its capital was a large modern city of more than a million people. Its ruling elite was Armenian; an Armenian intelligentsia of considerable power had been forged; and the republic could boast one of the most highly educated populations in the Soviet Union. But the revolutionary aspirations of its founders were never realized. Instead of a higher form of democracy and egalitarian society, Soviet Armenia, like much of the rest of the Soviet Union, had become a run-down version of a developing country. The achievements for a society that had suffered revolution, civil war, and state terror were impressive, but by the 1980s the economy that the Soviets had built was in decay. Armenian production could not be easily disaggregated from the rest of the Soviet economy, and output collapsed rapidly. Armenia's principal capital remained its people. On the political front the Soviet system had pacified the Armenian population for many years, but given a possible opening Armenians immediately mobilized one of the most effective nationalist movements in the USSR. The Communist Party fell from power in a peaceful transition, and a democratic nationalist government took its place. But the loss of the empire led to new, unanticipated conflicts. Soviet imperialism had managed a rough peace throughout the Soviet Empire, both within the USSR and along its borders, that precluded interethnic warfare and interstate hostilities. With the end of Pax Sovietica each republic was confronted with internal ethnic problems and external security threats that it would have to deal with on its own. Armenia entered its second period of independence in the twentieth century with war raging on its frontiers.

Bibliography

Libaridian, G.L., *Modern Armenia: People, Nation, State* (New Brunswick and London: Transaction Publishers, 2004).

Matossian, M.K., *The Impact of Soviet Policies in Armenia* (Leiden: E.J. Brill, 1962).

Mouradian, C., *De Staline à Gorbachev: Histoire d'une République Soviètique, L'Arménie* (Paris: Editions Ramsay, 1990).

Suny, R.G., ed., *Transcaucasia, Nationalism and Social Change: Essays in the History of Armenia, Azerbaijan and Georgia* (Ann Arbor: The University of Michigan Press, 1983).

—— *Looking toward Ararat: Armenia in Modern History* (Bloomington and Indianapolis: University of Indiana Press, 1993).

—— 'Soviet Armenia', chapter 11 in R.G. Hovannisian, ed., *The Armenian People*, vol. 2 (New York: St. Martin's, 1997).

Torosian, S. 'Soviet Policy in the Armenian Question', *The Armenian Review*, vol. 2, no. 2 (Summer 1958), pp. 27–39.

Walker, C.J., *Armenia: The Survival of a Nation*, revised second edition (London: Routledge, 1990).

—— ed., *Armenia and Karabagh: The Struggle for Unity* (London: Minority Rights Publications, 1991).

7 Armenians in diaspora

Susan P. Pattie

Following the 1915 Genocide, the numbers and nature of the Armenian diaspora changed dramatically. Always diverse, the diaspora has become more radically dispersed and attained a greater sense of fragile permanence. Today reliable figures are difficult to find but it is generally agreed that at least one half of Armenians in the world live outside the Republic of Armenia.[1] With recent migrations away from that state, it is probable that the balance has shifted to a majority in diaspora, including what many call the 'internal diaspora', other states in the former Soviet Union (FSU). The approximate figures are some five million in diaspora and under three million in the republic. The focus in this chapter will be on the diaspora outside the FSU, providing information about the context of the present diaspora, a description of some of its communities, and an analysis of issues raised.

Origins of the contemporary diaspora

Historical roots

There has been an Armenian diaspora for over seventeen hundred years. Before the twentieth century, the Armenian diaspora was formed by forced

---

1 No reliable census has been undertaken in the Armenian diaspora and figures are therefore approximate. Economic problems in the new Republic of Armenia have encouraged both temporary and permanent migration, especially towards Russia and California. The 2002 census in Armenia showed a population of just over 3 million, nearly 25 per cent below the last Soviet census in 1989. However, many observers believe the number is even lower. Other approximate figures for main regional centers: Los Angeles area, Fresno, San Francisco, CA (up to 1 million); rest of US (500,000); Canada – Toronto and Montreal (45,000); S. America – Argentina (100,000); France – Paris, Marseilles (200,000); UK – London (15,000), Greece (15,000); rest of Europe (10,000); Turkey – Istanbul (50,000); Lebanon – Beirut (100,000?); Syria (120,000); Iran (100,000); other Middle East (Kuwait, Cyprus, Israel, Jordan, Gulf States, Iraq, Egypt) (25,000); Bulgaria (15,000); Australia (20,000). Probably over 1 million Armenians live outside Armenia in the former Soviet Union (Russia, Georgia in particular). Main source: R.H. Dekmejian, 'The Armenian Diaspora', in R.G. Hovannisian, ed., *The Armenian People,* vol. 2 (New York: St. Martin's Press, 1997) pp. 413–43.

migration under the rule of various empires, by survivors escaping the attacks of invaders, by families sending out representatives along trade routes, and by those seeking educational opportunities. Rouben Adalian writes that progressive relocations from early times each 'opened a new chapter in the history of the Armenian diaspora'.[2] Many Armenians living in the contemporary diaspora have their origins in the lands that are now central and southern Turkey, Syria, and Iran, outside what is considered as the ancient Armenian homeland. Their ancestors had migrated or been moved to these places, for example by the Byzantines following the depletion of those areas through wars with the Arabs. It is the blossoming of the trade networks and economic migration in the tenth century which, Adalian believes, brought with them the beginnings of a concept of diaspora. At that point people living in such communities began to speak of themselves as living in exile or colonies. The word for colony is the same as that used today for local community (*gaghout*, from a Semitic root meaning stranger) and has only recently been replaced in common usage by *spiurk* or diaspora.

Legacy of the Ottoman Empire

The Ottoman period is crucial to understanding the present diaspora. The *millet* system of organizing the peoples of the empire by religion effectively enforced and extended the religious aspect of identity, consolidating political power around the Armenian Church. Constantinople remained the leading centre of intellectual life and, with the introduction of vernacular printing, the dialect of the capital influenced the linguistic standard of Western Armenian. Finally, the increasing insecurity and dangers of the last century of Ottoman rule pushed Armenians to look towards education to secure their place in society. In the countryside and city, Armenians began sending both boys and girls to 'national' Armenian schools or to those organized by Protestant missionaries. Though the missionaries were disappointed in the low conversion rate, they had an important effect on the population through the new attitudes towards learning, increased Western influences, and the further opportunities introduced. A significant number of young people went on to become doctors, nurses, and teachers. Equally important, by the time of the Genocide, education was seen by many intellectuals as the way to reclaim and reform Armenian identity.

Genocide and dispersion

The Genocide of the Armenians by the Ottomans is described in chapter 5. In addition to the physical decimation and dispersion, the Genocide is

---

2   Rouben Paul Adalian, 'The Historical Evolution of the Armenian Diasporas', *Journal of Modern Hellenism*, no. 6, 1989, p. 81.

significant for the ways in which it overshadowed most of twentieth-century
Armenian life, both public and private. Jenny Phillips, studying Armenians in
Boston, suggests that Armenians have a root paradigm of an endangered
people.[3] They live as if they, as individuals and a group, are constantly threatened. Nearly every family in the Western diaspora has been directly touched
by the loss and trauma of the Genocide period. The psychological burden of
what these people witnessed and experienced remained with them and was
passed on to the next generations in a variety of ways. Many took their own
survival as a message that they must work hard for those who were
'martyred'. New sacrifices must be made by the survivors in the rebuilding of
communal life. In the third generation, young people are still pushed hard to
achieve and most consider it important to remember the Genocide and
demand recognition from Turkey, the successor state to the Ottoman Empire.
Meanwhile, a narrow focus on Genocide issues and the related fostering of
hatred of Turkey and all things Turkish are themselves debilitating.

Post-Genocide

During the First World War and the Genocide many Armenians fled the
Ottoman Empire for the relative security of the Russian Caucasus. With the
declaration of independence of the Republic of Armenia in 1918 (see
chapter 5), immigration continued though Armenia itself was impoverished
and stricken by famine. When Armenia entered the Soviet system, the repercussions were felt around the diaspora, and there emerged a new version of
the East/West divide, with the Armenian Revolutionary Federation (ARF or
Dashnaktsutiun) leading the anti-Soviet or pro-free, independent, unified
Armenia movement. Ramkavars, Hnchaks and other anti-Dashnak organizations led a looser movement that was more conciliatory towards the
Soviets, accepting foreign rule as necessary for protection and aid. This
opposition intensified as the political parties vied for control of the new
diaspora communities, their churches and schools.

The Soviet authorities introduced a 'repatriation' movement (*nerkaght*) to
encourage diaspora Armenians to immigrate to the Republic of Armenia.
This was to have important short- and long-term consequences for families
and whole communities in diaspora. For diaspora Armenians the decision to
immigrate was based on a dream of 'Return' to a homeland, and the nature
of Armenian family life meant that very few would dream of making that
'Return' alone. Thus, families (including extended families) were forced to
negotiate between members torn in opposite directions. Usually, the young
gave way to the old but were among the first to return to the West when the

---

3   Jenny Phillips, *Symbol, Myth, and Rhetoric: The Politics of Culture in an Armenian-
     American Population* (New York: AMS Press, 1989).

opportunity later arose (taking parents with them). The communities they left behind were affected by the scale of the migration, with some struggling to piece collective life back together.

Many, though not all, of the migrants were from lower economic levels and were attracted not only by ideology but also by a promise of better opportunities. Instead, they found themselves on the fringe of an unexpectedly different and closely knit society. Worse, they were resented as a new burden on already scant resources. The example of the first president of the new republic, Levon Ter Petrosian, a child in that early repatriation, is enough to show that integration did occur, in spite of these initial difficulties. However, differences and some prejudice still persist between descendants of these groups in Armenian society today.

The diaspora passed on to another phase of further and more permanent settlement in the new environments. Repatriation continued sporadically until the early 1960s but word had reached the diaspora that integration into Armenian society was not easy and, at the same time, economic conditions in the diaspora improved for most. More importantly, fewer families were able to persuade all their members to uproot themselves from countries where they had become increasingly 'at home'. In many countries the Second World War forged a further integration of the second generation into the mainstream through their war service to the host country.

Post-Second World War

The Cold War years were marked by bitter and open rivalry between diaspora political parties and their sympathizers. The Dashnak party demanded a 'Free, Independent and United Armenia', continued to fly the flag of the short-lived pre-Soviet republic and taught their young people revolutionary songs. The leadership feared the infiltration of the Soviet system into the hierarchy of the Church, the Catholicos being based in Etchmiadzin in Soviet Armenia. Historically, there is another Catholicos, based in the Western diaspora, which administers churches in the Middle East. During the 1950s the Dashnak party consolidated its influence on this, the Holy See of Antelias (outside Beirut). The Dashnaks formed a parallel and rival system of churches in the New World, most importantly in the United States. To this day, most American Armenian communities have two churches, one affiliated with Etchmiadzin, the other with Antelias.

The anti-Soviet fervour of the Dashnak side was met with equally ardent sentiment against the Dashnaks themselves. The Ramkavars, Hnchaks and sympathetic clubs and organizations took an opposite stand regarding Soviet Armenia. They believed that Armenia should be supported, no matter who ruled it. Though a few were Communists or Marxists, the great majority were not. This view maintained that the diaspora would soon die out through assimilation and physical threats and that the republic was the only viable long-term solution for an Armenian future. These organizations regularly hosted guests from Soviet Armenia, whether visiting artists, academics, or political speakers. Teachers went there for training and some students to university.

From the 1970s onwards, with the thawing of the Cold War, the two sides were less diametrically opposed and began to take similar stands, particularly regarding the state of Armenia. Today young people are even less interested in the bitter internal political battles of the past. In the late 1970s and early 1980s small but very visible groups turned to terrorism to make their cause heard and a number of Turkish diplomats were killed or wounded. This ended with internal fighting and a diaspora divided over these methods. It has been suggested that these groups were equally motivated by the desire to awaken what they called a 'sleep-walking' diaspora to political activism on a larger scale. This activism was to be aimed primarily at obtaining admission of the Genocide by Turkey and restoration of certain of the old homelands.

Each year all those who died during the Genocide are commemorated on 24 April. The services and events range from church mass to evenings with speeches and poetry and music to protests and marches in front of Turkish embassies. In some communities, where young people especially have tired of hearing political speeches, new activities have begun, such as organizing blood donations for current victims of ethnic cleansing and massacres. In some communities these are jointly sponsored events, in others the political divisions continue and each side organizes its own. The purpose of such events is threefold – to honour the dead, to put pressure on Turkey, and to try to forge ties among the dispersed Armenian people.

Today relatively few diaspora Armenians till the soil, though most were farmers at the time of their dispersal from Western Armenia. Instead Armenians have become known as merchants, traders, skilled artisans, and professionals. Earlier in this century, in the Middle East, Armenians were prominent in photography and other modern, technical professions, while today they can be found in all the arts. Like other diaspora peoples, Armenians pursue a host of other mobile professions, increasingly varied as generations pass. Education remains highly desirable, but tension emerges between the pressure for traditional Armenian-language based schooling and a more Western-oriented, often English-based education that is seen as providing more sophisticated job opportunities.

Armenians are a people proud of their ancient past and concerned about their collective future. As the twenty-first century begins, Armenians appear to be thriving in many places but, at the same time, there is a sense of threat to the collective. In physically secure countries, where there is little pressure on the group, assimilation is seen as taking a faster pace. Where physical insecurity looms, many people are considering the option of further emigration. The earthquake in Armenia in 1988, independence of the republic in 1991, and the struggle for Karabagh (Artsakh) have all sent tremors around the diaspora. In some cases there has been a reawakening of connections and a mobilization of professional services previously unseen in community work. The outpouring of people from the republic post-independence has also affected the diaspora and forced rethinking about the future.

Links and divisions in the contemporary diaspora

'Ours is a story of moving, rebuilding, moving again,' say Armenians. In fact, some who have migrated to Europe or North America will have made three or four attempts to make a permanent home in their own lifetime. For example, someone who survived the Genocide may have settled in the French mandate until its demise, then left for either Cyprus or Beirut, then been displaced again by communal conflicts in those places. Those who fled the Genocide to Cairo later moved on at the height of Arab nationalism. In Western countries life feels more secure, but at the same time new problems arise, such as adjusting to new surroundings and trying to maintain aspects of a shared culture once taken for granted. The world is also changing in ways that appear to give those in the diaspora certain advantages, as globalization favours cosmopolitan, mobile lifestyles and people with international networks. While present life for many appears comfortable, there are always some within each community whose arrival or departure reminds the rest of the precarious position of a people in diaspora.

Armenian communities have developed in significantly different ways within the constraints and opportunities found in particular host cultures and countries. Though there is a strong ideology of 'Armenianness' and desire for unity among the politically active, there are several important internal divisions. The most obvious is between the East (Iran, former Soviet Union) and the West, including different dialects (though mutually intelligible), traditions, and attitudes. These variations developed over centuries of living under different, sometimes opposing empires, the Byzantines and later Ottomans in the West, Persians and Russians in the East. Other major divisions in the diaspora are based on further regional variation, age and/or place of birth (i.e. whether the person was born in or near the old homelands), political sympathies, and so on. The most significant political division has been between the Dashnak party (and its sympathizers) and the anti- or non-Dashnak people.

Overlaying these divisions are very strong ties, practical, symbolic, and emotional, that bind Armenians around the world to each other and to the idea of an Armenian people or nation. Family networks, based on blood and marriage, form the basis for diaspora connections and for the passing on of attachment to the larger ethnic group or nation. Institutional life, primarily the national Church, political parties, and some charitable and cultural groups form trans-national links and provide continuity in a fluid world. These institutions and the intellectual and politically active elite also construct a framework of ideas that informs private as well as public constructions of belonging. Moving from one country to another,

Armenians can find a familiar base from which to begin again. They can often also find practical aid and certainly useful information to help in that process. In the past, and still to a large degree today, the local church serves as a focal point for newcomers, a place to seek out others and learn about the community.

Until recently there has been no centre and periphery in the Armenian world, and it is only with the independence of the former Soviet Republic of Armenia in 1991 that there is increasingly a focus on one place as a symbolic homeland. The Republic of Armenia is a small corner of the historic home-land and, until the recent emigration of perhaps one million of its inhabitants, very few in the diaspora traced their origins to that territory. Instead, thoughts of 'Return' were also directed at the lands lost during the deportations and Genocide of the early twentieth century. Equally, many did not think of return at all but were pleased to be given a new start in coun-tries where they felt more secure. These 'Western' Armenians speak (or spoke) the Western dialect and their recent ancestors lived in the Ottoman Empire. The diaspora also includes Armenians living in (or immigrants from) Iran and now the former Soviet Union.

The rapidly increasing use and extension of all forms of Internet com-munication is changing the ways in which the diaspora is organized, enab-ling older institutions to reach their members (and others) more quickly and, perhaps more importantly, allowing the mass communication of non-institutionally based individuals and small groups. The word 'democracy' is heard often in this context, but it remains to be seen how far these new methods of communication will extend Armenian institutional life beyond a freer exchange of information

Description of selected major centres

Middle East

After the Genocide, survivors fled first to Aleppo and then onwards around Syria, to Lebanon, Iraq, Iran, Palestine, and Egypt, enlarging already existing settlements of Armenians and creating new ones. These countries closest to the old homelands were until recently the amorphous centre of the Armenian diaspora. As Adalian notes, 'the role of [these] communities in the modern Armenian diaspora cannot be over-emphasized' (p. 102). While influenced by the colonial powers in the region, Armenians in these coun-tries developed a modern identity with considerable continuity with the past in the same region, surrounded by many of the same peoples. Armenian language use not only continued but actually increased, through mass education and literacy. An ethno-religious identity was encouraged by many of the legal systems of the region, continuing Ottoman traditions. Armenian survivors settled near each other, usually around churches initially, and began to build compact, interwoven networks of family, trade, and friendship. With populations of over 100,000, the major communities in Iran, Lebanon, and Syria could be stable and self-sufficient to a certain degree. The majority of children in each of these countries still attend at least primary school in Armenian, though there has been (and continues to be) variation at secondary level, both for internal and external reasons. A high rate of literacy in Armenian permitted a lively output of prose and poetry and numerous daily and weekly newspapers and literary papers. Beirut, Cairo, Isfahan, Tehran, and Istanbul at different times have all been known for their rich artistic life. Unfortunately, the Middle East has also been subject to periodic turmoil, from nationalist movements to inter-communal troubles and war. Though Armenians in each country have generally maintained non-aligned or apolitical stands, these new pressures have forced successive waves of Armenian migration.

Turkey In the Republic of Turkey some 50,000 Armenians remain in Istanbul. Since the 1970s Istanbul has received a steady flow of Turkish-speaking Armenian families from eastern Anatolia. There they gravitate to the churches and the Patriarchate of Istanbul maintains contact with several churches and small communities in eastern Turkey. With the lay community, the Patriarchate has had to find a balance between pursuing ethnic or communal interests and demonstrating that Armenians are citizens loyal to the Turkish state. When fellow Armenians around the diaspora protest against Turkey, there is concern about repercussions. The demands of the secular constitution of Turkey allow the authorities to intervene in what could otherwise be seen as the internal affairs of the community and Church, resulting in, for example, buildings falling into disrepair or patriarchal elections being postponed. However, Istanbul is a familiar home and Armenians who have remained are attached to this city where their ancestors have lived for well over a thousand years. The daily Armenian language newspaper *Marmara* continues as a staple on the intellectual scene, now joined by a new, lively bilingual paper, *Argos*. In the past Armenians have made great contributions to the city, particularly in architecture. Today some of the best-known entertainers in the Turkish media are of Armenian heritage.

Iran The Persian or Iranian Armenian communities have a long history, having come initially through trade, exile, and forced migration. Later connections with the Russian Empire promoted a certain continuity between those living under the neighbouring empires. During the twentieth century the population has developed an urban and bourgeois face with its centres in Tehran, Isfahan, Tabriz, Abadan, and Rasht, though previously many lived in villages and small towns. During the Pahlavi dynasty, many Armenians thrived in the oil-based free market economy and a virtually autonomous communal life supported a lively arts and cultural programme. The intellectual and artistic life of the community was well integrated with that of the

Iranian majority, but following the Islamic Revolution the Armenian population of Iran has been much reduced. Periodic pressures force new and stricter laws concerning education in particular, but, as Dekmejian points out, the Church has expanded its authority under Islamic Shari'a law and the Armenians remain Iran's largest non-Muslim minority.

Syria and Lebanon The first stopping point after the massacres and Genocide, the Armenian population of Syria expanded rapidly and remained one of the world's largest centres until later Arab nationalist movements. Syria especially became a minefield for the otherwise pro-Arab Armenians, as the government became aligned with the Soviet Union during the Cold War and the large Dashnak contingent, thought to be pro-Western, suffered repression. Increasing nationalism brought new restrictions on schooling, including less Armenian and an increase in Arabic language classes. However, over 70,000 Armenians remain spread between Aleppo, Damascus, Deir ez-Zor, and Latakia and the more secular government of Hafez Assad, himself from a minority group, encouraged community life again, and this continues with his son.

In Lebanon the clear centre is Beirut. Indeed, Dekmejian calls Lebanon itself 'a most ideal setting' until the civil war. The vitality of this community is enhanced by the proximity of the Catholicate of Cilicia in neighbouring Antelias. In addition, the political organization of the country encouraged ethnic alignment and participation in the country's political process. Local economics enabled a remarkable generation of wealth for some. Armenians were living in this area before the Genocide survivors arrived, but the community was radically transformed both by the sheer numbers of the newcomers and by participation in the new state of Lebanon. In Beirut it is still possible to go from kindergarten through university in Armenian institutions, as Haigazian University is located there. Some of the diaspora's best-known schools, newspapers, artists, and political activists thrived in this environment. Dekmejian's claim that 'Lebanon became a second homeland' is not an exaggeration, and it remains to be seen how many Armenians will return to the state as rebuilding follows the end of the civil war.[4]

Both Syria and Lebanon retain a rural element: Anjar, in the Bekaa Valley, is made up of former residents of Mount Moussa (Musa Dagh or Musa Ler, see chapter 5). In Syria, on the Turkish border, are their former neighbours in Kessab. Sima Aprahamian writes of the 'multitude of collective identities' juggled by the residents of Anjar. Like Bakalian, looking at a broader spectrum in the United States, Aprahamian observes that, depending on the situation, a person might stress, for example, rural roots, a

---

4   R.H. Dekmejian, 'The Armenian Diaspora', in R. Hovannisian, ed., *The Armenian People: From Ancient to Modern Times*, 2 volumes (New York: St. Martin's Press, 1997), p. 426.

local (Mt. Moussa/Anjar) tie, a socialist political stand, particular needs and interests of a family or gender role, dialect, or religion. Aprahamian also clearly outlines the sympathy of the people of Anjar for 'historic resistance', due to their successive uprootings.[5]

North America

Population shifts from the Middle East and, more recently, from the Republic of Armenia have resulted in North America having the largest diaspora population outside the former Soviet Union. The diversity of the diaspora is clear even within the borders of one country, perhaps most obviously so in the United States. Regionally, there are marked differences between the east and west coasts. To some degree this mirrors the difference perceived generally in American culture but it also reflects a much higher Californian intake of the newest waves of immigrants over the past decade. Today perhaps the largest diaspora settlement anywhere in the world is the Los Angeles area. This has redefined community profiles and priorities, provoking both regeneration of identity as well as resentments between the newcomers and the older families.

In spite of its smaller population, the east coast of the United States is the base of numerous cultural organizations and intellectual institutions. The Boston area alone is home to newspapers, the National Association for Armenian Studies and Research (NAASR), ALMA museum, Project Save (photographic archive), Armenian International Women's Association, and others. Washington, DC is the natural home for active and successful lobbying groups, such as the Armenian Assembly. The world's largest Armenian charity, the Armenian General Benevolent Union, is based in New York City, though its membership is found in local chapters around the world.

The patterns of life and living conditions are quite different on the west coast. Certain areas such as Glendale or Hollywood have a high percentage of Armenians and one can easily sit in a park or walk through a shopping centre and overhear conversations in Armenian all around. Ararat Home, equipped for active retirement and for those needing medical care, is a very popular, well-designed institution. Compatriotic societies continue to link people with a local homeland ('the old country'), the most active perhaps being the Kessab Education Association, with an annual address directory and new social hall north of Los Angeles, modelled on a building in Kessab itself. Television and radio programmes are at least as popular as the newspapers and magazines and probably this is the one Western city that most resembles the Middle East in possibilities for self-containment within an Armenian environment. One can shop, attend school, be entertained, and

---

5   Sima Aprahamian, 'A Multitude of Overlapping Identities: a Lebanese Armenian Community in the Beka'a Valley of Lebanon', *Armenian Review*, 43:1/169, Spring 1990, p. 68.

gossip with neighbours entirely in Armenian. There are also a number of Armenians serving time in jail, a fact that greatly distresses older Armenian American families.

If the processes of acculturation and assimilation continue as they have in the past, the new Armenian American will also take on a hyphenated identity, pursuing what Bakalian calls symbolic ethnicity. Armenian language knowledge is generally not retained beyond the second generation and, as in the case of the Jews, there is a considerable exogamy in that generation. However, there is also a strong desire to remain connected to the people who call themselves Armenian and this is maintained through family, through new and old institutions, life-cycle events, attendance at camps or seminars, and annual regional and community events such as the ARF (or AGBU) Olympics. Professional affiliations have also emerged both as aid agencies and as career and friendship networks. The Church (Apostolic and Protestant) remains an important symbol of community life and the most meaningful link for many.

Though ethnic politics and the state formulation of a plural society differ in Canada, generally there are broad similarities with the situations, issues, and attitudes found in the United States. The centres of Canadian Armenian life are found in Toronto and Montreal.

Europe and Eastern Europe

France In addition to Paris and its suburbs, Marseilles and Lyons have the largest concentrations of Armenians. A colonial and intellectual metropolis, France attracted Armenian settlers before the Genocide. Equally importantly, it exerted considerable influence on the elite of Istanbul, Cairo, Lebanon, and elsewhere, encouraging a tilt towards Paris rather than the New World for many. The population of French Armenians has been estimated at roughly 300,000 but pressure to become first a citizen of France has promoted a very different environment from that of the Middle East. Dominique Schnapper states that the nation-state tradition of France assumes that 'political unity would, or could, be made to coincide with cultural unity'.[6] The powerful Jacobin tradition is behind Schnapper's assertion that 'as a host country for immigrants, France can have no policy but that of continuing the integration of its foreign populations through its universal institutions'.[7] This is a proactive project, more so in the past than in the present European context. At the same time, France is host to a number of important Armenian cultural institutions, such as the highly

---

6   Dominique Schnapper, *La France de l'intégration: sociologie de la nation en 1990* (Paris: Gallimard, 1991), p. 353.
7   Ibid., p. 360.

regarded newspaper *Haratch* (the only Armenian language daily in the West), other media, dance and music ensembles of high quality, and a number of distinguished Armenian artists. Some of the latter have changed their names, such as Charles Aznavour and Henri Verneuil, fitting in with the pattern mentioned above. However, Aznavour was very active in fundraising following the 1988 earthquake in Armenia and Verneuil has produced a celebrated film about his Armenian roots. Similarly, political activists in France have organized European-wide protests against Turkish denials of the Genocide and have initiated salvage work on vernacular and church architecture in the diaspora and Armenia.

In her ethnography of three generations of Armenians, Martine Hovannisian outlines continuity and change in detail, sometimes illustrating Schnapper's points but often demonstrating that state ideology is not entirely successful. The life histories and interviews illustrate the French experience as well as the broader influences of the West and modernization. In addition, Hovannisian probes the reverberations which changes in Armenia have produced in the diaspora. 'From their very beginnings, the events of the 1980s in Soviet Armenia have had a completely unexpected effect, mobilizing and disturbing the community in France.'[8] In a series of excerpts from interviews, Hovannisian highlights the conflicting emotions and opinions within a community as well as the ambivalence felt by individuals.

Italy Though the Armenian population of Italy has never been large, like that of Venice, it remains important in diaspora history as an intellectual and spiritual centre. In Venice the island of San Lazzaro is home to an Armenian monastery of the Mekhitarists, Armenian Catholics. It houses a magnificent museum, important library, and printing presses. Mismanagement of funds in the 1970s and 1980s put the holdings of the Venice Armenians at risk, but these have since been put on a sounder footing and the academic and cultural work of the community is continuing.

Britain Another small community, estimated at approximately fifteen thousand, the British community began in Manchester, where textile merchants gathered to expedite trade with their home communities. London's emergence as a world financial and trade centre continued to attract some Armenians, but the population remained small until the mid-1950s when people began migrating from Cyprus and Palestine, where Britain had colonial ties. This has been followed, as elsewhere, by a larger intake from Lebanon and Iran (and now the former Soviet Union). Until recently Britain has appeared to itself and to outsiders as predominantly 'English'. However, as many Londoners will attest, this is changing radically and, while struggling with its

---

8   M. Hovannisian, *Le Lien communautaire: trois générations d'Arméniens* (Paris: Armand Colin, 1992), p. 278 (my translation).

European identity, Britain is emerging as a visibly multicultural country. Young Armenians mention that this combination, of an increased embracing of multicultural life (not only tolerance) and a future with Europe, makes it easier to feel comfortable as both Armenian and British.

Belgium, Germany, Switzerland   These communities have grown rapidly and host active organizations, not all of which are connected with international umbrella institutions. Individuals gathering together have managed to promote aid and relief to Armenia, the beginnings of a forum for European Armenians to meet and discuss their interests, exhibitions, and other important events.

Eastern Europe   Romania, Poland, Bulgaria and Hungary have all had flourishing Armenian populations in the past, dating back to the eleventh century. Those in Orthodox countries survived longer than those pressured by Catholic regimes, but all are at present considerably smaller than in the past. Very few Armenians remain in Poland or Hungary, but one can still find active community life in Romania and Bulgaria today.

Russia and the Caucasus   As one of the empires competing for the territory of Armenia, the Russians exerted considerable influence even before the twentieth century. In addition, Armenians migrated to Russia, seeking refuge. Trade communities and networks were established, and intellectuals and political activists also travelled to Russia for education. Major centres outside Moscow can be found in Petersburg, Sochi, and Rostov. It is estimated that perhaps 2,000,000 Armenians live scattered throughout the former Soviet states, in Central Asia, the Baltic states, and Georgia. Earlier there were also many Armenians living in Azerbaijan but, in the wake of the forced population exchange during the recent war, few if any remain. Georgia is especially interesting as this was formerly the intellectual and artistic centre of Armenians in the Caucasus. It was only in the early twentieth century, with the establishment of Armenian, Azerbaijani and Georgian republics, that nationalist causes (and Soviet nationality policies) provoked the intense identification of each ethnic group with a particular territory in the Caucasus. However, many Armenians continued to live in Georgia: some 400,000 before the collapse of the Soviet Union.

Today there remain profound differences between what many call the 'internal diaspora', those people living in the former Soviet Union, and the rest. As Tamara Galkina points out, for Armenians in the former Soviet Union relations with other Armenians tend to be with Moscow or Yerevan rather than the Western diaspora.[9] The crushing economic needs and the very different

---

9   Tamara Galkina, 'La Diaspora Armenienne dans l'espace ex-Sovietique', *Revue du Monde Armenien*, vol. 4, 1998.

allegiances and influences make communication difficult. Outside the Soviet Union, Armenians lived and operated within varied forms of capitalism, whatever their personal beliefs. Those who immigrate learn from the system they observe operating around them. Those who remain are part of the building of new states and new economic systems, none of which can yet be relied upon to be part of a particular pattern for any length of time. In addition, there is a difficult cognitive transition for those living in the former Soviet Union, from being an Armenian living in the USSR, all of whose republics were part of the same state as Armenia and whose inhabitants all had the same citizenship, to being an Armenian in one of the new independent states (Russia, Ukraine, Turkmenistan), which have much weaker ties with the Republic of Armenia. Diaspora arrived even if the person stayed still.

South America

The largest population is found in Argentina, where some 80,000 Armenians live. The core of the population came from Cilicia following the massacres in Adana in 1909 and the Genocide of 1915 and, as elsewhere, many of the early settlers became merchants. Hekimian notes an earlier study by Binayan which states that by 1974, though a very small minority in Argentina, Armenians controlled 'one-third of the textile industry, fifty percent of the rug industry, and ten percent of the shoe industry'.[10] Churches and full-time schools have been built and Hekimian notes that they and other cultural institutions are flourishing.

Australasia and India

Though India represents one of the most interesting and historic of diaspora communities, its time is now effectively over. Very few Armenians remain there. The Australian community, by contrast, is growing and enjoying the trend towards increased state support and interest in multicultural life. Most Armenian immigrants are first or second generation, from a variety of countries.

Contemporary social and institutional life in the diaspora[11]

The public institutions of diaspora life are struggling to come to terms with the kind of response appropriate to the new and changing environments

---

10 K. Hekimian, 'Armenian Immigration to Argentina: 1909–1938', *Armenian Review*, vol. 43, no. 1/169 (Spring 1990), p. 109.

11 As noted in the section on diaspora centres, the social and economic situation in the former Soviet Union is substantially different from the (loosely termed) Western diasporas. This section treats the Western diaspora only, where sufficient research has been done to allow some broad generalizations.

Established in another place and another time, they have generally been slow to change, missing out on the impact that Western (or Westernized) educational systems have had on the new generations. However, political parties, churches, cultural organizations, and clubs continue to be active and provide a framework for amorphous and floating family networks. Social and political structures are necessarily loose and overlapping in a diaspora context. The cement of diaspora life is the family network within which some connection to being Armenian is established and nurtured.

Family

Marriage traditionally was between two families as well as two individuals, with mutual social obligations, potentially helpful in times of need, generally forming a social network. This continues to some degree. There is still pressure to choose an Armenian spouse, but not from a particular town or family as before. However, with increasing intermarriage, there is less chance of a household creating the connections described above. Family relations also change in the Western countries, whereas Arab, Persian, and Turkish neighbours share many of the same values and reinforce those of the Armenian communities in the Middle East. In the West there is an emphasis on the individual that is at odds with the traditional focus on the family unit. Higher education and diverse professional jobs have also served to encourage a focus on the individual and his or her personal satisfaction. Ties with one's family become narrower and with the community more tenuous. However, the importance of family remains and interdependence is encouraged, though to a lesser degree.

The Armenian family of the last century and earlier is often thought of as 'patriarchal', or having its authority based in the male line and the father figure. Certainly public life was and remains male dominated. Many people, men and women, however, speak of having been influenced by the strength of female relatives. In a world where the home and family were agreed to be the focus of life, power was shared by women working within and men working outside for the home and the shared life of family. This shifted radically with dispersion and uprooting and also with the rapid adaptation to modern life. The role of women within the home became secondary, as did the need for certain local knowledge and maintenance of family networks. Thus this source of power became greatly diminished. Increasingly, women around the diaspora are working outside, as well as inside, the home in a variety of careers.

Certain aspects of home life continue to anchor new generations in a sense of belonging to a people called the Armenians, though their own lives may not often intersect with many other members of the group. The most obvious among these is food and the importance given to hospitality and the sharing of food on a daily basis within the family. Like others around the Middle East, Armenians always welcome guests with a heavily laden table.

This continues in varying degrees around the diaspora. Reciprocal hospitality is a way of binding people together, whether or not they are members of the same community. For many families it is common to have visitors or house guests from abroad. In this way, as well as through the telephone, post and email, Armenians maintain contact with each other. Children grow used to meeting many new people and through them are also introduced to political problems around the world in a very direct manner. This then ties in with the sense of precariousness they begin to associate with being Armenian.

Institutions

Numerous 'cultural' organizations still link people and communities. Most of the traditional ones are associated with or sympathetic to one of the political parties. The Dashnak party and cultural organizations in its circle such as the Hamazkaine and Armenian Youth Federation (AYF) have by far the largest membership. Much to the dismay of political activists on every side, the most popular community events are dinner-dances, picnics, and bazaars. These serve as a way to bring people together who are otherwise scattered around large cities or regions, and who in earlier times would have shared a neighbourhood.

Education remains very important and continues to influence direction and alignments. In the Middle East most children attend Armenian schools at least at primary level. Elsewhere in the diaspora such schools are not widely available. Today the prime purpose of the Armenian school is to provide a specifically Armenian education, emphasizing language and history. It may also provide an environment that parents believe is 'safer' from perceived new physical threats, such as drugs and gangs, and from assimilation. Other parents feel strongly that their children must learn how to fully function in the host culture and that local rather than ethnic schools are the key to that process.

At the level of higher education, individual scholars in the Middle East and Europe are pursuing Armenian studies. In America a number of chairs of Armenian studies have been established at universities (for example, the University of California at Los Angeles and Fresno, the University of Michigan, and Harvard). The motivation for this is to encourage further learning and research, particularly in history and literature, to legitimize the field, make academic links, and reach as many Armenian students as possible. The great majority of American Armenians do not attend Armenian schools and thus university classes respond directly to the anxiety that new generations may grow up knowing nothing about their past, and also to the fear that Armenians are being forgotten by a world where 'no one knows about us'.

In recent years email and the Internet have had a great impact on communication and education. News agencies provide instant information and many young people who would never subscribe to the ethnic press follow events regularly. Equally importantly, new websites emerge daily on a wide variety of subjects, some representing organizations, others individuals. One of the most creative is Narod, which links Armenian schools around the diaspora and the republic with interactive projects.

The Church remains important to Armenian identity for a number of reasons. It provides a link with the ancient past and preserves the classical language. Its political role, solidified during the Ottoman Empire, continues, and it acts as a link to Europe through shared Christianity. Its structure connects people throughout the diaspora. Throughout this century the Apostolic Church has been regarded as a key symbol of survival and continuity. The Church itself has emphasized this and sermons are frequently heard praising the resurrection of the people and urging the congregation to go forth as soldiers for the nation. This has resulted in a national Church which some have accused of focusing on survival of the ethnic group rather than a particularly spiritual message. Some call it a national museum. While still proclaiming that the Armenian Apostolic Church is one of the cornerstones of Armenian identity, the population is increasingly abandoning the Church in all practical terms.

In Europe the secularization of society in general continues to grow, an ironic turn as it is through Christianity that Armenians have most strongly identified themselves with Europe. In the United States a very different social environment prompts other changes. There, some have emphasized Christian education for children or introduced English into part of the mass, though such changes arouse heated controversy. The Church is caught in a double bind, representing continuity and links with the past in its seemingly 'unchanging' structure, while losing people because they say it does not speak to their present needs. In addition, the needs (and opinions) of new waves of migrants are quite different from those of the third and fourth generation Armenian Americans. It is important to note that there are two small but important religious minorities within the Armenian population: the Protestants and the Catholics.

Security versus assimilation

Security remains a problem and events continue to occur which nourish such concerns. With the Lebanese civil war, the revolution in Iran, war between Iran and Iraq, and communal troubles in Cyprus, thousands of Armenians migrated to Europe, Australia, and the Americas. An earlier exodus had followed unrest in Istanbul, Egypt, and Palestine but many of these people had moved elsewhere in the Middle East only to be uprooted again. In addition to these conflicts, the immensity of the devastation of the 1988 earthquake in Armenia, in which some 25,000 people were killed, also contributed to the feeling of constant danger and insecurity. Though Armenians in the diaspora were not harmed, they felt the impact of these shocks. The pogroms against Armenians in Azerbaijan during the late 1980s and early 1990s fitted into a pattern of persistent threats to the Armenian people as a whole, raising again the notion of an endangered people.

Living in the Middle East had allowed people to remain quite close to their original homes and the historic lands. They were familiar with the Arab and Turkish worlds and felt part of them, while connected to Europe through their Christian faith and through education. The further migrations from the Middle East to the West meant a further transformation of the diaspora, and a new form of insecurity. Assimilation or, as the Armenians call it, 'white massacre' (*jermag chart*) replaced physical survival as the main concern in the stable Western environments. During centuries of living with mostly Muslim neighbours, Armenians maintained friendly social relations with them but religious differences prevented nearly all intermarriage and set a cap on the kinds and levels of inter-communal interaction. In Christian or, equally importantly, secular settings this changed and barriers to inter-marriage and social interaction were brought down, encouraging a marked increase in participation in activities and organizations outside the Armenian community sphere.

Secondly, speaking Armenian was the norm in the Middle East, where Armenians regularly speak several languages. However, in many Western countries monolingualism is normal and young Armenians have followed this pattern. Learning Armenian means attending Saturday or Sunday schools, or a private day school, but even after such efforts are expended, it remains difficult to practise the language on a daily basis. Readers and writers of Armenian literature are decreasing more rapidly.

Through political rhetoric, poetry, novels, sermons, newspaper editorials, and other means, the intellectual elite of the diaspora (of all political shades) has tried to counter the problems of dispersion and mobility by shaping a new identity that is not based on locale or kin. The 'real' Armenian in this version is someone who speaks the language, knows the history, is a member or supporter of the Apostolic Church, and shows active commitment to these being perpetuated in the wider community. There is also an intensification of the identification with Europe or European culture that produces another important side effect, that of rejecting the Muslim world and thus further distancing the Middle Eastern past. This is empha-sized by the Russian orientation of the former Soviet and present Republic of Armenia, which finds its way into all aspects of culture.

Anny Bakalian, in her study *Armenian-Americans: From Being to Feeling Armenian,* documents the drift from an identity that is taken for granted to one which is more conscious, situational, and symbolic. The narrowing of identity described above has proved to be alienating to those who do not fit into the categories but do feel themselves to be Armenian. The public image of 'Armenianness' as an unchanging core does not fit easily with the flexible, changing realities of lived experience. This conflict can be found in views on language, church affiliation, or political activity but also more generally, for example in gender issues or sexual orientation. A debate led by Anahid Kassabian and David Kazanjian in the first issue of *Armenian Forum* brings out, among other points, the tendency of nationalist discourse to be male-centred and to picture women as ideally wives and mothers, devoted to producing new members of the nation.[12] As Avakian says, an essentialized, universal Armenian image reduces many to 'total invisibility'.[13] But Avakian also reminds the reader that feminism and femininity are interpreted in various ways around the Armenian world, though people may assume (wrongly) that all Armenians share a particular set of standards and symbols.

Issues raised

A discussion of diaspora usually includes ideas about a homeland, whether it includes a dream of actual return or not. In the Western Armenian case, there have been several visions of homeland, the most evocative having been the homes that were left behind during the Genocide, now in eastern Turkey. Iran also has sentimental and historic importance for its Armenian citizens and their own diaspora. With the establishment of independent Armenia in 1991, however, the focus is rapidly changing to an idealized homeland on that soil. As with Israel and the Jewish diaspora, relations between homeland and diaspora reflect differences in historical experiences, current political situations, and mutual expectations.

Following *glasnost* (see chapter 6) and especially beginning with the rebuilding following the earthquake, diaspora funding has been channelled away from its own institutions and towards Armenia. For some, the existence of a free Armenia means there is no further need for diaspora public life. Armenia should serve as anchor and focus of all future Armenian life. This overlooks the very different historical and contemporary experiences of the Western diaspora and assumes that the political agenda and cultural attitudes of the state and its citizens are similar to those of the diaspora. In fact they are often quite far apart or even opposed. In the future, the Republic of Armenia will increasingly become a kind of standard of 'Armenianness', which, again, those living in diaspora will find unfamiliar. The September 1999 Armenia-Diaspora Conference and the second conference two years later were important symbolic events and could serve as a starting point for more formal, sustained attempts at coordination, cooperation and less judgemental communication. Reaction in the diaspora ranged from hopeful to sceptical, with most remaining strikingly indifferent. It seems clear that the republic sees itself as a

---

12 Anahid Kassabian and David Kazanjian, ' "You Have to Want to be Armenian Here." Nationalisms, Sexualities, and the Problem of Armenian Diasporic Identity', *Armenian Forum*, 1:1, 1998, pp. 19–36.

13 A. Avakian, 'Validated and Erased: A Feminist Views *Back to Ararat*', *Armenian Forum*, vol. 1, no. 1 (1998), p. 62.

natural centre for a peripheral diaspora but whether the diaspora will be shaped into satellites of the republic will depend on whether or not the diaspora organizations and institutions retain and reflect their local bases.

This in turn depends greatly on whether the institutions manage to change themselves. Having emerged and come of age in very different times and social environments, they struggle to attract young people, even in the Middle East. Hovannisian gives an example of this disenchantment, quoting from a 1976 article in *Culture arménienne*: 'What is common to all these organizations is that they have aged, the leaders have not been replaced by younger ones, and their discourse remains the same.'[14] Bakalian relates identical findings from the United States and my own research has also revealed profound dissatisfaction. However, one can still attend a meeting of the Armenian Youth Federation in California, for example, and discover hundreds of enthusiastic, excited teenagers. The institutions are not dead but the older leaders need to pay attention to the younger voices in the diaspora as well as to the changing relations between Armenia and diaspora.

A number of issues are raised concerning the public treatment of the Genocide and reactions to its denial. While there is widespread support for Genocide recognition, the massacres are also a more personal memory for most in the Western diaspora. Given that the survivors of the physical traumas re-established themselves and were often flourishing again by the second generation, in what ways is psychological trauma passed on through generations? On a community level, how can memory be honoured without forever defining future relations and, equally important, without constantly confirming victim status for the survivors? How can ethnic or national groups that have become locked in battle find a way to live and work together again?

Finally, as Robin Cohen points out in *Global Diasporas*, diaspora life fits well with the mobility and flexibility required by globalization and modern life. Ironically, both the lack of physical threats in the West and the easy fit of globalization produce another danger, that of further dispersion and assimilation. How can one balance flexibility with continuity and connection? What are the dangers of the shift of emphasis to the individual from the family and community? More than the loss of the Armenian language, this steady drift towards a group of loosely affiliated individuals will have the furthest-reaching ramifications for Armenians in the diaspora. H. Aram Veeser's vision of contemporary home living rooms as parallel public spheres recognizes not only the ability to create Bakalian's notion of symbolic (and situational) ethnicity alongside a non-Armenian world, but also the increased introversion of families and individuals.[15] Veeser also notes that the current trend towards interpreting diasporas as global tribes

---

14 Hovannisian, *Le Lien communautaire*, p. 286 (my translation).
15 H.A. Veeser, 'International Nationalism: Living Lack, Muzzled Cohort: Most at Home when Furthest Abroad', *Armenian Forum*, vol. 1, no. 1 (1998) p. 55.

was predated by William Saroyan's main body of work, which celebrates the detachment from territoriality that goes with movement into social rather than physical space. Saroyan optimistically predicts that Armenians will continue to re-create themselves as a people wherever they are found and under whatever circumstances. Nationalists are scathingly sceptical, looking now towards an independent nation-state as salvation. Examining simultaneously his own experience and the state of theorizing on diaspora, Khachig Tololyan writes that 'at its best the diaspora is an example, for both the homeland's and hostland's nation-states, of the possibility of living, even thriving in the regimes of multiplicity which are increasingly the global condition.'[16] Today personal and collective belonging are constructed through such multiple connections. The nation-state is only one dimension of this process. For Armenians, the diaspora is the other – in all its diversity and richness.

Bibliography

Adalian, R.P., 'The Historical Evolution of the Armenian Diasporas', *Journal of Modern Hellenism*, no. 6, 1989, pp. 81–114.

Aprahamian, S., 'A Multitude of Overlapping Identities: a Lebanese Armenian Community in the Beka'a Valley of Lebanon', *Armenian Review*, 43:1/169, Spring 1990, pp. 67–83.

Bakalian, A., *Armenian-Americans: From Being to Feeling Armenian* (New Brunswick: Transaction Publishers, 1993).

Cohen, R., *Global Diasporas* (London: UCL Press, 1997).

Dekmejian, R.H., 'The Armenian Diaspora', chapter 13 of R.G. Hovannisian, ed., *The Armenian People: From Ancient to Modern Times*, vol. 2 (New York: St. Martin's Press, 1997), pp. 413–43.

Hovannisian, M., *Le Lien Communautaire: Trois générations d'Arméniens* (Paris: Armand Colin, 1992).

Miller, D.E., and Miller, L.T., *Survivors: An Oral History of the Armenian Genocide* (Berkeley: University of California Press, 1993).

Mirak, R., *Torn between Two Lands: Armenians in America, 1890 to World War I* (Cambridge, MA: Harvard University Press, 1983).

Pattie, S.P., *Faith in History: Armenians Rebuilding Community* (Washington: Smithsonian Institution Press, 1997).

—— 'New Homeland for an Old Diaspora', in Andre Levy and A. Weingrod, eds, *Homelands and Diaspora: Holy Lands and Other Places* (Stanford University Press, 2004).

Tololyan, K., 'Rethinking Diaspora(s): Stateless Power in the Transnational Moment', *Diaspora*, 5:1, Spring 1996, pp. 3–36.

---

16 K. Tololyan, 'Rethinking Diaspora(s): Stateless Power in the Transitional Moment', *Diaspora*, vol. 5, no. 1 (Spring 1996) p. 7.

8 The Karabagh conflict

From Soviet past to post-Soviet uncertainty

Marina Kurkchiyan

Although the tensions underlying the Karabagh conflict can be traced much further back, the issue became global news only during the late 1980s. Its emergence was triggered by the announcement of the new policy of *perestroika* (see chapter 6) in the USSR. *Perestroika*, or restructuring, was a set of promises: Soviet society would be liberalized, social problems were to be treated more effectively, and political decisions would henceforth be approached in a more democratic fashion. The First Secretary of the Party, Mikhail Gorbachev, intended the innovation to be a signal that the authorities in Moscow were willing to transform the entire country into an open society. In his USSR the right of the people to spell out their needs and to lobby for their interests would be fully protected, and furthermore the public could expect the Kremlin not just to listen to popular demands but to respond to them.

These promises aroused hopes within the Soviet Union's many nations that it would now be possible to review various conflicts of interest that until then had been suppressed. People gained the impression that justice could be achieved simply by attracting the attention of the Kremlin and then backing a given claim with formal arguments and mass support. For people to interpret the intentions of the Communist Party leaders in this way was exceptionally naive, but it happened. *Perestroika* provoked spontaneous political activity on a scale never seen before in the USSR, and the resulting mass demonstrations – notably in Armenia – created opportunities for new organized movements to form and for new leaders to emerge and lead them. All this in turn loosened the monolithic authority of the old repressive regime so that the bearers of non-Communist Party interests and concepts got their chance to enter the political arena, spread their ideas, and mobilize the population.

The unprecedented permissiveness of the Soviet Empire's ruling elite brought crowds on to the streets of Stepanakert, the capital of Karabagh (more formally called the Nagorno-Karabakhskaya Avtonomnaya Oblast or 'Mountainous' Karabagh Autonomous Region), on 13 February 1988. Their demonstration was an outburst of intense frustration, long accumulated but bottled up by the rigid Soviet system of government. Mountainous

Karabagh was a small enclave in Azerbaijan with a population of 160,000 people, of whom 75 per cent were ethnic Armenians. The demonstrators demanded that Karabagh be separated from Azerbaijan and annexed to Armenia, after its 'national council' applied officially to the governments of Azerbajian and Armenia for a grant of sovereign power.

That brief turbulence in early 1988 not only escalated the tension among all the parties to the Karabagh conflict, but also kick-started change within the domestic politics of both Armenia and Azerbaijan. It marked the starting point of the first violent conflict of the post-Cold War era, while also placing the 'Karabagh movement' at the centre of further political development in Armenia itself, thereby determining the Armenian way of post-Soviet political and economic transformation (see chapter 9). Although the two processes, the Karabagh conflict and the Karabagh movement, are too closely linked within the real world of politics to be separable, for analytical purposes it is useful to consider them as distinct. In this chapter only the conflict will be discussed.

The background to the conflict

Since at least the fourteenth century, the Southern Caucasus has formed an arena for vicious power political competition between a long series of Turkish, Persian and later Russian empires. The peoples living in the region found themselves repeatedly taken under the control of one or another of the three dominant powers without any chance to establish and sustain a state structure of their own. Among the many unfortunate effects of this history was its impact on the location of borders, which carved up the land and communities without regard either to the ethnic structure of the population and historic settlement patterns, or to the preferences of local people. The boundaries were imposed after the external states had fought battles and signed treaties according to who won and who lost.

In the Caucasus the local people were affected culturally as well as militarily by the misfortune of living within the boundary zone contested by two major spheres of influence. The contrasting implications of Russian hegemony from the north and Muslim hegemony from the south were sufficient over time to convert the sequence of imperialist battles into a full-scale confrontation of civilizations. The Armenian populations tended to regard the Russians as safer for them, whereas the local Muslims felt more secure when the laws were made by their co-religionists. The effect was that military gains and losses were usually followed by population movements. In each territory conquered by the Tsarist army, Armenians would move in as the Muslims moved out, and vice-versa. These intermittent migrations caused the population in any given part of the region to fluctuate substantially.

But it was also the case that not everyone on either side could either manage to move or choose to move as the imperial armies marched back and forth across their land, and the consequence was substantial ethnic mixing across the region. In some localities, groups belonging to different communities co-existed for centuries; Armenians and Muslims certainly had that experience. However, proximity did not always instil a culture of sympathy or of shared values. In some cases two or more different ethnic groups came to focus their territorial self-identification on the very same territory, thereby creating passionate disputes in which each group insisted on the rightfulness of its claim.

As Russia and Turkey, defeated states of the First World War, briefly collapsed into revolutionary turbulence, a power vacuum opened in the South Caucasus. For a few short years the Armenians found their sovereign voice, set about creating an independent state, and immediately ran into disputes with the Azeri communities about where the borders should be (see chapter 5). The issue was complicated both by the overlapping ethnic attachments to the land and by the competing needs for security. Although the people of Karabagh were predominantly Armenian (93 per cent Armenian-speaking in 1919 is the accepted figure), the territory was claimed by the newly formed states of both Armenia and Azerbaijan. Argument about the boundaries was accompanied by armed confrontations, confused by a Turkish invasion, and finally suspended in the face of the advancing Red Army in 1920.

Once all the new states had been sovietized, the Caucasian Bureau of the Soviet Communist Party decided in 1921 that Karabagh would be included in the territory of Azerbaijan. Officially there were economic grounds, but it is clear that the Soviet government was more concerned with politics. Moscow was careful to do nothing that might jeopardize future relations with Turkey. The decision met resistance on the Armenian side, and in 1923 Karabagh was granted the status of an autonomous region. It was to have a limited form of self-governance, although it would remain subordinate to the government of the Soviet Republic of Azerbaijan.

The Armenian population of Karabagh never accepted this decision as a just and final one. At least five times during the 70 years of the Communist regime, signatures were collected in the oblast and petitions delivered to the Supreme Soviet in Moscow. The Armenian population of Karabagh complained repeatedly about the conduct of the Azerbaijani authorities and asked for the revision of Karabagh's administrative subordination. Under the totalitarian regime these actions made no impression, and it was understood that any attempt to mobilize the population would be suppressed even before it could manifest itself.

Interpretations of the problem by the main parties involved in the conflict

Taking decision-making prerogatives away from the people of the region and replacing them with Soviet rule from the centre effectively stopped the disputes and violent conflicts that had plagued the region in the first two decades of the twentieth century. Although stories circulated continually in both republics about cases of ethnic discrimination, the facts were that when the open dispute began in 1988, around 185,000 Azeris lived in Armenia and 360,000 Armenians lived in Azerbaijan, some 120,000 of them in Karabagh. Armenians made up a significant part of the population in many Azerbaijani towns, including a long-established community in the capital Baku, while numerous villages on the Armenian side of the border had an ethnically mixed population. Although mixed marriages were not common, they enjoyed social tolerance in both republics. Ethnic problems were not a subject of discussion in the tightly controlled Soviet media and there was no deep or widespread awareness in either republic of the accumulated frustration in Karabagh. From the 1920s to the 1980s the region therefore appeared on the surface to be a peaceful place where ethnic tolerance was generally practised.

But that was a misleading impression. The reality was that the continuing mutual suspicions and frustrations were pushed underground where they accumulated and festered, while on the surface the relationship between Azerbaijan and Armenia developed in accordance with the official doctrine of 'friendship of the peoples'. When the events of February 1988 occurred in Karabagh, they caught many people by surprise, especially on the Azeri side, and provoked a variety of explanations of what was going on and why. Poor reporting and inadequate mass communication forced many people to rely on hearsay, while the lack of democratic means of public debate facilitated the rapid growth of stereotypes, prejudice, tunnel vision and hostility. Conflicting beliefs were formed on the two sides of the dispute, and in the absence of corrective interpretation they grew into 'truths'.

The contradictory images of Azeris and Armenians were not frozen constructs, and they evolved in parallel with the development of the conflict. At the outset in 1988 the main components of both opposed images were the historical legitimacy for their own claim to Mountainous Karabagh, and the explanation of the opposition's behaviour by means of a grand conspiracy theory. On the one side, the enemy was regarded as inspired by Pan-Turkish goals; on the other, by the ambition to restore the Greater Armenia of ancient times. As the state-building project got underway after 1991 in both countries, the security issue came first: each side stressed the military threat directly posed by the capabilities and intentions of the other. But despite the shifting emphases of the two images, the mutual misrepresentation persisted, together with the continuing stubbornness of the opposed convictions.

The Armenian version of the conflict

The land of Karabagh is the historic motherland of the Armenian people, and the roots of the culture and religious traditions are to be found here.

The numerous ancient monuments – the Christian churches and ceme-teries – built on the territory of Karabagh prove this. The majestic church at Gandzasar, finished in 1238, is a good example; in contrast, the Muslim population has only two notable monuments in Karabagh, both nineteenth-century mosques.

The conflict in Karabagh was only a new stage in a continuous fight for independence by the Karabagh people that had been under way for centuries. The decision made in 1921 by the Communists was a historic error, committed under Moscow pressure and ordered by Stalin himself. The 1988 decision of the Karabagh authority to seek a reunification with Armenia was an expression of the will of the people who live in Karabagh. Furthermore, it was their constitutional right as a group to claim self-determination if they chose so to do, and their universally acknowledged individual human right also.

Throughout the seventy years of the Communist regime, the Soviet authorities in Azerbaijan operated a policy designed to expel Armenian people from Karabagh. That explains why the Armenian proportion of the population decreased from 95 per cent in 1921 to 75 per cent in 1988.

The policy of displacement was carried out by means of social, economic and cultural discrimination against the Armenian section of the population. All the financial resources allocated to Karabagh were put into the develop-ment of villages with a predominantly Azeri population. No books were published in the Armenian language. Cultural links with Armenia were very difficult. Appointments of staff to all professional positions, including civil servants, medical staff and teachers, were referred for approval to Baku, the capital of Azerbaijan. This significantly reduced the opportunities for Armenians to secure employment and education in Karabagh, compelling them to leave their country.

If Karabagh had been allowed to remain within Azerbaijan, the repres-sion of the Armenian people there would have continued and intensified in independent Azerbaijan. Quite soon all the Armenians would have been forced out of their homeland, and ethnic cleansing would have been effec-tively completed – as had already happened in another disputed territory, Nakhichevan, which like Karabagh was placed under Azerbaijan's juris-diction in 1921. The policy of gradual ethnic purification carried out by Azerbaijan is part of a wider policy of Pan-Turkism designed to rebuild a vast Turkish state.

The Azeri version of the conflict

What happened in February 1988 was an insurrection, orchestrated by external intervention or, at the very least, manipulation. The Armenian government and overseas Armenian communities were involved. The Karabagh authority's demand for secession was a clear act of rebellion, and its provocation of the mass demonstrations was sedition. It deliberately mobilized the Armenian population of this country against its sovereign integrity. The claim that the Armenians own the land is historically shallow; they began to settle in the territory in significant numbers only in the nineteenth century.

According to accepted international norms, the ethnic composition of a state cannot be regarded as a sufficient justification for changing its borders. To change that principle would destabilize most states in the world, because the presence of several national groups inside one set of borders is the norm, not the exception. There was no objective reason to suspect the existence of a deliberate policy of discrimination against ethnic minorities in Azerbaijan; all citizens were equally required to have their appointments approved in the capital. In any case, the Armenians of Karabagh occupied a considerably more privileged position than many minority groups in the Soviet Union in having a constitutionally guaranteed degree of administrative self-government.

There was never any justification for the Armenians to speak of a 'historic error' committed by the Communists in the early twentieth century. The decision on the status of Karabagh was legal and just. It was made principally for an economic reason; the undeveloped Karabagh needed to be linked to the industrial region of Baku, which was much more advanced at that time. The decision was taken in the interests of the Armenian population, and the proof that it was a sound decision is self-evident: it provided them with a better standard of living.

There were no grounds for the Armenians to complain about economic, social or cultural discrimination. The region contained Armenian schools and an Armenian theatre. The emigration of some people from Karabagh was normal. It is expected that there will be migration from the peripheries to the centre, and from the rural areas to the cities. Certainly, there were some administrative problems, especially in terms of an authoritarian style and in central government interference in the internal affairs of an autonomous region – but that was how things were done throughout the entire USSR. Everybody suffered from it, not just people in the region.

Looking back, one can see that the whole Karabagh 'problem' was dreamed up and then stirred up by the Armenian chauvinists, and particularly by their most fundamentalist group, the Dashnak Party. The so-called 'question' of Karabagh was actually nothing more than the aggression of these Armenian extremists, who managed to brainwash the population of Karabagh and manoeuvre them on to the streets. The Dashnaks had aims reaching far beyond the enclaves of Azerbaijan; they wanted to reconquer the territories held by their ancestors a thousand years ago so as to restore the legendary 'Greater Armenia from Sea to Sea'.

Dynamics of the conflict

Over a three-year period from its beginnings as a series of peaceful demonstrations and legal requests, the Karabagh conflict degenerated into war. It was accompanied, as wars often are, by passionate commitment, close-quarters combat, wicked acts against civilians and political crises behind the lines of battle. As it passed through several stages of development, the conflict seemed to acquire a life of its own, and changes occurred in all its major aspects: the nature of the relationship between the parties involved, the identity of those parties, and the strategies adopted by them.

The nature of the conflict and the parties involved altered dramatically. Initially all the events took place on Soviet soil, but, when the USSR collapsed, Russia became an intervening external state. Meanwhile, the newly independent Republic of Armenia became directly engaged alongside Karabagh in its fight with Azerbaijan. From the early 1990s various foreign governments and international organizations played a role. Over time, therefore, a domestic conflict was transformed into an international conflict. The issues disputed between the two sides also changed. At the outset, the legality within the Soviet constitution of a union between Karabagh and Armenia was the principle at issue, but by the end Karabagh claimed full independence and had acquired a political identity distinct from Armenia.

Chronologically, it is useful to divide the Karabagh conflict into three relatively separate phases: (a) the dispute between the two Soviet republics, 1988–91; (b) the war between Azeri and Armenian armies, 1991–4; and (c) the negotiations, from the cease-fire declaration in 1994 onwards.

The first phase

The clearest starting point is the formal appeal of 20 February 1988 by the Karabagh local authority for a change of legal status for the region and its unification with Armenia. This was backed up by a mass demonstration in Karabagh, and further backed up by an even bigger demonstration in the capital of Armenia. The demonstrations stopped only after Gorbachev promised to negotiate about the problem by holding a summit meeting of all the appropriate authorities.

On 28 February, the eighth day of the dispute, there was an event that in many ways determined the entire future development of the conflict: a murderous assault carried out on the Armenian residents of the Azerbaijani city of Sumgait. This pogrom lasted three days and was stopped only by the intervention of the Soviet Army. It left at least 31 people dead (according to official reports), many injured and thousands in panic. There followed an outflow of terrified refugees heading for Armenia.

For Armenians, the fast-spreading news of the Sumgait pogrom evoked emotive memories and the agonizing personal distress of the Genocide. The widespread assumption was that the ethnic cleansing that had been conducted with such marked efficiency in Western Armenia almost seventy-five years before was about to be repeated in the East. The Sumgait attacks were presented in Armenia as a 'Pan-Turkish threat to the whole nation' or as 'the Turkish model of behaviour when dealing with Christian Armenians'. In the Armenian perception, the identification of Soviet Azerbaijan with Ottoman Turkey was quickly made – however misleading.

The pogrom in Sumgait had an immediate and profoundly negative effect on the conflict. It fomented hostile attitudes and emotional confrontation from the beginning, and made it impracticable to hold serious discussions about alternative policies or possible compromises. The National Council of Karabagh repudiated its constitutional subordination to the Azerbaijan government and declared a state of siege.

Escalation then set in. A refugee flow poured out of both Armenia and Azerbaijan, and tension within Karabagh and along the Armenia–Azerbaijan borders intensified. Cases of violence remained local, but there were frequent incidents of cattle theft and blockades of roads. The leaders of the national movement organized boycotts of the authorities in an attempt to force them to ask Moscow to give in to popular demands. In return Moscow prevaricated, trying to keep a balance without taking any decisive steps. Its inaction gave rise to criticism not just in Armenia but also in Azerbaijan, thus contributing to the collapse of the legitimacy of the authority of Moscow as a whole.

In April to May 1991 the first military actions took place just after an anti-communist political group won power in Armenia's first free elections. The Azerbaijani authorities, backed by Soviet troops in an action known as 'Operation Ring', began to deport the Armenian population from Shahumian and Getashen, regions bordering Mountainous Karabagh. At that early stage, there was resistance by Armenian guerrilla groups, though it was unsuccessful. As one of the Armenian leaders remarked in an interview: 'We were aware that we were fighting against the Russian Army. Certainly we were losing, but we learned to fight. That was the very period when we began to create our own army. It gave us the advantage of starting earlier than Azerbaijan in building our own regular army.'[1]

---

1   All the interviews referred to in this chapter were conducted by the author as a part of the EU-INTAS project on 'Conflicts in Post-communist Societies' in 1996.

This stage was terminated by the formal disintegration of the USSR between August and December 1991. 'The putsch in Moscow in August was our salvation', as another Armenian leader commented in an interview. Until this point the dispute had been considered to be an internal problem within the Soviet Union; only Moscow officialdom fulfilled the roles of mediator and arbiter. Its attitude throughout had been exceptionally rigid. Its pronouncements had often come with vital delays and more often had the effect of pouring oil on the fire than suppressing it. The first reaction of the Soviet government in 1988 was to deny the existence of ethnic tensions in the Soviet Union, and to attempt to close down the issue by promising additional finance for the development of the region. When that did not work, the party leaders resorted to a more traditional method: an attempt to suppress the dissent by sending a large contingent of armed forces to the region. The troops stayed in and around Karabagh from March 1988 until the Moscow putsch in August 1991.

The only radical Soviet effort to pacify the region was the decision to impose direct rule from Moscow, by means of the 'Special Administrative Commission on Mountainous Karabagh'. Established in January 1989, this unrepresentative governing body reported directly to Moscow and was required to co-ordinate its actions with Azerbaijan. Its incompetent administration consisted mostly of delays followed by emergency actions, provoking distrust and suspicion among Azeris as well as Armenians. The fierce resentment persuaded Moscow to abolish the Commission in November 1989 and replace it with direct military rule in Karabagh.

Officially, the contingents of armed forces dispatched to the region were there to prevent violent confrontation between the parties and to guarantee law and order, and indeed they did so in the initial stages, albeit using harshly repressive methods. But as an anti-Soviet mood developed in the region in 1989 and 1990, their priority shifted and they slowly became an occupying force whose job was to suppress the increasing irritation of the people in both republics with the USSR itself. When the anti-communist agitation increased in Armenia, where the political changes generally were more rapid than those in Azerbaijan, the actions of the troops were visibly pro-Azerbaijan. As soon as Armenia's new nationalist leaders took office in August 1990, the army assisted in the deportation of the Armenian population from the Karabagh border zones. That action was interpreted in Armenia as a sanction against Yerevan's new anti-communist authorities. But the same Soviet troops also used force to suppress the anti-Soviet movement in Azerbaijan. An example was the action in 1990 known in Azerbaijan as 'Bloody January', when soldiers entered Baku nominally for the purpose of stopping another anti-Armenian pogrom and protecting people who were fleeing the town. The military operation went far beyond that, using violence as a deterrent in an (unsuccessful) effort to crush the pro-independence movement in Azerbaijan.

The second phase

With the disintegration of the Soviet Union in the autumn of 1991, the drastic change in the legal environment brought about the second phase of the conflict. All the parties involved in the dispute began to act as independent entities, and their relationship quickly escalated into full-scale violent warfare. Armenia and Azerbaijan were immediately recognized by the international community as states within their existing borders. Karabagh started to behave as a *de facto* sovereign state, although it went unrecognized by any country. The new situation significantly changed the character of the conflict, including the arguments used and even the political positions of those directly involved.

Independent status made it possible for Azerbaijan to invoke the international norm specifying that recognized borders must be respected, and in November 1991 its new parliament abolished the autonomous status of Karabagh and refused to acknowledge any dispute as to its status. A blockade was imposed of all transport and energy across the entire border between Azerbaijan and Armenia. The deprivations caused by this became a major factor contributing to the catastrophic Armenian post-communist economic decline.

In Karabagh itself the dissolution of the Soviet constitution provided an ideal opportunity to proclaim that the Politburo decision of 1921 on its status had lost its legitimacy, and that the territory had acquired the right legally, as well as morally, to decide its own fate. The Karabagh authority withdrew its initial demand for transfer to Armenian jurisdiction and declared full independence instead. To demonstrate the determination of people in Karabagh, a referendum was held on 10 December 1991 and recorded an overwhelming vote for independence. Thereafter Karabagh engaged in an active programme of institution building designed to equip the emergent state with the full range of governmental structures: a constitution, an elected president and parliament with supporting bureaucracies, administrative agencies and most significantly a strong army.

Finding itself in both a suddenly created new legal environment and a radically altered political situation, the Armenian government under Levon Ter Petrosian acted with relative caution. It declared repeatedly that although it was not directly a party to the conflict, it would continue to act as a guarantor for Karabagh and would give full backing to whatever decision the people of the territory chose to make about their future.

These changes in the international position of the conflicting parties came at a time, in 1991–2, of increasing emotional tension between them and a growing consciousness of national insecurity. The earlier experience of the strategy adopted by Moscow, which was a manipulative technique of playing one local party against another in order to preserve its own dwindling influence, contributed to a growing conviction in Baku, Stepanakert and Yerevan that the issue could be settled only by the parties themselves, and by forcible means.

There was no shortage of armaments in the region. After the disintegration of the USSR the Soviet forces began to disband or retreat, leaving behind great stockpiles of arms and equipment. From the winter of 1991–2 on, direct military actions began between Azerbaijan and the Karabagh forces, which were supported by Armenia. The intensity of the battles increased and their locations spread beyond the borders of Karabagh. Early in 1992 and for two years beyond, clashes between armed forces occurred all round the fringes of Karabagh and along all the borders between Armenia and Azerbaijan.

The major military operations lasted for about two years, with alternate advances and retreats along the front lines separating the two sides and frequent cease-fires, which lasted only a short time before they were violated. In due course the Armenian/Karabagh army prevailed. During the spring of 1994 it took control of the territories bordering Karabagh on the Azeri side, together with all the land that had previously separated it from Armenia. By the time the final cease-fire was signed on 12 May 1994, the Armenian army controlled 15 to 20 per cent of Azerbaijan's territory, including almost the whole of Karabagh itself. One of the Armenian leaders commented on the factors that influenced the decision to agree to an armistice: 'Our army was advancing and it was in the clear interest of the Azeris to sign the armistice to stop the continual losses of territory. We also had to sign, because we were losing international prestige, and it was not good for us to go on from the political point of view. To break the peace was not in the interest of either of the parties.'

Against the background of the armed conflict between 1991 and 1994, repeated efforts at mediation were made by foreign countries and international organizations. Most of them were in the form of short-lived initiatives, such as the so-called Zheleznovodsk initiative jointly undertaken by the presidents of Russia and Kazakhstan in September–November 1991, or the mediation attempt by the Iranian government in February–May 1992. All such efforts had an incidental character and made virtually no impact on the conflict.

However, a more persistent attempt to bring the conflict to an end was undertaken by the Minsk Group of the Conference on Security and Co-operation in Europe (CSCE), a permanent international body that became the Organization for Security and Co-operation in Europe (OSCE) in December 1994. The CSCE became involved in the mediation in March 1992, after both Armenia and Azerbaijan joined the organization. The Minsk Group consisted of nine officially 'neutral' countries plus the two recognized parties, Azerbaijan and Armenia. But although the mediation effort by the CSCE/OSCE was always present and had promising moments, little progress was achieved overall. Its pacific intervention was undertaken when the conflict had just reached the point of open warfare and for some years both parties were hopeful of the prospect of military success, rather than inclined to compromise.

The role played by Russia also reduced the chances that any mediation process could succeed. The Russian withdrawal from the region took about two years. But Moscow began thereafter to interfere in the politics of the former Soviet territories, which it now called the 'near abroad'. This time its influence was exerted as an ally of Armenia. While the Minsk Group was arguing for step-by-step demilitarization under the umbrella of international peace-keeping forces, in late 1993 Russia introduced a contradictory proposal for a Russian or Russian-led CIS 'separation force' to be deployed between the warring sides. This manifested the tension among the mediators themselves, thereby offering the conflicting parties diplomatic room for manoeuvre. It took a year to reach a compromise, when the Budapest Summit of the Heads of the OSCE Participating States recognized Russia as a permanent co-chair of the Minsk Group from December 1994. That made it possible to co-ordinate different initiatives under the OSCE umbrella.

Russian mediation did, however, facilitate the cease-fire that was finally reached on 12 May 1994. The war ended leaving around 20,000 casualties, numerous refugees in Azerbaijan from the territories conquered by the Armenian army, prisoners of war badly mistreated on both sides, stories of atrocities against civilians on both sides and deep reciprocal distrust. The cease-fire itself proved to be long lasting, but, in the absence of an agreed final settlement, the Karabagh peace remained a fragile hostage to the self-restraint of local politicians.

The third phase

The 1994 armistice did not bring a conclusion to the undeclared war between Azerbaijan and Armenia: borders stayed closed, mines were left uncleared in the fields, refugees were forced to continue to live in 'temporary' camps, and the embargo along the Azeri and Turkish borders was extended year after year. With the situation on the ground completely frozen, the conflict moved into a phase of formal negotiations under the auspices of the OSCE Minsk Group, which proceeded at a snail's pace.

The negotiations were complicated by a confused overlap of goals, claims and attitudes among the various parties. The core issue was the fixed insistence of the Karabagh Armenians on their right to self-determination, which Azerbaijan refused to consider. In the Azeri view, the nationalist leadership in Karabagh was nothing but a puppet regime manipulated by the Armenian state. Azerbaijan therefore considered that the Armenian state was its opposing party in the conflict, not Karabagh.

Armenia itself continued to maintain its 1992 denial that it was a party to the conflict between Karabagh and Azerbaijan, although it supported the Karabagh claim to sovereignty. It insisted that it had no territorial claims and that the military occupation of Azerbaijani territory was carried out by Karabagh forces and was intended merely to protect the Armenians in Karabagh from Azeri threats. It countered Azerbaijan's allegation of aggression with the assertion that Armenia itself was the victim of aggression in the form of a punitive blockade by Azerbaijan and Turkey.

The Turkish and Russian positions in the mid-1990s were resonant of the imperial chess-playing attitudes of earlier centuries. Turkey denied having any involvement at all in the conflict, and justified closing its Armenian borders as an act of solidarity with its co-ethnics and co-religionists in Azerbaijan. It accused Russia of fomenting and extending the conflict by its support for Armenia. Russia, in its turn, alleged that Turkey was exploiting the situation as an opportunity to enlarge its sphere of influence in the Transcaucasus. Overall, the complex claims and counter-claims in the early years over who was responsible for which damaging actions had the cumulative effect of pushing the mediation effort into an impasse. The negotiations were trapped at the preliminary stage of identifying the parties involved, debating the legitimacy of their authority, and then agreeing on their status in the process.

However, the objective circumstances surrounding the dispute after 1994 were quite different from those prevailing in the dying years of the USSR. If the transformation of the conflict during the second phase was determined by the radical shift in the legal environment, in the third phase it was the realistic appreciation of the economic interests of the newly independent states that became more prominent, and began to hold out the prospect of an eventual settlement.

With independence, the interests of Azerbaijan rapidly developed far beyond military success in Karabagh. The government recognized the need to normalize internal social conditions, to receive international loans, and to develop the country's oil resources with the help of foreign investors; and the main requirement for all these was stability. Such considerations encouraged the Azeri side to avoid further armed confrontation and to continue to negotiate. An additional factor that reinforced the tendency to talk indefinitely was that Azerbaijan secured international recognition of its 'territorial integrity', Karabagh included, in the 1990s and therefore felt more secure.

The scope of Armenia's interests also changed in the 1990s. As GDP crashed to a fraction of the 1990 level and half the population slid into poverty (see chapters 11 and 12), the absolute priority of the national economy became self-evident. Closure of the borders with both Azerbaijan and Turkey inflicted immense damage on the economy and left Armenia dependent on long and expensive routes to the outside world through Georgia and Iran. The need to subsidize virtually all economic activity in beleaguered Karabagh also conflicted with the economic interests of the republic. There followed a determined attempt by Yerevan to distance itself as far as it could from the conflict by repeatedly stressing that Armenia had no claim on Azerbaijan.

As an independent player in the 1990s, Karabagh was able to give expression to its own interests, which were not always in harmony with those of Armenia. Since the declaration of independence Karabagh had developed a full state structure with an elected parliament and president, and it had achieved *de facto* independence. The military successes in 1993–4 gave it a strong position, and it exerted considerable leverage on the government in Armenia. The political leadership felt able to reject any compromise prior to recognition of Karabagh's status as a party to the negotiations, and by 1997 it had effectively succeeded in becoming a party to the OSCE negotiations. With the significant exception of Azerbaijan, it became generally accepted that any agreement must be signed by all three main actors: Azerbaijan, Armenia – and Karabagh.

Inevitably, the great potential of Caspian oil reserves became a major factor in the negotiation process, but its effects were mixed and confusing. On the one hand, it seemed to encourage Azerbaijan to settle with its rebellious province, because genuine political stability in the whole region was essential if foreign investors were to be convinced that it was safe to commit themselves. On the other hand, it encouraged procrastination. Oil wealth would one day turn Azerbaijan into the 'new Kuwait', so time was on Azerbaijan's side. Why agree to a compromise when the country's position would improve so much in the future? On the opposite side of the table, the Armenian delegation was conscious of equivalent implications. Believing that soon Armenia would have to face a stronger, wealthier enemy that would eventually resort to force, the government in the mid-1990s committed scarce resources to a further build-up of its already substantial military machine and set about securing Russian support.

As the negotiations progressed, the practical questions that needed to be settled were formulated. These were the determination of the political status of Karabagh, the withdrawal of Armenia's army from Azerbaijani territory, the return home of refugees, establishing a guarantee of the security of the Karabagh population, and the timing and sequencing of all these actions. In an attempt to lead the parties towards an agreement, the OSCE mediators used two approaches alternately, 'the step-by-step' and 'the package deal'.

The step-by-step approach consisted of separating the many aspects of the conflict into smaller, distinct issues that could be resolved one at a time, with the most difficult left to the end. The peace process would begin with demilitarization of the conflict zone and proceed to deal with the humanitarian issues – safe return of refugees, prisoner release, restoration of communications. The much trickier subject of what to do with Karabagh would follow. This approach was dominant around the negotiating table throughout the second phase of the conflict, first introduced formally by the mediators as the 'Timetable of Urgent Steps' in November 1993. It called for the withdrawal of the Karabagh army from the territories around Karabagh in return for the lifting of the blockade. This would then be followed by the return of refugees. CSCE monitors would observe compliance. This proposal was rejected by Azerbaijan on the basis that the withdrawal of the army should be unconditional. The Armenian side, however, immediately rejected unconditional withdrawal, and the proposal hit deadlock.

In February 1995 the mediators dropped the step-by-step approach and introduced the 'package deal' approach – the principle that nothing is agreed at all unless everything is agreed. The plan was that the parties should negotiate an agreement about each key issue in turn, but not implement it until all the other issues had been discussed and a final 'Big Agreement' could be put into action. This approach dominated the sessions for almost two years but did not achieve any breakthrough, despite the noticeable increase in diplomatic activity.

A heavy blow was struck against Armenian diplomacy at the OSCE Lisbon summit in December 1996, when it failed to prevent a vote in favour of the principle that the territorial integrity of Azerbaijan should be preserved. Armenia had consistently argued that this should not be a precondition to the negotiation on the status of Karabagh. The Lisbon declaration did not release the peace process from its deadlock, but rather the opposite because it magnified the suspicion and distrust in the Armenian delegation's perception of the mediators. In the domestic political arena, however, it shook the already weak position of the Armenian leadership as public opinion grasped the failure of their foreign policy in general and specifically its inability to stand up for Armenian interests.

In 1997 the step-by-step strategy came back into diplomatic circulation when the Minsk Group submitted its next proposal: withdrawal of the armed forces from seven Azerbaijani provinces, then border reopening, then refugee return, and finally the key discussion on the status of Karabagh. By this stage, four years into talks, it was generally understood that the agreement on status would have to incorporate two principles: territorial integrity, leaving Karabagh *de jure* as part of Azerbaijan, and self-determination, giving the region *de facto* self-government. This time both Azerbaijan and Armenia accepted the proposal, at least as a basis for further talks, and there was optimism that a settlement might at last be within reach.

The softening of the Azerbaijani position was probably derived from a hard-headed reassessment of its gloomy prospects for economic development. It became clear that expectations of an oil boom were exaggerated, and that to date the Azerbaijani economy as a whole had benefited little from the country's considerable oil potential. Its hot/cold war over Karabagh was thought to be a reason for that, though clearly not the sole reason. The global petroleum industry was suffering from over-production and hard competition, the Azerbaijani oil fields were too remote from their Western markets, and flourishing corruption among Azeri leaders discouraged many companies from co-operation.

It seems likely that Armenian acceptance, in contrast, was motivated more by politics than by economics. The troubled campaign for the presidency in 1996 was followed by a suspect election, and questions were raised not only about the effectiveness of President Levon Ter Petrosian but also about his legitimacy. He had urgent need of a positive step that might restore his progressive image, bring economic and social benefits, and open the door to a more active foreign policy. He therefore insisted that Armenians had to accept the 'phase-based' proposal, despite the uncertain future status of Karabagh.

But he did not convince the public. He used the economic arguments: that the economy as a whole was struggling, that living standards had fallen and that Armenia desperately needed to open its borders. But by that time the Armenian economy had become sustainable despite being poor; its income was derived to a large extent not from production but from the export of labour, together with foreign aid and gifts from the diaspora. The people were by that time fully aware of how minimal their economic performance had become, but they inclined to the explanation that the cause was to be found in government incompetence and corruption, not in the embargo. Ter Petrosian's readiness to accept the demilitarization of the conflict zone as part of the step-by-step proposal did not win significant backing in Armenia, among either the politicians or the public.

Moreover, the Karabagh leadership rejected the proposal, and did so fiercely. From their perspective, to pull back the army without a security guarantee would cancel out the whole sacrifice of the war and return them to the conditions of the 1980s. An attempt by the Armenian president, who had already lost his popularity at home, to put pressure on the Karabagh leadership backfired when key ministers and most parliamentary deputies sided against him, leading to his forced resignation in February 1998. He was replaced as President of Armenia by Robert Kocharian, one of the hard-line nationalist leaders of the Karabagh struggle and a former president of Karabagh. Kocharian, together with the Armenian military, represented the faction most hostile to the phased approach. As a result, by 1999 the negotiation was pushed all the way back to its starting point with a draft 'package deal' on the table.

The first three years of Robert Kocharian's presidency were marked by an increase in the frequency of direct meetings between the presidents of Armenia and Azerbaijan. The fact of the sessions was announced, but the talks themselves took place under the cover of secrecy, which was said to be required for productive dialogue. Although no tangible progress had been made by late 2000, both presidents claimed to remain committed to the negotiation process. Every meeting between them or with international bodies closed with public statements referring to 'substantial progress', 'optimism' and even 'agreement'. But despite these promising, if bland, signals, only a few officials and observers expected that a solution would be agreed upon soon.

To reach a settlement, several conditions would have to be in place at the same time. One prerequisite was a genuine political commitment by the leaders of all three parties to make the compromises necessary for an agreement. Those leaders would need the empowerment given by political stability in their own countries so that they could overcome the inevitable domestic opposition to change. They would also need to resurrect the optimistic atmosphere and trusting public opinion that marked all three societies at the end of the 1980s. And finally, a stable settlement would be dependent on firm and principled commitment on the part of the mediators – who would themselves need the backing of international pressure and assistance.

Robert Kocharian and Heidar Aliyev appeared to be acting upon a shared understanding that unyielding attitudes to the conflict were equally damaging for both the Azerbaijani and Armenian economies, and that the two countries could get full benefit from the global market only as a region, not as separate countries, much less as unstable ones. Each leader also brought a personal stake to the bilateral summits, wanting to see the troublesome issue resolved before leaving office. The aging Aliyev made it clear that he wanted his son (his choice of successor as president) to be free of the burden of it. The newcomer Kocharian saw his presidency as a unique opportunity to achieve a settlement. His combination of Karabagh origin with the Armenian presidency gave him the authority to speak for both Armenia and Karabagh, and he was determined to use it. As he himself put it: 'If we don't solve this problem, then who else will? Taking into consideration Heydar Aliyev's background, and my background related to the Nagorno-Karabakh problem ... we feel a great burden of responsibility lying on ourselves.'[2]

This mixture of realism and personal commitment did make it possible in the late 1990s to envisage the making of real concessions, at least in principle. Aliyev announced in 1997 that he would concede the highest possible autonomy for a Karabagh that would remain within the territorial space of Azerbaijan – although he did not specify what kind of autonomy he had in mind. Kocharian's reciprocal acceptance of *de jure* Azerbaijani authority, provided it guaranteed *de facto* Karabagh self-governance, was an appropriate response. He deployed terminology like 'horizontal relations' and 'common state'.

By April 2001 these exchanges brought the two presidents closer to signing a peace agreement than ever before, following an intensive round of negotiations first in Paris, France, and then on the island of Key West, Florida. Although the content of the so-called 'Paris Principles' was not made public, it was understood that the two sides had agreed the fundamentals of a settlement, leaving the details to be negotiated later.

Unfortunately, the potential benefits of compromise were lost to view as soon as abstract principles had to be applied to concrete practicalities. Although each president had good justification to lead his country into a settlement, it became apparent that each would face severe 're-entry' problems when he attempted to convince his electorate of the need for it. As a result, the Azeri leadership later denied that any agreement had been

---

2   Radio Liberty, Armenian Service report, 15 August 2002.

reached in Florida, and each side publicly blamed the other for destroying the progress made at that meeting. By mid-2002 it had become clear that the momentum lost in 2001 was vital. Presidential elections were approaching, in February 2003 for Armenia and in October 2003 for Azerbaijan. Neither Kocharian nor Aliyev was inclined to risk an unfavourable outcome by making radical decisions before the votes had been safely cast. Although the two leaders continued to meet each other, smile and shake hands, nobody any longer expected a peace deal on Karabagh until the election dust had settled.

In the event the 2003 elections brought no surprises. Heydar Aliyev expertly passed the presidential office on to his son, Ilham Aliyev, while Robert Kocharian manoeuvred himself into a second term. Sadly for the Karabagh issue, the campaigns imposed a chauvinist tinge on the political climate of the whole region, and by the end of the year the negotiation process was again deadlocked. Ilham Aliev judged that he had to take a harder position than his father had because he was more vulnerable in the domestic political scene. During and immediately after the election Ilham made speeches ruling out major concessions to Armenia. His Foreign Minister, Vilayat Guliev, declared that: 'We do not exclude starting from scratch, because Ilham Aliev is a new president. He may have new ideas.'[3] Against this, Kocharian was beginning by 2004 to feel the time pressure of his second term, insisting that the peace agreement already reached in April 2001 should be revived and refusing to go back to the starting point. The contradictory positions brought about the postponement of previously scheduled summits and the freezing of the negotiation process, with further damage to the economies of both countries.

Over the fifteen years of the war and its aftermath, the public psychology suffered as much as the economy did. Dislike and suspicion hardened into fear and hatred. The effort and sacrifice, the casualties and displacements, the atrocities and stories of atrocities, the hardship and the hard-summoned determination, had all implanted a deep conviction that for such a great project there had to be a fitting reward; something visible and valuable had to be won. The Azeris, as the losers in the military exchanges and with the larger number of refugees to accommodate, felt themselves to be the innocent and mystified victims of an almost feckless campaign of aggression. For them, only something that could feel like a victory, in whatever form, could compensate. On the Armenian side, the images of the conflict conjured up vivid folk memories of the entire dreadful history of Armenian suffering at the hands of the Turks. Within all three of the territories involved, the undeclared but all too real war created a gap between the leaders and their publics so wide that any compromise would be seen as a 'sell-out'.

---

3   Radio Liberty, Armenian Service, 11 December 2003.

What these problems meant for Azerbaijan and Armenia was that the Karabagh dispute had, by the first decade of the twenty-first century, become what in peace studies is known as a 'protracted conflict': a pile of tangled, embedded layers of ethnically predetermined attitudes, pressure group activism, outside manipulation, simplistic ideology and contingent error, each layer compounding and inflaming the next. It seemed likely that even if both countries remained stable and undisturbed by any unexpected crises, an effective peace settlement could still take several years to formulate, agree and implement.

Bibliography

Chorbajian, L., ed., *The Making of Nagorno-Karabagh: From Secession to Republic* (Basingstoke: Palgrave, 2001).

Cornell, S.E., *Small Nations and Great Powers: A Study of Ethnopolitical Conflict in the Caucasus* (Richmond: Curzon, 2001).

Herzig, E., *The New Caucasus: Armenia, Azerbaijan and Georgia* (London: Royal Institute of International Affairs, 1999).

Hovannisian, R. G., *The Republic of Armenia*, Vols 1–4 (Berkeley, Los Angeles: University of California Press, 1971–96).

Libaritian, G., ed., *The Karabagh File: Documents and Facts on the Question of Mountainous Karabagh 1918–1988* (Cambridge and Toronto: Zorian Institute, 1988)

Suny, R. G., 'Living with the Other: Conflict and Cooperation among the Transcaucasian Peoples', *Caucasian Regional Studies*, 2, Issue 1, 1997.

de Waal, T., *Black Garden: Armenia and Azerbaijan through Peace and War* (New York: New York University Press, 2003).

Walker, C.J., ed., *Armenia and Karabagh: The Struggle for Unity* (London: Minority Rights Publications, 1991).

9   Politics in independent Armenia

Edmund Herzig

Introduction

In 1991 Armenia became, for the second time in the twentieth century, an independent state. The life of the first Armenian Republic of 1918–20/21 (see chapter 5) had been short-lived and fraught with crisis and war. Post-Soviet Armenia has certainly experienced its share of problems and conflict, but after ten years of independence it was evident that the political as well as the social, economic and international foundations of its independence were far more resilient than those of its precursor.

The September 1991 referendum on secession from the USSR, the presidential election the following month and then the December dissolution of the USSR allowed Armenia to achieve its independence relatively smoothly. In neighbouring Azerbaijan and Georgia the first months and years of independence were marked by coups, secessionist rebellions and the collapse of central authority, but in Yerevan the 1988–91 period had prepared the ground for the transition from Soviet to post-Soviet politics (see chapters 6 and 8), and President Levon Ter Petrosian was able to take up the reins of government without conflict or major disruption. There were, however, some immediate problems to tackle: first, the human and material costs of the Karabagh conflict, which soon escalated into an undeclared war (see chapter 8); second, the precipitate decline of the economy (see chapter 11), owing to the dissolution of the USSR in December and the blockade imposed by Azerbaijan (and supported by Turkey); third, the task of reconstruction following the 1988 earthquake; and fourth, the urgent need to accommodate several hundred thousand refugees from Azerbaijan as well as those displaced by the earthquake. This was not the most favourable backdrop against which to attempt to develop political and state institutions and to cultivate unfamiliar traditions of democratic politics and civil society.

As the first decade of independence progressed, the successes of Armenia's governments were in consolidating the new state's independence and international standing, and in building a state institution that was increasingly capable of securing and running the country – guarding borders, maintaining law and order, collecting taxes, maintaining macroeconomic stability, holding elections, accommodating diverse political opinions and groupings, and managing political change. Armenia's political leaders also played their part in reaching and maintaining a cease-fire with Azerbaijan (though, at the time of writing, neither side had yet made the major compromises needed to turn cease-fire into peace). Government was far less effective in reaching down to touch ordinary people's lives in a positive manner. Far from fulfilling hopes of a better life, the experience of independence left many Armenians disillusioned and impoverished. Unemployment was rife, and the education, medical and welfare services that were taken for granted in Soviet times withered away, threatening the medium-term social capital of the country (see chapter 12). In the first ten years of independence as many as one million Armenians (25 per cent of the total population), mostly men of working age, often with good qualifications, emigrated to search for work in the Russian Federation and elsewhere.

The first few years, 1991–4

At the outset the Armenian government's top priorities were survival, stability and Karabagh. The immediate challenge was to consolidate control over the territory of the Republic of Armenia and over whatever coercive and material resources could be mustered in the aftermath of the Soviet collapse. Armenia's first post-independence government was assisted in this by the fact that historical consciousness had instilled in Armenians the belief that weakness and internal squabbling would leave them, or their Karabagh compatriots, vulnerable to attack and annihilation. As long as the war continued, this engendered some measure of national consensus and helped Levon Ter Petrosian and his government survive in spite of their growing unpopularity. The civil conflicts and chaos that characterized Georgia and Azerbaijan in this period also had a sobering effect on Armenia's politicians, persuading them that the complete collapse of government and the social order was a real danger for Armenia as well.

This modicum of national unity in the face of war also helped the country's new leaders, who had emerged from the Soviet-era nationalist opposition, to find compromises with the old Soviet elite. At the national level, the main political positions were occupied by members of the new nationalist elite, but many major enterprises were still headed by their former directors from the Communist era, while at regional and local levels much of the old Soviet elite stayed in place in the political, economic and social spheres.

The creation of a national army capable of defending the country and covertly assisting the Karabagh Armenians in their secessionist struggle was one of Levon Ter Petrosian's first priorities. Even prior to independence, work had begun on the task of subordinating the various militias and armed gangs to a single, central political authority. Now Vazgen Sarkisian, another member of the former Karabagh committee, became Minister of Defence and is credited with building Armenia's army into one of the most effective in the former Soviet Union. In a period when the government's resources were meagre in the extreme, the Defence Ministry was always assured of relatively generous funding, and its needs and concerns gained a higher priority in the government's agenda than those of ministries. The task of building the national army was made easier by the recruitment of a large number of Armenian officers who had served in the Soviet army, as well as by the support of Russia in training and equipment.

In the late Soviet and early independence periods, the old Soviet law enforcement system was paralysed by the political turmoil, providing the opportunity for the underworld of organized crime to expand its activities and operate more openly. In the years immediately before and after 1991 the streets of Yerevan witnessed numerous 'turf' wars, with gun battles and assassinations, for control over sections of the informal economy. Gang leaders, and their patrons in the worlds of politics, law enforcement and national security, competed to monopolize sales of, for example, cigarettes or scarce petrol in certain parts of the country. Levon Ter Petrosian appointed another former Karabagh committee member, Vano Siradeghian, as Minister of the Interior, giving him the resources and political backing to restore the law enforcement forces to effectiveness. Here again the policy met with some success: the activities of the criminal underworld were curtailed or driven underground, and law and order returned to the streets; but Siradeghians's methods and style sowed the seeds of later political problems. He was accused of having simply taken over rather than defeated organized crime, of using the forces at his disposal to pursue his personal gain and vendettas, without regard to legality or respect for human rights. And his arrogance and shamelessness – building a luxurious new home in Yerevan at a time when most were struggling to survive – aroused public revulsion and tarnished the image of the government and the ruling party, the Armenian Pan-National Movement (ANM).

The ANM had grown out of the Karabagh committee and its supporters but had since been joined by many former members of the Soviet elite, and others who simply wanted to associate themselves with the ruling power. If consensus on the need to maintain some degree of stability and national cohesion helped prevent the rifts in Armenian politics from undermining the state and its institutions, that is not to say that the politics of these years were harmonious. On the contrary, the mood of permanent crisis and the sense that poor decisions or leadership could lead to disaster tended to intensify political contestation and criticism of the government. Levon Ter Petrosian soon found the wave of support that had swept him to victory with more than 80 per cent of the vote in the 1991 presidential election ebbing away. One of the most damaging developments was the defection of prominent former allies in the Karabagh movement: among others Vazgen Manukian and Ashot Manoucharian, who went on to become the leaders of opposition parties or movements and two of the severest critics of the president and the ANM.

Opposition to the government was expressed in parliament – the Supreme Council, the successor to the Supreme Soviet, was replaced in 1995 by a new parliament, the National Assembly, elected under new laws – and on the streets of Yerevan. The main parties in this period, apart from the ANM, included the Communist Party, several parties that had remained active in the diaspora since the beginning of the century, among them the Dashnaktsutiun or Armenian Revolutionary Federation (ARF), the Ramkavar or Liberal Democratic Party and the Hnchak or Social Democratic Party. On the whole, however, parties were not the principal political actors and were prone to frequent splits and defections. Prominent individuals (many of whom had their own parties to provide a platform) dominated the scene, and their disputes often had a strongly personal flavour as former friends and colleagues fell out, becoming bitter rivals and trading accusations and recriminations. Soviet political culture, with its sharp black-and-white division between the ruling Communist Party and the dissident counter-elite, neither of which recognized the legitimacy of the other, left Armenia's politicians ill prepared for democratic politics, which recognizes the legitimacy of multiple parties and ideologies, and in which the cut and thrust of political contest is the norm. The politics of the Armenian diaspora, moreover, were scarcely a better preparation (see chapter 10).

Karabagh remained a key political issue throughout this period. President Ter Petrosian's government provided substantial moral and material support for the separatists, but denied (although with little credibility) direct military involvement. It dropped its demand for unification with the enclave, stating that it would accept any settlement that satisfied the Karabagh Armenians, and refused to recognize the independent 'Republic of Nagornyi Karabakh' (declared in December 1991). This exposed it to frequent attacks from the opposition, which accused it of being lukewarm in its support of the Karabagh cause. Criticism was particularly strong following the launch of an intensive counter-offensive by Azerbaijani forces in June 1992, which resulted in several thousand people being expelled from Karabagh, exacerbating the already serious refugee crisis in Armenia. In mid-August the opposition held mass rallies in Yerevan in protest at the situation in Karabagh and the worsening economic crisis.

The dismal state of the economy was an important political issue in its own right. Especially in the winter of 1992–3, when the economy seemed at a complete standstill and the supply of electricity was restricted to an hour or two a day, if that, leaving the population burning furniture and books to keep warm. While it was recognized that the problems were caused by the collapse of the Soviet command economy and the Azerbaijani and Turkish blockades, the government's failure to tackle the problem or provide support for the suffering populace led to increasing criticism. In fact, the government adopted radical economic policies aimed at speeding the country's transition to a market economy through privatization and deregulation (see chapter 12).

These did produce results: the 1992 land privatization (the first in the former Soviet Union) was quickly followed by an increase in agricultural production, and in 1994 Armenia's economy became the first in the CIS to return to positive growth. But any upturn was insignificant compared to the previous collapse and did not make much of a difference to most ordinary Armenians. They, on the contrary, felt their standard of living continue to slide, while they watched corrupt officials and their entrepreneur friends flaunt the wealth amassed through abuse of office, the illegal sale of state assets, and the proceeds of rigged privatization. The growing sense of sleaze and the belief that the economy was being managed for the benefit of private interests rather than for the national good were undoubtedly major factors in undermining the credibility of Levon Ter Petrosian's presidency.

Another important political issue in this period was to do with the conduct of politics itself. In these early years Armenia, like most other post-Soviet states, was operating without a proper constitutional framework. In theory the 1978 Soviet constitution was still in force, except where superseded by new legislation, but in practice the constitutional rules of the game were uncertain. Early in his presidency Levon Ter Petrosian began to be accused of authoritarian or dictatorial tendencies. The executive, it was argued, was too strong, and the legislature and the judiciary too weak. Ter Petrosian and his supporters justified this by stressing the need for strong government in a period of emergency, when state and nation were threatened, but this special pleading became increasingly threadbare as the government's hold on power was consolidated and as the danger of national disintegration receded. A tradition of harassing and persecuting opposition politicians and journalists, and of occasional apparently politically motivated killings, began this period and has continued, with some recent amelioration, to the present day.

It was not only the way the government governed but also its handling of the constitutional question that exposed it to accusations of dictatorial tendencies. In 1992 and 1994 two draft constitutions were made public. The first was the official draft, produced by the parliamentary constitutional commission, which outlined a political system in which a presidential executive enjoyed extraordinary powers compared to international norms; the other draft was produced by a coalition of opposition parties and envisaged a parliamentary system. Nationalist opponents of the government also argued for a clause in the constitution about seeking international recognition for the 1915 Genocide, and another to make it easy for diaspora Armenians to acquire citizenship. It was the government's draft that eventually won approval in a referendum in 1995 (see below), but the constitutional debate remained alive, and in February 2001 a presidential commission submitted proposals for reform that involved amendments to nearly half of the articles of the 1995 constitution.

By the time the Karabagh cease-fire came into force in May 1994, the euphoria of independence and the sense of national unity that had characterized the end of the Soviet period and the elections of 1991 had entirely evaporated. To a great extent the government was alienated from the people and from the intellectual community in Armenia, but it had the support of the new state structures, notably the army and law enforcement forces, as well as the new economic and administrative elite, who were a composite of the nationalists who had swept to power in 1991 and those of the former Soviet elite who were flexible enough to join forces with them. Until 1994 the war and the sense of imminent threat had kept political discord within certain bounds, but, during the fragile peace that followed, the political struggle intensified.

In foreign affairs Ter Petrosian sought to develop normal relations with neighbouring countries and the international community. Armenian–Russian relations were especially strong, both countries having a particular interest in security and military co-operation and viewing each other as strategic partners. Armenia needed a safeguard against a potential Turkish threat and to gain equipment, training and expertise for its own nascent armed forces, while the Russian Federation was interested in retaining control of the former Soviet external borders and in maintaining a forward air-defence zone. Independent Armenia's relations with Iran were also generally cordial, despite tension during the Karabagh war, when Armenian victories threatened to send many thousands of Azeri refugees into Iran. Armenia's relations with the USA and the countries of the European Union – major donors of humanitarian assistance and loans – also developed rapidly. The presence of the Armenian diaspora, which lobbied effectively in Washington, was an additional factor in strengthening US–Armenian ties.

By contrast, relations with the two most important neighbours from an economic perspective remained suspended owing to the Karabagh conflict. The nationalist opposition criticized Ter Petrosian for his pragmatic policy towards Turkey, accusing him of ignoring the historic issue of the 1915 Genocide for the sake of contemporary economic and political benefits. Ter Petrosian remained convinced that Turkey and Azerbaijan would eventually become Armenia's key trading partners, and that all possible steps should be taken to normalize relations and end the blockade. This pragmatic policy produced few tangible results. While the approach was appreciated by Turkish officials and an informal dialogue was maintained, the Turkish government still insisted that the establishment of diplomatic relations and the opening of the border were conditional upon the resolution of the Karabagh issue.

An early priority was to gain international recognition and become a member of the international community, in order to symbolize and consolidate Armenian independence. Though the referendum on independence was held in September 1991, Armenia won international recognition only after the dissolution of the USSR in December of that year. Armenia was one of the original signatories of the Almaty (Alma-Ata) Declaration that established the Commonwealth of Independent States. In February 1992 Armenia was admitted to the Conference on Security and Co-operation in Europe (which subsequently became the Organization for Security and Co-operation in Europe or OSCE), and in March to the United Nations. In international forums, and in its bilateral relations, an important priority was to put the Armenian case in the Karabagh conflict and prevent international isolation on the issue. Already in these years, Yerevan began to work towards the goals of membership of the World Trade Organization and the Council of Europe.

The twilight of the Ter Petrosian presidency, 1994–8

In July 1995, in the country's first post-Soviet general election, the Republican (Hanrapetutiun) bloc, an alliance of six groups led by the ANM, won 119 of the 190 seats in parliament (which was now known as the National Assembly). In a simultaneous referendum, 68 per cent of voters (56 per cent of the electorate) voted to adopt the new constitution. As noted above, the new constitution concentrated power in the hands of the executive, leaving both the legislature and the judiciary weak by comparison. It also reinforced the capital's control over the regions by introducing a system of local government based on ten large provinces (*marz*), each headed by a governor enjoying wide powers and appointed from Yerevan. Then, in September 1996, Levon Ter Petrosian was re-elected president, defeating Vazgen Manukian in the first round of a presidential election, although he gained only slightly more than the 50 per cent of the votes required to avoid a second round.

The 1995–6 elections and constitutional referendum were marred by electoral malpractice. The refusal of the Central Electoral Commission to register a large number of opposition parliamentary candidates, the government's monopoly of television and radio, and falsification of results were among the most serious abuses. Voters' choice was, in any case, significantly reduced by the suspension in December 1994 of the ARF (the most blatant example to date of the government's preparedness to exclude dangerous political opponents) and the prosecution on a variety of charges of a number of prominent ARF party members. International observers dubbed the 1995 election 'free but not fair'. Although the presidential election of 1996 was better conducted than that of the previous year, the narrowness of the margin of victory left the result open to question and allowed the defeated candidate, Manukian, to stage mass demonstrations supporting his claim to have been the real winner. A few days after the election, opposition demonstrators attacked the parliament building (which also housed the Central Electoral Commission), breaking in and beating the chairman and deputy chairman of parliament. After the attack the government imposed martial law for a short period to restore order, Yerevan's residents being shocked to experience the presence of armoured vehicles in the streets and military checkpoints at every major road junction. Several unpopular ministers were replaced, but this was not enough to rebuild the popularity and legitimacy of President Ter Petrosian and his government.

In the period 1995–7 President Ter Petrosian's government attracted increasing criticism from both the domestic opposition and the international community for its authoritarian tendencies. Attacks and harassment of opposition activists and journalists continued, as did the intermittent murders of public figures. The trials and imprisonment of ARF members also dragged on until 1997, contributing to the political malaise of the last years of Ter Petrosian's presidency. The ARF was permitted to re-enter politics only in February 1998, after Ter Petrosian's resignation.

Foreign policy in this period continued the main trends of the previous years. Relations with Russian and Iran were further consolidated. In 1994 and 1995 a series of agreements was signed, giving Russia 25-year military basing rights in Armenia. The 1995 opening of a permanent bridge over the Araks/Aras river greatly facilitated trade relations with Iran and helped to alleviate the impact of the blockade, while the linking of the two countries' electricity grids in 1997 further consolidated ties. During the Soviet period road and rail traffic between Armenia and Iran had all gone through the Azerbaijani exclave of Nakhichevan.

The development of the Western track in foreign policy also continued. In October 1994 Armenia joined the North Atlantic Treaty Organization's (NATO's) Partnership for Peace programme of military co-operation, though security relations with Russia remained of paramount importance, and in April 1996 the country, together with Azerbaijan and Georgia, signed an agreement on partnership and co-operation with the European Union. The stalemate over Karabagh meant that relations with Azerbaijan and Turkey remained on ice and the blockade in place.

Levon Ter Petrosian's political demise was precipitated in the latter part of 1997, when growing splits with the leadership in Karabagh over what constituted acceptable terms for a permanent settlement of the Karabagh conflict became clear. The president's prestige had suffered a knock the year before when the Lisbon summit of the Organization for Security and Co-operation in Europe had given support for Azerbaijan's central demand that its territorial integrity should be preserved in any resolution of the conflict. The discord between Yerevan and Stepanakert in turn engendered divisions within the government. The loss of the support of Robert Kocharian, the Prime Minister since March, Vazgen Sarkisian, the Minister of Defence and one of his oldest political allies, and Serge Sarkisian, the Minister of Internal Affairs and National Security, as well as the defection of a large number of his parliamentary supporters from the ANM to the recently formed Yerkrapah parliamentary faction (which was loyal to the Defence Minister), were decisive in persuading Ter Petrosian that he had no choice but to resign in February 1998.

Levon Ter Petrosian, Armenia's first post-Soviet president, was the son of Syrian Armenians, who brought him to Armenia in the late 1940s, when many diaspora Armenians immigrated, mainly from the Middle East. Educated in Armenia and Leningrad, Ter Petrosian worked as an academic until the late 1980s, when he became a member of the Karabagh Committee. A stirring speaker at demonstrations, Ter Petrosian personified the determination, seriousness and idealism of the national independence movement in Armenia.

His political talents were tested to the full in the last two years of Soviet rule, when he was speaker of the Armenian Supreme Soviet. His vision for Armenia's future was as a strong independent state, at peace with its neighbours (including Turkey and Azerbaijan), integrated with the world economy, but maintaining a special relationship with Russia. Ter Petrosian was adept at balancing the powerful competing forces within the regime, but he failed to tackle the corruption and high-handedness of ministers. In the last year or two of his presidency he appeared increasingly aloof and withdrawn from the political arena. The death of his brother Telman in 1997 and the resignation of his long-standing advisor Gerard Libaridian left him increasingly alone and apparently reluctant to engage in the constant politicking necessary to keep supporters loyal. But it was the defection of Vazgen Sarkisian, the long-standing Minister of Defence, a colleague from Karabagh Committee days and in the opinion of many the most powerful man in the country, that fatally weakened Ter Petrosian's position. Many Armenians felt that by this time he had completely lost touch with his electorate, and that he was now more interested in talking to foreign statesmen and negotiating over Karabagh than in trying to solve domestic problems. Certainly by 1997 he bore little resemblance to the popular demagogue who had stirred the hearts of crowds of tens of thousands in the early days of the Karabagh movement.

Subsequent to Ter Petrosian's resignation, his former senior advisor Gerard Libaridian wrote an analysis of Armenian politics that suggested that the central ideological issue at stake in post-Soviet Armenia was whether Armenia could emerge as a 'normal' nation on equal terms with the other members of the international community, with its sovereignty and government serving primarily to secure the interests of its citizens, as in any other nation. According to Libaridian, this was the vision of the national democratic movement of the late Soviet period and of Levon Ter Petrosian and the ANM in the post-Soviet period, which underpinned their pragmatic domestic and foreign policies. Their opponents, whether on the right or left of the political spectrum (including the Communist Party, Vazgen Manukian's National Democratic Union and the ARF), had a different vision, conditioned by Armenia's history of victimization, and saw Armenian statehood primarily as a vehicle to advance a higher purpose, the Armenian Cause, central to which are recognition of the Genocide, the righting of historic wrongs and national unity for all Armenians, in both the homeland and the diaspora.[1]

---

1   Gerard J. Libaridian, *The Challenge of Statehood: Armenian Political Thinking since Independence* (Cambridge, MA: Blue Crane Books, 1999).

While Libaridian's division of Armenian politicians into two distinct camps of pragmatists and visionaries may be an oversimplification and coloured by special pleading for the president he served, there is at least a kernel of truth in his analysis. The nationalist discourse remains prominent in Armenian politics and is powerfully shaped by a historical consciousness of the Armenians as being special, different from other nations, on account of their unique historical experience, particularly the Genocide.

The Kocharian presidency

In the presidential election that followed Ter Petrosian's resignation in early 1998, the prime minister and acting president, Robert Kocharian, won a large majority over his main challenger Karen Demirchian, Armenia's Communist Party First Secretary for much of the 1970s and 1980s. Armenia's first post-Soviet change of president was achieved smoothly and within the framework of the constitution (although Ter Petrosian did not lose office through the electoral process). While the defeated candidate's supporters alleged that the 1998 presidential election had been rigged, international observers, while noting continuing abuses, considered the election to be a marked improvement on that of 1996.

Once in office, Kocharian continued many of the policies of his predecessor. Initially, it seemed likely that he would adopt a tougher line on Karabagh, but in fact there was little difference of substance. Yerevan's position continued to be that it would accept any settlement that was acceptable to the Karabagh Armenians, and Kocharian, like Ter Petrosian, refrained from recognizing Karabagh's independence. Kocharian certainly was more successful, however, in keeping the policy of the Armenian and Karabagh leadership in harmony, and in general enjoyed a close relationship with Arkadii Ghukasian, the president of the unrecognized republic. In domestic affairs Kocharian professed a stronger commitment to open and democratic government, and his personal style was certainly more populist, but he soon found himself accused of the same authoritarian tendencies as his predecessor. Economic and social policy remained essentially unchanged.

In foreign policy also most of the trends of the previous administration continued. President Kocharian gave great emphasis to the importance of the European orientation of the country's foreign policy, and in June 2000 the Parliamentary Assembly of the Council of Europe accepted Armenia's application for membership. Relations with the USA remained warm, while Russia continued to be Armenia's closest partner. Armenian–Russian military co-operation continued into the twenty-first century with the implementation of a new joint air defence system in May 2001. There were limits, however, on how far Armenia would go in its relations with Russia, and in 2001 Robert Kocharian followed Ter Petrosian in rejecting Armenian membership of the Russia–Belarus Union, which had its advocates in both

Armenia and Russia. The same year he also turned down a proposal to make Russian Armenia's official second language.

As prime minister, Robert Kocharian had disagreed with Ter Petrosian over relations with Azerbaijan and Turkey, arguing that Armenia could survive even if the blockades continued, and that rooting out corruption and more vigorous reform were the keys to economic revival and attracting investment. As president, however, he came to appreciate the importance of the blockades in stifling Armenia's economic development. One issue on which his policy differed from that of his predecessor was in the priority it gave to seeking international and, ultimately, Turkish recognition of the 1915 Genocide. Kocharian's government also laid greater emphasis on fostering relations with the Armenian diaspora. In both these respects, Kocharian's policies marked a shift towards a more nationalist position.

The parliamentary election of May 1999 was won by a new force in Armenian politics, the pro-government Unity bloc, the principal components of which were the Republican Party of Armenia (RPA), unofficially led by the Minister of Defence, Vazgen Sarkisian, and the People's Party of Armenia (PPA) of Karen Demirchian. Following the election, in which the Unity bloc won 55 seats in the 131-seat legislature, Sarkisian became Prime Minister and Demirchian was elected Chairman of the National Assembly. Unity's cohesion, however, soon began to crumble. In the months after the election differences, apparently having more to do with the control of political and economic resources than with policy issues, emerged between Sarkisian and Demirchian, the latter realizing that he had gained relatively little in exchange for offering his party's support during the election. Sarkisian's dominance of real power within the state became increasingly apparent; by comparison, the President appeared weak and isolated. Sarkisian had the army, the Yerkrapah and the RPA as a power base. Demirchian had the PPA and his considerable popular appeal – his relative successes as a Communist Party boss twenty years before had convinced many that he was the leader best suited to set Armenia's economy back on track. This gave him a sense of his own importance and made him reluctant to play second or third fiddle. By contrast, though President Kocharian had the presidency, a reputation as an effective leader in Karabagh and some support from Karabagh Armenians and others in Yerevan, he seemed to recognize the limitations of his power and was ready to make the necessary compromises with Sarkisian. It seemed only a matter of time before these splits would come out into the open in some new political crisis, but on 27 October 1999 events took a dramatically different course. Sarkisian and Demirchian, as well as six other deputies and officials, were assassinated when gunmen stormed the Armenian parliament. The loss of the two leaders left both the Unity bloc and the government in disarray.

The murdered premier's younger brother, Aram, was appointed Prime Minister in early November, but tensions between the president and parliament soon emerged, with the president coming under attack over the handling of the investigation into the assassinations (there were implausible rumours that the assassins had not been acting alone, but on the orders of powerful political figures in the president's camp), over allegations of corruption, over continuing failure in the social and economic spheres, and over rumours that he was planning to sell out Karabagh in his negotiations with President Aliyev of Azerbaijan. In the last months of 1999 and in early 2000 President Kocharian was threatened with impeachment but was able to recover the political initiative. He dismissed Aram Sarkisian and appointed Andranik Markarian, the leader of the RPA, as Prime Minister and Serge Sarkisian (no relation and a Karabagh Armenian like Kocharian) as Defence Minister in May 2000.

For the rest of their first term in office Kocharian and his government were generally able to muster support in parliament, counting on the votes of most deputies of the Unity bloc, the ARF and the Stability bloc (the second largest parliamentary bloc). They suffered some defeats, however. In April 2000 parliament voted for a moratorium on the proposed privatization of the energy distribution networks, and in May 2001 the government could not secure the necessary votes for parliamentary approval of its fulfilment of the 2000 budget. Parliamentary politics remained fluid throughout this period, with new parties and groupings emerging and old ones declining or disappearing. Among the most significant developments were the fading away of the Yerkrapah and simmering differences within the Unity bloc between the RPA and PPA. The RPA was generally supportive of Kocharian, while the PPA became increasingly critical of both the government and its Unity bloc partner. Eventually, in September 2001, the PPA split from the Unity bloc, though some of its MPs left the party to continue to support Unity. Aram Sarkisian, the dismissed brother of the assassinated prime minister, started a new party called 'Republika' and immediately became one of the harshest critics of the president. At the same time, the parties on the left wing of the political spectrum, led by the Communists, began to make more serious efforts to co-ordinate and to work as a parliamentary bloc opposed to the government's social and economic programmes. Nevertheless, Kocharian faced up to all the growing opposition and was re-elected to the presidency in March 2003, winning a second term with 67 per cent of the vote.

In the course of the campaign, Stepan Demirchian emerged as the main challenger to the president, identifying himself with populist themes such as anti-corruption and justice. He also linked up with Aram Sarkisian, like himself a family member of one of the leaders assassinated during the attack on the parliament in 1999, in an effort to expose the plot behind the murders. Together they resurrected the rumours that had circulated at the time of the incident, hinting that Kocharian himself might have been involved. Faced with such accusations in addition to criticism on a variety of other grounds, Kocharian increased the governmental pressure on the media. On the eve of the election, the two most critical TV stations, Noyan Tapan and A1+ , were taken off the air. The rest of the electronic media quickly fell into line, leaving only a handful of press outlets to give publicity to opposition statements. In the two rounds of the election itself, officialdom once again resorted to systematic irregularities such as stuffing ballot boxes and intimidating voters, despite the fact that the incumbent was known to have strong electoral support beforehand. In the eventual assessment of the OSCE and Council of Europe observers, the entire electoral process was once again judged to have fallen short of democratic standards by a considerable distance.

The opposition leadership refused to accept their defeat and challenged the results in the Constitutional Court. In its findings the Court did acknowledge that serious violations had taken place, but it nevertheless ruled that the result should stand. This self-contradictory judgment satisfied only the government, so that from the very start of his second term in office Robert Kocharian was confronted by serious questioning both at home and abroad of his legitimacy, as well as by opposition demands for his resignation.

The next blow struck the opposition in the parliamentary election of May 2003, when pro-presidential parties took a comfortable majority of seats. Inspired by the success of the peaceable 'rose' revolution in neighbouring Georgia, the leaders of the opposition started to rally together, hoping and even expecting that public dissatisfaction would express itself in mass demonstrations and ultimately in open rebellion.

Conclusion

After more than ten years of independence, Armenian politics had been transformed from the late Soviet pattern, in which the Communist Party monopolized the formal structures of power. The nationalist opposition had successfully challenged that monopoly through mass demonstrations, street democracy and a network of informal social, political, economic and military institutions. By 2004 independent Armenia had held no fewer than seven parliamentary or presidential elections, as well as a constitutional referendum. If none of these elections fully conformed to democratic norms, at least they took place on schedule, without large-scale violence (except in the aftermath of the 1996 presidential election) and were all seriously contested by multiple parties and candidates. Observers of the elections, moreover, judged that each election marked an improvement on the last in terms of adherence to democratic norms. Opposition candidates' access to electronic media improved in the period 1995–8, and the sustainability of democratic reform grew, with opposition political parties, NGOs and the independent media gradually developing their capacity to monitor the electoral process and challenge abuses. Elections unquestionably provided an opportunity for genuine political mobilization. Incumbents may have enjoyed significant advantages, but the outcome of elections could not be taken for granted and active campaigning for public support was essential. A mandate from the electorate played an essential role in legitimizing power. Ter Petrosian was seen as a lame-duck president after his controversial re-election in 1996, and the presidency of Kocharian became shaky after his notorious second election in 2003. If parliament was weak in constitutional terms, from the mid-1990s it began to play an increasingly important part in national politics. Loss of support in parliament was an important factor in forcing Ter Petrosian's resignation in 1998. The Armenian National Assembly also developed a growing professionalism in the way it handled its legislative workload, conducted its debates and carried out its committee work.

If the institutions of democratic government gradually stabilized and consolidated in the first ten years of independence, there was less evidence of the kind of broad-based socio-political developments required to underpin political structures in a democratic society. At the end of the decade, Armenia still lacked a judicial system capable of defending the rights of citizens against arbitrary government action, an independent, economically viable media, and NGOs capable of lobbying on specific issues and mediating between government and society. Political parties remained, for the most part, vehicles for political mobilization in support of their leaders in the capital, rather than for the political expression of the interests of a broad-based membership. With one or two exceptions, mostly among the longer-lived parties such as the ARF and the Communist Party, Armenia's political parties remained weak and poorly defined in terms of ideology and support base, and prone to defections and splits. In short, the institutions and traditions of civil society had scarcely taken root, and the political arena was still, in the public perception, a different world, disconnected from ordinary people's lives and needs.

Bibliography

Dudwick, N., 'Armenia: Paradise Lost?', in I. Bremmer and R. Taras, eds, *New States, New Politics: Building the Post-Soviet Nations* (Cambridge: Cambridge University Press, 1997).

Herzig, E., *The New Caucasus: Armenia, Azerbaijan and Georgia* (London: Royal Institute of International Affairs, 1999).

Libaridian, G.L., *Modern Armenia: People, Nation, State* (New Brunswick and London: Transaction Publishers, 2004).

Masih, J.R., and Krikorian, R.O., *Armenia at the Crossroads* (Amsterdam: Harwood Academic Publishing, 1999).

Suny, R.G., *Looking toward Ararat: Armenia in Modern History* (Bloomington and Indianapolis: University of Indiana Press, 1993).

—— *The Revenge of the Past* (Stanford: Stanford University Press, 1993).

10 Media and democracy in Armenia

Mark Grigorian

History

The history of the Armenian press goes back to the end of the eighteenth century. It did not, however, begin anywhere in the historic territory of Armenia. At that time the land between Lake Van and the foothills of the Caucasus mountain range was an impoverished battlefield, repeatedly fought over by Turkey, Persia and Russia. Instead, the early Armenian language press was initiated within the diasporan Armenian communities around the world, where people took refuge away from the troubled homeland and had to struggle to establish their cultural centres and to maintain community ties sufficient to preserve their national identity.

The first diaspora grouping to create its own proto-newspaper was that of Madras, in India, which succeeded in bringing out *Azdarar* (The Herald) between 1794 and 1796. It was a substantial monthly issue, 40–66 pages in length, with large sections on different aspects of community life, including news reports, politics and business. The newspaper was published in the classical Armenian language, Grabar.

At approximately the same time, in 1799, the Armenian newspaper *Taregrutiun* (The Chronicle) was launched several thousand miles to the west, in Venice on the southern fringe of Europe. *Taregrutiun* was issued by the Mekhitarists' Congregation in the modern Western Armenian language, Ashkharabar. It was put together in the printing house on the Venetian isle of San Lazzaro. By the beginning of the nineteenth century Armenian communities as far apart as Bombay and Calcutta in India, Astrakhan in Russia, Vienna in Austria, and Constantinople and Smyrna in the Ottoman Empire were all enjoying the opportunity to read locally produced newspapers in their native Armenian language.

Nearer to the ancient homeland itself the first Armenian newspaper to appear was the weekly *Kavkaz* (Caucasus). It was produced in Tiflis in Georgia, the capital of Transcaucasia in the Tsarist period, where Eastern Armenian intellectual and cultural life was able to develop more rapidly than in Armenia itself. One hundred issues of *Kavkaz* were prepared between 1846 and 1847, using the printing house facilities of the Nersisian

School, a college famous in that region. During the second half of the nineteenth century about a hundred Armenian newspapers were published in Tbilisi, one replacing another. Some of them came out in Russian.[1]

On the territory of today's Armenia, newspapers as a means of communication were introduced almost a century later than in the diaspora. The first of them, *Ararat*, was founded in the town of Etchmiadzin, the spiritual centre of the Armenian Church. It commenced publication in 1868 and kept going until 1919. A decade after *Ararat*'s first issue the citizens of Yerevan also began to get used to having their own local press with the appearance in1879 of Yerevan's *Haykakan Ashkharh* (Armenian World).[2]

Despite these Caucasian developments, the most prominent growth in the Armenian periodical press in the mid-nineteenth century all took place outside Armenia proper. For Western Armenians, the most notable publications appeared in Constantinople, and for Eastern Armenians in Tiflis. From 1832 until the mid-1860s about fifty Armenian newspapers appeared regularly in Constantinople, among them several written in the Turkish language but printed with Armenian letters.

Trouble began for the national press in Constantinople in 1865, when the Turkish authorities enacted the 'Basic Law on the Press'. This measure established an Office of the Press that was granted extensive rights of censorship. When it came into full operation in 1867, this organization began a regime of tight censorship. Day by day, it scrutinized the entire range of newspapers and magazines produced by all the national minorities in Turkey, including those issued in Armenian.[3]

Overall, the early period of development of the Armenian press lasted from the end of the eighteenth century until the middle of the nineteenth, and its overall character can be summarized as having a cultural and educational orientation. Although there was no master plan and no nationalist direction from the centre, a common sense of purpose inspired virtually all the editors of the many local publications, each of which served a particular group of Armenians among the numerous scattered communities of the fragmented people. Their vision was that by providing reports about whatever was 'Armenian' in the local scene, their journal would be able to bring background knowledge and current information to all their fellow-nationals in the community.

The flavour of 'cultural education' began to fade away in the Armenian press towards the end of the nineteenth century, as the various settlements matured, stabilized and began to look for rewards of a more tangible kind

---

1   Vahan Zardarian, *Armenian Journalism in the Caucasus 1846–1880* (Cairo: Gratun, 1932) (in Armenian).

2   Grigoris Galemkarian, *A History of Armenian Journalism from the Beginning to the Present Day*, Vol. 1, (Vienna: Mkhitarian Congregation, 1893) (in Armenian).

3   See V. Ghukasian, *The Formation of the Armenian Press and Armenian Publishing in Constantinople*, (Yerevan: Academy of Sciences of Armenia, 1975) (in Armenian).

than sentiment and the artefacts of culture. As the twentieth century loomed, political parties were formed in many of the various communities and began to crystallize the vague aspirations of their followers into concrete objectives – material, political, ideological and territorial. In response, the press became politicized and in a remarkably short period acquired a strong ideological colouration. The social-democrat Hnchak (Bell) Party issued its party newspapers (all called *Hnchak*) in Constantinople, Geneva and London. The nationalist Dashnaktsutiun party competed for the hearts and minds of the people directly through its organ *Droshak* (Flag), which commenced publication in Geneva, and less obviously by means of its sponsorship of a series of journals such as *Alik* (Wave), *Gorts* (Work), *Azatamart* (Struggle for Freedom) and others. To compete with this flowering of opinion-formation by both the moderate centre and the hard-right nationalists, the Marxists produced their own ideological mouthpieces, *Proletariat* in 1902, *Kayts* (Lightning) in 1906, and several more in the same vein.

Armenia's press therefore began as a mosaic – culturally uniform possibly, but multiparty most certainly, and that characteristic was evident even after the country declared its independence in 1918 (see chapter 5). The novelty in terms of media development came with the introduction of Armenia's first official state newspapers, the titles *Karavarutian Lraber* (Government Bulletin) and *Hayots Azgayin Khorhrdi Lratu* (Bulletin of the National Council of Armenia) marking the arrival of state formation in Armenia.

Compared with this relatively insignificant change in the world of Armenian media, the arrival of Communism was explosive. In 1920 the republic collapsed and the people found themselves under Soviet rule. Throughout the entire seventy years of the Soviet regime that followed, the press shared the fate of all print and electronic media across the entire Soviet Union. It completely lost its independent reporting functions and became a medium of official propaganda. Everything concerning the press, including who should publish, with what frequency and what kind of material should appear on the page, was strictly controlled by Communist Party regulation and censorship.

According to the directives 'from above', in each republic, including Armenia, there had to be two republican newspapers: one in Russian and the other in the local language. Komsomol, the Communist youth organization, was also expected to exert editorial control over two newspapers. In addition, every town was instructed to establish its own local newspaper, and another one was to be set up to cater to the needs of each administrative district (*rayon*) within the republic. And finally, every large organization – defined as any enterprise or institution that employed 300 or more members of the Communist Party – was also to issue its own newspaper. With such extensive bureaucratic direction, the Soviet press became an obedient instrument of the policy requirements of the ruling party. In Armenia it continued to play that role until 1988, when the Karabagh movement (see chapter 8) 'broke the ice' and a radically new pluralism of opinions poured out into the press.

Independent media in the making: 1988–92

The spectacular weakening of the Soviet regime during the 1980s triggered the rapid development of an alternative, non-communist press all over the Soviet Union. The turning point in Armenia, both in socio-political life and in the culture of the media, has an unusually precise date: February 1988. That was the month in which people crowded in tens of thousands into the streets of Yerevan, demonstrating about a controversial political issue on a scale unprecedented in Soviet times. They wanted to show their enthusiastic support for the national movement demanding reunification of Karabagh with the Republic of Armenia.

There followed a disconcerting kaleidoscope of events. The awesomely large mass meetings and demonstrations in Yerevan were accompanied by protests and hunger strikes in support of the demands of the people of Karabagh for independence. Rumours and news of the pogroms in the Azerbaijani town of Sumgait, partly brought by frightened refugees, spread rapidly through the population and were discussed throughout Armenia in incendiary terms reminiscent of the Genocide of three generations before.

The insensitive authoritarian response shown by the Communist leadership in Moscow to all these happenings put the entire society into a turbulent mood not experienced since the Bolshevik Revolution. The tightly controlled Soviet media, both in Moscow and in all the cities and regions of Armenia, reflected the Karabagh events incompletely and inaccurately. The concern of the media was to construct an image of events that would be in line with the official ideology, rather than to report the events factually as they occurred and then discuss their implications. Inevitably, the disparity between this official line and the news arriving by word of mouth (and confirmed by the international media) added fuel to the fire already lit by nationalist emotions. The popular claim that the time had come to 'tell the truth' stimulated the emergence in Armenia of what was known as *samizdat*, the uncensored press that was distributed illegally. Even as late as the closing Soviet decade, to engage in this enterprise automatically placed the journalists under threat of arrest and punishment.

Dozens of *samizdat* newspapers, bulletins and leaflets appeared in 1988. This burgeoning of free speech became a real alternative to the state press. Curiously the *samizdat*, despite resting upon a long tradition in Russia and in Eastern Europe, had been almost non-existent in the Caucasus region before the social turmoil of the late 1980s prompted its sudden, and short-lived, efflorescence.

The appearance of the *samizdat* as an expression of mass dissatisfaction with officialdom took place in a kind of parallel contradiction with Moscow's new policy of liberalization of the press, known as *glasnost*. The

USSR law passed in 1989 'On the Press and other Mass Media' was intended to implement the new policy in practice. It effectively legalized s*amizdat* and eased control over the formal press. According to this law, a newspaper with a circulation of more than 1,000 copies had to be registered only with the Ministry of Justice. No longer was special permission required from the Communist authorities in Moscow, and if the circulation was lower than that, the newspaper could be issued without registration.

The origins of the loosening of Soviet control were by no means entirely political; a technical revolution was occurring at the same time. By 1990 it had become possible to issue handwritten newspapers, or to print them on a typewriter or on a computer. Because photocopying machines had by the end of the 1980s become sufficiently numerous to pass beyond the practical control even of the KGB, there was no difficulty for any would-be publicist to print and distribute a relatively small number of copies of a publication with any content imaginable. As of May 1991 there were more than two hundred immature publications in Armenia that could be charitably classified as newspapers.[4]

The first independent newspaper registered under the law was *Hayk*, the newspaper of the Armenian National Movement or ANM, at the time of its first publication on 2 November 1989 the leading political force in the emerging democratic system. Its first issue was devoted to the founding general meeting of ANM and was printed in 50,000 copies with the aim of building up a large readership. However, the authorities then intervened vigorously to block the printing of the newspaper, and the second number was not issued until January 1990. Events were moving quickly in the USSR, and by that date other political organizations, such as the Constitutional Rights Union and the Union for National Self-Determination, had already launched their newspapers and achieved a wide circulation without formal registration.

The political landscape, and subsequently the media landscape, was then transformed with the return to Armenia in 1989–91 of the traditional political parties that had been founded at the end of the nineteenth century and had successfully kept going in exile throughout the entire seventy years of the Communist regime in Armenia. Newspapers launched by those parties played a dominant role in the development of the Armenian printed press in the 1990s by introducing Western experience, which significantly changed the manner of reporting.

Overall, the period from 1990 to 1992 can be regarded as Armenian journalism's 'Golden Age' in terms of freedom of expression and the scale of the popular demand for the product. Free from the suffocating ideological pressure and confining censorship of the Soviet period, the journalists gloried in

---

4   See N. Hayrapetyan, *A Bibliography of the New Armenian Periodical Press, 1987–1999* (Yerevan: Girk Publishers, 1999) (in Armenian and English).

the opportunity to present their views openly and often in a publication with which they fully sympathized. Large circulations combined with cheap and freely available newsprint, of which extensive stocks remained from Soviet times, to make the newspaper business uniquely profitable.

The downside of the booming media industry of the 1990s was that its output quickly fell to an extremely low quality. The professional standards achieved by the writers, reporters and editors fell to a level well below the acceptable threshold – even of the not very demanding requirements of Soviet professionalism. The decline in standards occurred largely because the dramatic increase in the number of printed media outlets could only be staffed by a very substantial number of journalists. That opened up employment opportunities for many ambitious young people with poor writing skills, only a slight knowledge of journalism, virtually no systematic training and inadequate supervision.

The early post-Soviet idealism and the widespread urge to make their voice heard in public were other factors that attracted many people to contribute to the print media. Their passion led to an emphasis on the quantity of the written words, rather than on the elegance and concision of the style, and still less the strength of the arguments. The apparent ease with which it was possible to set up, publish and manage a newspaper encouraged a virtual army of non-professionals to venture into the print media industry in order to see if they could quickly turn themselves into press barons.[5]

The situation in the electronic media was very different. Both television and radio stayed under strong and continuous state control throughout the whole period. Tight direction of policy and scrutiny of content by local, Armenian authorities simply replaced Soviet censorship. TV and radio continued to be perceived as legitimate tools for propaganda, although in the new age not for the Communist ideology but instead for the interests of the ruling party of independent Armenia. Despite the contradiction between this line and democracy, and despite also the striking contrast between the electronic media output and the products of the new freedom of the press, the nationalistic ethos of TV and radio propaganda was regarded as a progressive achievement by most people in Armenia. It provoked no criticisms, no strong dissatisfaction and no sign at all of popular resistance.

Summing up this stage in the development of the Armenian media, from late *glasnost* to early independence, it is important to mention that the period was significant in laying the foundations of the media industry in Armenia that is currently in place. The industry was, and remains, intensely politicized. Every organ of the media, press, radio and television was founded and is sponsored by a particular political force. It openly speaks for and actively promotes the interests of that individual, party, group or organization. Even

---

5   See Y. Lange, *Media in the CIS: A Study of the Political, Legislative and Socio-economic Framework* (Brussels: European Institute for the Media, May 1997), p. 41.

small political organizations, counting only several tens of members, have attempted to set up their own newspapers in order to propagate their ideas and convey an image of size, influence and success. In combination with the historical accident of low journalistic standards, the popularity during the years surrounding independence of the practice of buying a propaganda machine ensured that the Armenian mass media for the decade to come would be an arena devoted merely to fighting out political issues. There would be no restraint imposed by conscientious media self-regulation, and no effective code of journalistic ethics.

From economic crisis to political repression: 1992–4

Between the end of 1992 and the end of 1994 political and socio-economic life in Armenia underwent rapid deterioration. Collapsing industry put the great bulk of the population, perhaps more than 50 per cent, out of a job. The conversion of the currency from the Soviet rouble via the 'post-Soviet rouble' to the Armenian dram caused inflation, followed by hyperinflation. The imposition of a tight blockade on communication routes and energy supplies by neighbouring Azerbaijan and Turkey left the republic with poor travel and transport facilities and temporarily without any sources of electricity and heating. In addition to all these tribulations, the military operations in Karabagh, which reached their peak of violence at the same time, contributed even more distress to the overall suffering, depression and misery.

Inevitably, this conjunction of crises had a powerful impact on the media industry. During the winter of 1992–3 almost all the newspapers had to suspend printing because of the shortage of energy. Television and radio became inaccessible to most of the population. Power cuts were frequent, with engineers bewildered by their service's inability to meet demand. They were forced to switch off supplies of electricity for hours at a time in each district in turn, cutting off both the television broadcasting stations and private apartment neighbourhoods – but often not at the same time so that the combined effect tended to double the duration of the cut-offs. The television and radio station employees commonly ate and slept at their workplaces to ensure that broadcasting would go ahead during the limited periods when power was available, but even so the television service was on the air for only two hours per day.

A joke was popular at that time. Opening the programme, the announcer would say: 'Good evening, dear Mr President and dear owners of energy generators', reflecting the widespread belief that electricity was supplied only to the residence of the president, and those few rich people who could afford private generators.

Nevertheless, newspaper editors did their best to find ways to print. For example, the opposition publication *Golos Armenii* (Voice of Armenia) was typed out on an ordinary typewriter, and then duplicated as a newspaper on a photocopying machine dating from the 1960s. The effort involved meant that this procedure did not last long – only for a couple of weeks. Politically, the significance of the crisis period was the lesson learned by the political elites. By the time the energy supply situation had been more or less stabilized by the reopening of the country's nuclear power station in 1995, the officials had realized that electricity supply could be used as a powerful tool for manipulating the press. The frequent, unpredictable electricity cut-offs had made life very hard for the opposition newspapers. Only a few of the richer newspapers had managed to maintain publication throughout the period of acute crisis. The leading example was *Yerkir* (Homeland), the organ of the Dashnaktsutiun or Armenian Revolutionary Federation (ARF) Party, which was able to rely on its own electricity generators supplied by wealthy patrons who could also arrange printing facilities on a private basis.

The energy crises and power cuts in residential districts deprived people of the most familiar and inexpensive sources of information: television and radio. The effect was that, by the beginning of 1994, newspapers became the main, and for many people the only, source of news, background information and commentary. In consequence the major newspapers built up relatively high circulations. For instance, in 1993 the circulation of the most popular title, the daily *Yerkir*, reached 50,000 copies, and *Azg* regularly exceeded 30,000 copies.

However, as the middle years of the decade approached, a series of negative factors combined to gradually reduce the profits that the newspapers had been able to make in the early years of the transition. There were sharp rises in the price of paper, and a progressive diminution of the purchasing power of the population, as poverty began to displace the relative material comfort that most people had enjoyed under Communism. By the end of 1994 there were no self-sustaining titles still operating. Only the newspapers that could call upon generous subsidies from their sponsors or founders managed to survive. Mostly, they were the ones supported by political parties or by individuals with political interests or connections. Even this group experienced a continuing decline in the size of their print runs. By the winter of 1994–5 a circulation of 10,000 copies was considered to be very large.

With the reduced availability of newspapers, the importance of television as a source of information began to increase again by the beginning of 1995. But now the popular attitude to the government-controlled media began to shift in response to the deteriorating circumstances. After only half a decade of independence, people became increasingly frustrated by their incompetent government and shocked by the deepening corruption among the ruling elite. By the end of 1994 the near-universal trust and admiration accorded to the national heroes who took office in 1991 had vanished altogether, to be replaced by a sullen populace inclined to harsh criticism of the government and its policies.

Faced with growing opposition and the threat of direct confrontation, the first rulers of independent Armenia adopted authoritarian methods. On 28 December 1994 President Levon Ter Petrosian announced a decree suspending the activities of the most influential opposition party, the ARF. Together with the party itself, thirteen media outlets and a printing house were closed.

This political turn marked a radical change of environment for the media in Armenia. By the act of banning a popular political party, the president's decree did much more than limit the right of the citizens of Armenia to make their own political choices. Because of the media's dependence on the widespread links between parties and publishers, it also damaged freedom of speech generally in the republic. Newspapers that were offering alternative points of view were silenced, and the number of opposition newspapers went down. Finding themselves once more under political repression, journalists instinctively ducked under cover. The majority of them, right across the political spectrum, went straight back to the traditional Soviet practice of self-restraint and voluntary censorship whenever they were writing about the internal political life of Armenia.

The political pressure imposed on the media from the mid-1990s onwards took a great variety of forms, from the direct physical abuse of journalists to the institutional ban on opposition outlets, together with a more sophisticated array of economic sanctions. During the period immediately following the ban on the ARF there were several cases in which journalists who criticized the rulers for their incompetence and corruption were harassed and beaten. At about the same time, the offices of several opposition newspapers were attacked and their equipment sabotaged.

But rather than attacking the employees and their workplaces, an even more effective means of manipulating the media was to exert control over the printing process. In fact, the newspapers were squeezed between two powerful agencies of the state: a newspaper delivery organization and the government-owned printing house that produced most of the newspapers in the country. It became a common pattern that the delivery agency would owe large sums of money to the newspapers, which meant that the latter were not able to pay the printing house on time. This gambit effectively manoeuvred the newspapers into the position of dependent debtors, and kept them there indefinitely. On this basis the printing house could at any time refuse to print an edition of any title – a potent sanction that was frequently deployed in practice and with predictable political arbitrariness.

As a result of this sustained government strategy to undermine its independent critical function, the Armenian media became by the end of 1994 considerably less free than it had been during its short flowering after the collapse of the USSR. In the early months of 1995 it reached its lowest point in the decade of independence.

Run-up to national elections: 1995–7

The military operations in Karabagh ended in May 1994 with the signing of a cease-fire agreement. That freed the attention of the public, the politicians and the media to allow a new focus on domestic politics and in particular the parliamentary election scheduled for 1995, to be followed by a presidential election in 1996. An additional matter absorbing the nation's attention was a referendum on the controversial proposal for a new national constitution (see chapter 9), to be held on the same date as the parliamentary election.

Although the balance of political power was significantly distorted by the repressive policy of the ruling party, the opposition was neither demoralized nor destroyed. Backed by the support of the population, which was alienated by the corruption and ineptitude of its leaders and tired of the material hardships that had resulted from the total collapse of the Soviet economy and its associated institutions, the opposition still represented a considerable threat to the governing forces. Political tension ran high in the mid-1990s, and that was reflected on the pages of the newspapers.

But the newspapers were less and less concerned about their readers and progressively more committed to promoting the ideologies, policies and personalities of the parties or pressure groups that they represented. However, the rising economic pressures, on the one hand, combined with increasing prices in the printing industry, on the other hand, to create costs so high that not all the parties could maintain their own newspaper. By 1995 there were more than fifty political parties in Armenia, between them issuing not more than twenty publications.[6] Of those only *Hayk*, of the ruling party, and *Azg*, of the opposition Ramkavar-Azatakan Party financed from the diaspora, could support the regular publication of their titles.

At the same time, the various branches and layers of the state extended the spectrum of the country's journals and newspapers. The parliament had become the founder of the newspaper *Republic of Armenia* (*Hayastani Hanrapetutiun* in Armenian) and the co-founder of its Russian language edition *Respublika Armenia*; the Yerevan municipality and the various regional administrations launched their outlets; many of the individual ministries initiated their own newspapers, journals, bulletins and TV programmes. One might at first assume that this wave of official information was designed to make the work of the parliament and the state executive and administrative agencies more transparent. But in reality the new official press worked mostly as part of the president's party propaganda machine, and the editorial content was put together under strict censorship.

---

6   See M. Grigorian and A. Demurian, eds, *The Armenian Mass Media* (Yerevan: Team, 1996), pp. 105–8 (in Russian).

However concerned the elite might be about the traditional print media, the major influence upon the Armenian public remained that of nationwide television and state radio. Neither had ever been allowed to break free of official control, and in the period before the 1995–6 elections both continued to be tightly managed and directed by the ruling party.

Under such conditions, with the structure of political authority distorted by excessive executive power in the hands of the president and the media partisan to the extent that every single publication ruthlessly promoted the interests of just one particular party, it was impossible for the media to provide fair and unbiased information to its readers about an election campaign. The unfair coverage that occurred in practice was neatly described by the European Institute for the Media in its final report on the monitoring of the media coverage during the 1996 Armenian presidential elections:

> On the whole ... the dominant position of the state-controlled broadcast and print media, combined with their less than impartial coverage of the electoral campaign, show how a misbalance in resources can translate into a crucial advantage and tactical weapon to a national leadership faced with a serious political challenge.[7]

To demonstrate the point and to present a more vivid image of the media operation in the pre-electoral period, the results of the independent monitoring surveys provide convincing evidence. According to the reports, during the thirty days of campaigning for the 1996 presidential elections, the state television station dedicated more than 27 hours of editorial coverage to the incumbent president and leader of the ruling party, Levon Ter Petrosian. During the same thirty days his main opponent Vazgen Manukian received only 72 minutes.[8]

Against this background, the process of institutional development of the Armenian media was under way. The lesson learned by the community of journalists from the years of political pressure was that only mutual solidarity could protect them against political intimidation. This enforced move towards professional cooperation was strongly encouraged, but for different reasons, by international contacts. Western sponsorship of projects to promote democracy and freedom of speech in transitional countries was available mostly to organizations rather than to individuals. In response to these internal and external factors supporting non-governmental organizations, a number of professional institutions were formed in 1995 and 1996.

---

7   European Institute for the Media, *Monitoring the Media Coverage of the 1996 Armenian Presidential Election: Final Report* (Dusseldorf: The European Union, 20 January 1997), p. 38.

8   Ibid., page 39. See also M. Grigorian, 'Armenia's 1996 Presidential Elections Coverage in the Media', *Caucasian Regional Studies*, Vol. 2, Issue 1, 1997, pp. 65–81 (in Russian). For the English version see http://poli.vub.ac.be/publi/crs/eng/0201–00.htm.

The Union of Journalists of Armenia, which was an old Soviet organization that had been completely demoralized in the first years of national independence, managed to restore itself in the mid-1990s. Its revival and restructuring turned it into an NGO with a small budget, relatively modest programmes and close ties with journalists in the Armenian countryside regions.

A second professional NGO, the Yerevan Press Club, was established in 1995. Created as a union of the best Armenian journalists, it concentrated its activities on the organization of various workshops, seminars and conferences. The club issued a bulletin covering its work and highlighting some of the issues facing journalism in other countries. Within the next five years the Yerevan Press Club gained a membership of about fifty and, thanks to generous Western sponsorship, acquired an annual budget of about US $200,000, which made it one of the largest NGOs in Armenia.

The Association of Independent Media was created in the autumn of 1996. Its members were senior figures in the profession, mainly editors-in-chief of the majority of newspapers and news agencies. The main purpose inspiring its establishment was to eliminate the monopoly of Periodika, the only printing house in the country, by coordinating print orders and collaborating to raise funds that would eventually enable the association to set up its own printing capacity, free of government interference.

The last of the new institutions, the National Press Club, came into being in the spring of 1997. Its activities have been directed towards the protection of journalists' rights. Since its establishment several more organizations of journalists have officially declared their existence, but they tend to be more or less fictitious, and they are not visible in the media community.[9]

Overall, as the election season in Armenia came to an end in 1996, one could identify two tendencies in the development of the post-Soviet Armenian media. In respect of the media product, in other words its contextual aspect, it remained very much dependent on the political interests of its sponsors. Working journalists were required to ignore the basic rules of their profession specifying impartiality, objectivity and accuracy. Self-censorship was more apparent than self-regulation. There was no room for a binding code of ethics.

On the other hand, by 1997 the structure of the media institution had become much better organized. Its set of new representative groupings did allow it to gain a certain degree of independence and authority. It could henceforth demonstrate professional solidarity in cases in which the rights of journalists were violated.

But the most important advantage of the emergence of professional NGOs was that they opened up intensive communication opportunities with Western colleagues and international professional organizations. Through these contacts many journalists travelled to the West for conferences and visits to

9   Information on journalistic organizations can be found on the internet, at www. internews.am.

universities, governments and news organizations, took part in short training courses, got financial support for travel within their own region, and secured the opportunity to begin to improve the standards of the media in Armenia.

To sum up, by the time in 1998 when President Levon Ter Petrosian was forced to resign (see chapter 9), the media in Armenia had become even more partisan in terms of its crude dedication to the advancement of the interests of its political sponsors. But at the same time the institutional framework was being strengthened and the profession was becoming organized so that it might in due course become able and willing to resist pressure from the ruling power.

Ambiguity: the present period

Ter Petrosian's resignation in 1998 created a general expectation that there would be change for the better. Society and media alike were tired of his undemocratic governance, and there was an unexpressed but powerfully felt demand for a more liberal society, which would have space for much greater freedom of the media.

The first indication of liberalization was seen in the return to the political arena of the previously banned ARF party, together with *Yerkir*, which had been the most popular Armenian-language newspaper until its closure in 1994. During the 1998 presidential election campaign and at least the first few months in office of the new president, Robert Kocharian, media freedom was respected and journalists could breathe more easily in the knowledge that they would not be abused for a critical article in the way that they had often been before.

In the three years to the beginning of the new millennium, the number of cases of violence and outrage against media professionals declined significantly.[10] However, the number of court cases involving journalists increased, so it would be inaccurate to conclude that the media had been fully released from political pressure. The occasional exercise of monopoly power over the printing process has continued to be an effective lever against radical opposition. There have also been several instances of indirect pressure in a variety of forms, of which the most cunning is the instigation of repeated lengthy tax inspections.

The tension between, on the one hand, officialdom's attempt not to lose its long-established control over the media and, on the other, the emergent media institutions that are now capable of standing up for the rights of journalists became fully apparent for the first time in February–March 2002. A government-sponsored draft law on the media was confronted by decisive resistance from the journalistic organizations. According to the proposed law, a new government body was to be established to oversee the news organiza-

10 See David Petrosian, 'Violation and Outrage against the Armenian Media, 1994–1998', *Media Caucasica*, vol. 2 (Tbilisi: CIPDD, 1999) pp. 24–30 (in Russian).

tions and given the power to enforce its judgments by issuing and revoking licences to publish. The draft law also stipulated that newspapers would in future need the consent of officials and political figures before publishing their photographs or cartoons. Rightly interpreting the proposal as a legalization of censorship and a threat to press freedom, Armenian journalists launched a successful campaign to stop the bill. To assuage media anger, the bill in that form was withdrawn from discussion in parliament.

Yet, in response to the strengthening of the media sector as an institution in Armenian society, the means of political control over it has also become more sophisticated. This is especially the case in respect of the legal justification for whatever restraint the leadership might wish to impose. A good example of the new strategy was the use made of the 'Law on TV and Radio Broadcasting' adopted in the year 2000. That law required the establishment of a special committee to distribute frequencies for transmission. The committee was to consist of nine persons, all appointed by the president.[11] The exceptional concentration of power created by this arrangement was demonstrated in full in spring 2002 when two TV stations, A1+ and Noyan Tapan, were refused frequency licences despite having already proved themselves to be the most popular broadcasters. The only plausible explanation of such a decision was that both stations were known to be openly critical of the president. The action provoked local outrage and international condemnation. It made a significant contribution to the foreign observers' uniform assessment that the 2003 presidential election was undemocratic and unfair. Even so, the committee was undeterred, and when A1+ proceeded to submit a further six applications for the allocation of a frequency on which to broadcast, every one was refused.

This event damaged the media environment in Armenia to a significant degree. During 2003 and 2004 the surviving TV and radio stations began to impose self-censorship as a form of defence, despite being privately owned and financially independent of the government. The effect was that they became increasingly de-intellectualized and de-politicized. The deteriorating trend caused alarm among international media watchdogs concerned with press freedom, which voiced serious concerns about the status of the Armenian press, the lack of pluralism in the electronic media, and the criminalization of the offence of libel. For example, the globally respected NGO Article 19, scrutinizing the legal framework for Armenian media activities, commented that 'in some cases, the authorities have initiated retrogressive legislative measures which threaten to reverse some of the achievements'.[12]

The general characteristics of the media, however, continue relatively unchanged from the pattern established early in the first decade of

---

11 Under the first draft of the law only five members were to be appointed by the president, while the remaining four appointments would have been the prerogative of the parliament. But then Kocharian obtained the right to make all the appointments, through a decision of the Constitutional Court.

12 Reported by Radio Liberty, 23 March 2004.

Armenia's transition away from Communism. Virtually all the newspaper-publishing organizations remain strongly dependent on their patrons within the political structure, and they openly promote the interests of that sponsor. However, a few more encouraging changes are becoming evident in the electronic media. The technical quality of television broadcasts has improved, the state has given up the ownership of one of its two channels, and the number of privately owned TV stations has increased. In 2002 more than ten television companies were operating in Yerevan, and more than twenty in the rest of the country. The prominent American-sponsored radio stations Voice of America and Radio Liberty, both specializing in extensive news programming, have become available in the Armenian language on the local FM wavelengths and both are attracting a substantial audience.

The most significant response of the Armenian audience to the available media output is the number of sources, of widely assorted political orientation, that everyone tries to follow in order to build up their own understanding of events. It seems that this pattern of deliberately consulting a variety of different sources is a defensive response to the widespread impression that all news and information media are always and necessarily instruments of ideological manipulation. The instinct of most people in relation to any newspaper, radio station or television channel is to look behind the scenes in order to find out whose orders that particular source is following, who provides the finance for it, and in which direction that particular source might want to push the ordinary citizen.

The main criticism of the population is that the domestic media is not reliable, that it lacks convincing and interesting analysis, that any one source is always one-sided, and that the style of presentation is not professional enough. Armenia has no tradition whatever of investigative journalism, which weakens the role of the media in social and political life.

Despite the uniformly strong criticism of the domestic information sources, it is undeniable that recent years have seen some improvements. The fact that readers, viewers and listeners can now get an accurate picture of current events – even if doing so does require them to undertake the elaborate task of consulting a variety of sources, comparing the different versions, and then making up their own mind – is clear evidence of the positive trend. Competition also stimulates creativity and variety in the media output as a whole. Individual providers are keen to find new ways to attract and hold on to viewers and listeners. Some local channels have begun to strengthen their coverage of international news by transmitting shots from CNN, the BBC and other well-known international sources.

Conclusion

Within a decade of transition an institution of Armenian media has been created. It continues to develop, and there are strong relationships between the media and the centres of power in society, and quite different relationships between the media sources and their audience. The Armenian media has also developed a distinctive attitude towards news content and the various ways of presenting it. There remain certain taboo topics, issues that no one in the media yet dares to touch. Examples of these invisible and unremarked issues include life for soldiers within the army and aspects of how the military/defence institution is managed; criticism of the authorities in Karabagh; and the violation of the rights of religious minorities. Journalists also avoid reporting either on corruption at any level or on the dominant role of powerful 'clans' – informal social networks of patronage and protection – in government and the economy (see chapter 12 on social networks more generally).

The Armenian media is, ultimately, very much a post-Soviet phenomenon. It faces the same problems, or almost the same problems, as the media in the other countries of the former USSR. The problems are the low professional standards and skills of the journalists, the absence or near-absence of genuine news media, the prevalence of tendentious and opinionated reports, the state monopoly over nationwide television broadcasting, instinctive self-censorship, and the unsatisfactory provision of education in journalism.

But it is a developing system. It remains still heavily dependent on the grace and favour of the powers that be, but at the same time it is continuously stimulating the development of society and politics towards the ultimate goal of a more democratic Armenia, in which a diversity of viewpoints and ideas reaches a wide public.

Bibliography

Grigorian, M., and Demurian, A., eds, *The Armenian Mass Media* (Yerevan: Team, 1996, in Russian).

Hayrapetyan, N., *A Bibliography of the New Armenian Periodical Press, 1987–1999* (Yerevan: Girk Publishers, 1999) (in Armenian and English).

Lange, Y., *Media in the CIS: A Study of the Political, Legislative and Socio-economic Framework* (Brussels: European Institute for the Media, May 1997).

McCormack, Gillian, ed., *Media in the CIS: A Study of the Political, Legislative and Socio-economic Framework*, second edition (Brussels: European Institute for the Media, 1999).

UNDP, *Human Rights in Armenia: Progress but not Perfection* (Yerevan: UNDP, 1998).

11 Economic and social development

Astghik Mirzakhanyan

Background

The Republic of Armenia is a small, mountainous and landlocked country. Its land area is 29,800 square kilometres, of which only 55.7 per cent is habitable or agriculturally useable land. The average altitude is 1,830 metres above sea level and about 40.6 per cent of the country's territory is situated above 2,000 metres. The state's borders extend for 1,254 kilometres, of which 268 kilometres are with Turkey that lies to the west, 35 kilometres with Iran to the south, 164 kilometres with Georgia to the north, 566 kilometres with Azerbaijan to the east, and 221 kilometres with the Nakhichevan Autonomous Republic of Azerbaijan to the southwest. These geographical realities are important factors affecting the country's actual and potential economic development.

The administrative division of the Republic of Armenia underwent significant changes in 1995, when the Soviet-era system of 37 regions and 4 cities was replaced by a system which established 11 *marzes* or provinces. As of 1 January 2004, there were 48 cities, including the capital city Yerevan, which has the status of *marz*, and 952 villages mostly included in 871 rural communities. According to official statistics, the total population of Armenia in 2001, when the first post-Soviet census was carried out, was a little over 3 million – nearly 25 per cent lower than the 3.8 million recorded in the last Soviet census of 1989. Some 65 per cent of the population is urban. The capital of the Republic of Armenia is Yerevan (Erivan before 1936), whose population of 1.1 million accounts for over a third of the country's total population.

In general the country is considered to have few resources. There are exploitable reserves of metals and minerals such as copper, gold, blue vitriol, molybdenum, zinc, tin, iron and manganese. The land of Armenia is rich with stony materials such as tufa, granite, basalt, marble and onyx, sand and silicon earth. There are also beds of sodium chloride, pumice, perlite, barite, aragonite and diatomite.

The geographic situation of Armenia (the major part of historic Armenia is nowadays in Turkey and partially in Azerbaijan and Iran) at a crossroads of the overland trade routes of the Old World was favourable for the external economic activity of Armenians. The country served and escorted the caravans of foreign merchants, and exported goods and commodities of local production, such as dried fruits, wool, cotton, natural mineral colours, carpets, luxury goods, animals, etc. In pre-modern times Armenian merchants had direct trade links with the major commercial cities of the Mediterranean and Middle East – Constantinople, Aleppo, Cairo, Isfahan, Venice, Marseilles, and in the seventeenth and eighteenth centuries extended their commercial activities as far afield as northwestern Europe (Amsterdam), Russia (Moscow and Saint Petersburg), India, southeast Asia and the Philippines.

History of economic development

Before the twentieth century most Armenians were engaged in agriculture, though Armenians were also renowned for their trade and commerce and for their craftsmanship in textiles, metalwork and other industries. Modern industrial development in Eastern (Russian) Armenia started at the end of the nineteenth and the beginning of the twentieth century, though Armenian entrepreneurs and industrialists had played a significant role in the development of the Russian textile industry as early as the eighteenth century. The copper industry, managed by a French company, was a pioneer of large-scale industrial production in Armenia. In 1905–11 up to 28 per cent of the total copper production of Russia originated in Armenia. The second key industrial sector was the production of wines, vodka, spirits and cognac, which was established in 1887 by an Armenian entrepreneur, Nerses Tairov, though subsequently sold to a Russian businessman.

In addition to these more or less large-scale industries, there were also small plants processing agricultural products, which were mostly exported to Russia. Among these productions were cheese, processed cotton and wool. Thus, the pre-Soviet industry of Eastern Armenia consisted for the most part of traditional handicrafts and domestic industry. Only two branches, copper and wine-cognac, could be considered modern, capitalist industries, and both branches belonged to foreign capital.

Soviet period of industrialization

Soviet economic policy aimed essentially at the electrification and industrialization of the state. In Armenia, as elsewhere in the Soviet Union, industrialization started with the most capital-intensive branches of heavy industry such as the energy sector, heavy machine-building, chemical production and large-scale metallurgy. Policy makers assumed that the intensive development of those branches would help create the technical and technological basis for the industrialization of agriculture and of the handicraft production of other branches of industry.

The nationalization of land and industrial enterprises as well as the creation of the common Soviet monetary system laid the foundations for the implementation of the above programme. During the first phase of industrialization the policy was for Armenia to specialize in two important branches of heavy industry: non-ferrous metals and chemicals. In order to reach this objective, the resources of the Soviet Union were made available for the construction of new plants. Official statistics indicate that between 1928 and 1940 the volume of industrial output in Armenia increased 8–9 times as a result of the construction of about one hundred large industrial enterprises. In addition, the share of industrial production in the gross national product (GNP) increased from 23 per cent in 1923 to 78 per cent in 1940.

Based on this indicator, it would appear that Armenia had become an industrial country before the outbreak of the Second World War. But it would be a mistake to reach such a conclusion on the basis of a single indicator. In fact, in 1940 Armenia was still partly underdeveloped because a number of important sectors, such as communications, services and transport (at least in part), were not yet formed. The fact that the rate of industrial growth was several times higher than the rate of agricultural growth does, however, show that Armenia was undergoing a process of rapid industrialization in this period.

Armenia's economy scarcely suffered during the Second World War. In 1945 the GNP of the republic had decreased by only 7 per cent compared to 1940. In 1946 the level of development of the economy had already reached the pre-war (1940) level, while overall in the USSR the pre-war level was reached only in 1948. After the recovery of the volume of output, a new branch of industry, machine-building, was established. In the second phase of industrialization (1946–50), forty-one industrial enterprises were put into operation. More than half of them were in the machine-building sector, which developed three times faster than industry as a whole.

The period 1950–70 is characterized by structural changes in the food and light industries. Armenian light industry was considered one of the most highly developed sectors of the entire Soviet economy, using advanced technologies and highly skilled labour to produce goods for the military and consumer sectors. In 1970, for example, Armenia produced 42 million pairs of stockings and socks, about 60 million items of linen and underwear, and 10.3 million pairs of shoes. The production of consumer goods and commodities grew significantly, and Armenian production was able to meet a considerable part of the demand of the Soviet consumer goods market.

Characteristics of the economy before Gorbachev's reforms

In the period (1975–85) preceding the reforms initiated by Mikhail Gorbachev, Armenia's economy shared fundamental characteristics with the economies of the other Soviet republics.

Public ownership covered the whole national economy. Economic relationships were based on only two types of public ownership: state
(accounting for more than 90 per cent of the whole national wealth) and
kolkhoz, meaning collective or co-operative (which existed mostly in the
agricultural sector). The latter was also strongly regulated by the socialist
state.

The planning system was based on the development of five-year and one-
year strategic socio-economic plans, which were the only mechanism of
macro-economic policy in the republic. Plans were elaborated strictly
according to the ideology of the socialist state and following the main directives of the Congresses of the Communist Party of the Soviet Union. A
special government planning body, Gosplan, was responsible for the development and implementation of plans, as well as for development of the
methodology of planning.

The administrative-command system was effectively the sole tool of state
management of the national economy. All economic relationships were regulated through the decrees and decisions of the Central Committee of the
Communist Party of the Soviet Union, and of the Council of Ministers of
the Soviet Union, and, very occasionally, of the Supreme Soviet of the
USSR. There was no functional system of economic or commercial law.

The main indicator of macroeconomic stability was the relative size of
the two public funds allocated respectively to consumption and to 'accumulation', or money kept in reserve. The volumes and the structures of these
funds were prescribed annually by the centre and were distributed among all
the Soviet republics.

Central and republican budgets were powerful instruments for policy
implementation and economic management. The public expenditure from
republican budgets was determined and strictly supervised by central
government bodies (in Moscow). The mechanisms of subsidies and subven-
tions were extensively used in budgetary policy at all levels (central,
republican and regional). The centralization of management and the
concentration of production were characteristic of the Soviet economy.

The agricultural sector of the Armenian republican economy comprised
about 820 collective (*kolkhoz*) and state (*sovkhoz*) farms, which occupied
some 360 thousand hectares of agricultural land. The industrial sector was
made up of some 600–700 state-owned industrial enterprises. As mentioned
above, Armenia had specialized in the post-Second World War period as a
republic of science-intensive industries, utilizing highly qualified labour.
This development was underpinned by the intensive creation of scientific
industrial groups through the amalgamation of individual enterprises. By
1985 there were eighty-five such groups, which concentrated about 65 per
cent of the total number of industrial enterprises, 60 per cent of the industrial labour force, and 51 per cent of the total output of Armenia's industry.

Subordination to the Union on overall economic issues was significant.
For example, in the middle of the 1980s 51 per cent of the total volume of

industrial output in Armenia, about 55 per cent of the industrial labour force, and 72 per cent of fixed assets belonged to Union industries located in the republic. The great majority of these Union enterprises formed part of the military-industrial complex.

The territorial allocation of resources and production capacity was uneven, a fact that contributed to obvious per capita income differences between regions of the republic. The most intensive development was taking place in the Ararat (central) region and in Yerevan. This region covered only 20–21 per cent of the total territory of Armenia, but in it was concentrated 51 per cent of the total population of the country, 60 per cent of industry and 40 per cent of the agricultural production of the country.

Such were the main characteristics of the national economy of the Soviet Republic of Armenia, characteristics which were, to a great extent, shared by all the republics of the USSR. With the passage of time, the centralized system and mechanisms of socio-economic development became more and more ineffective. Rates of economic growth declined sharply through the 1960s–1980s, and the administrative-command system turned into a big and powerful 'administrative monopolist'. Enterprises lost their competitiveness because of the high costs. Soviet politicians and economists became increasingly convinced that the system was no longer working effectively, and that radical reform was needed for it to recover its efficiency.

Economic reforms under '*perestroika*'

The process of reform of the national economy in the Soviet Union as a whole and in Armenia in particular started in 1985 with Mikhail Gorbachev's policy of '*perestroika*', which initiated a process of shifting the state-owned enterprises to a self-financing, self-organizing and self-costing basis (Soviet economists also called that process the reforms of the three 'S's). These three elements of a free market economy were introduced into the existing socialist economic system at the microeconomic level.

Furthermore, the Soviet government decided to explore new directions for the gradual transition of the national economy towards a market economy at the macroeconomic level as well. The concept of the 'socialist market' was developed by the Commission of Economic Reforms under the Council of Ministers of the USSR. In essence, it was proposed to leave the state sector intact on one side, and on the other side to create new non-state market structures in order to strengthen the Soviet economy. Thus, a 'socialist market' was perceived as an economic area within the socialistic sector which would successfully compete with the private sector. This latter would emerge from the implementation of two very important laws: the Law on Co-operation (1987) and the Law on Leasing (1988).

In 1987–8 embryonic elements of private (non-state, to be more precise) ownership appeared. These were represented through co-operatives and leasing companies, which operated, in essence, in conformity with the rules of private and collective property. A newly created sector in Armenia was represented by more than four thousand co-operatives. In 1990 the non-state (co-operative) sector produced 6–7 per cent of total industrial production and absorbed 12 per cent of the labour force. The development of co-operatives progressed rapidly in Armenia, compared to the other republics of the USSR. However, as early as the late 1980s it became clear that developing and instituting a 'socialist market' was not possible. In fact, the monopolistic state sector with its extremely powerful administrative-command system started conducting unfair competition with the weak newborn non-state sector. As a rule, this was done in a very unfair manner, generating a growing 'shadow' economy, which became so large that it made the economy practically unmanageable.

Liberalization and privatization

Many of the economists and social scientists who did not believe that competition in the context of a 'socialist market' was possible proposed to concentrate all efforts on the creation of a 'normal' free market. To reach this objective it was necessary to conduct two essential economic actions: first, to liberate prices to ensure an economic environment for free and fair competition, and, second, to limit the importance of the state sector through the privatization of state assets. Moreover, it was argued that structural reform of the economy and the new market-oriented economic relationships required a new system of economic legislation.

Liberalization of prices and privatization of state property took place in Armenia in the early 1990s, just after the passage of the Declaration on Independence by the Supreme Council of the Republic of Armenia in 1990 (it has to be noted that an independent Armenia came into being when the Armenian people overwhelmingly voted in favour of independence in a national referendum on 21 September 1991).

Price liberalization started in April 1991, and most price controls were abolished in the great wave of price liberalization in January 1992. In October 1994 the prices of the remaining goods and services (such as bread, municipal transport and communal services) were liberalized, though some element of regulation (profit/trading margin controls on output) was retained.

Privatization in Armenia was implemented in a very peculiar manner, different from the process in other post-Soviet republics. Land was the first entity to be privatized, starting in January 1991 and being completed in a matter of months. In fact, by June 1991 more than seven hundred collective and state farms had been liquidated, and their agricultural land, as well as cattle and small animals, distributed to peasants.

Small-scale privatization (the privatization of trade and commerce, as well as public catering and services) followed land privatization and took 3–4 years in all. The first stage of small-scale privatization was conducted in

1991-2, the second in 1994-6. The privatization of housing was intensively carried out during the years 1993-5. By the end of 1995, the ownership of approximately 70 per cent of state-owned apartments had been transferred to their tenants free of charge, the apartments becoming their private property.

Industrial privatization started in April 1995 and continued into the twenty-first century. This was the most complicated stage of privatization, involving the restructuring of state-owned enterprises into joint stock companies. Vouchers (special privatization certificates) were issued to the employees of enterprises, and to citizens at large to allow them to purchase shares in the new companies. More than one thousand large and medium-sized enterprises were privatized in this way during 1995-7. The privatization of large enterprises caused particular problems, arousing public and political criticism of the governments of both President Levon Ter Petrosian and President Robert Kocharian on the grounds that national assets, such as the cognac factory (one of Armenia's historic industries), had been sold off cheap, and that foreign ownership of vital national assets, such as the telecommunications network and energy generation, represented a threat to national security.

Although price liberalization and privatization of the main sectors of Armenia's economy were carried out relatively quickly, the economic system of the country was still very far from being a 'normal' market economy. This was a common phenomenon among the post-communist countries, and the term 'transition economy' was widely used by economists and politicians to describe it. Armenia's economy is still in the process of getting through its very difficult transition period.

Economy in transition

The transition period for the Republic of Armenia as a newly independent country was characterized by fundamental changes in the political, social and economic systems towards: a) building a democratic state; b) forming civil society; and c) creating a market economic system. In due course, the political and economic transformations should ensure a transition from totalitarianism to democracy in all spheres of state and human activities. In Armenia the transition period was heavily influenced by a number of specific factors.

The collapse of the economic potential of the republic was precipitated before the beginning of the post-communist transition by a severe earthquake in December 1988. The earthquake caused numerous human losses and inflicted varying degrees of damage on around a third of the republic's productive capacities. Subsequently, the severe economic downturn and drastic energy crisis that occurred in the early transition period were in large measure the result of external factors, notably the armed conflict in Mountainous Karabagh and the blockade of road, rail and energy routes imposed by Azerbaijan and Turkey.

Armenia's economy in the Soviet era had been highly dependent on trade with other Soviet republics. For this reason, the dismantling of the common Soviet economic space and the breakdown of external trade relationships with traditional economic partners in the former Soviet Union affected Armenia particularly acutely. Added to this was the general impact of the overall economic crisis in all FSU countries, especially Russia, which persisted at least until 1993 when the unified rouble zone was eliminated.

The Armenian economy was also poorly placed to attract investment. There was a scarcity of domestic financial resources as a result of the deep economic recession of the production sector in 1990–4, while foreign investment was hard to attract to an economy lacking obvious exploitable natural resources and offering limited marketing opportunities (Armenia's population was small and impoverished, and the country was cut off from potentially more lucrative neighbouring markets by blockade and conflict). In these circumstances the Armenian government saw no alternative but to borrow money abroad, creating a high degree of dependency on external financiers, especially the big international financial institutions such as the IMF and World Bank. The level of foreign debt rose from US $35 per capita in 1993 to US $200 per capita in 1998 and in 2003 amounted to approximately US $1,090 million in total.

Moreover, in Armenia, as in the other non-Russian republics, the transition in the economy coincided with the recovery of state independence. Therefore, in addition to conducting economic reforms it was necessary to radically reform the political structures inherited from the Soviet system, to build new institutions (such as an army, a banking system, taxation and customs systems, etc.) in order to safeguard political and economic sovereignty. Thus, the transition period in Armenia occurred in an exceptionally difficult and complicated external and internal environment from both the political and the economic point of view.

Economic impacts of the transition period

Compared with the other republics of the Soviet Union, Armenia's experience of the transition was particularly painful. Between 1988 and 1993 industrial output declined by almost 64 per cent; GDP fell by more than 50 per cent; the output of the energy sector fell by about 60 per cent, and food production also fell sharply. Price liberalization led to hyperinflation, with prices rising thirteen- or fourteen-fold in 1992–3.

The economic crisis had a negative impact on state revenue and the balance of payments. In 1992–4 budget revenues (without grants) shrank to only 14–15 per cent of GDP. This was a result of falling tax receipts due to the widespread stagnation of production. The largest deficit in the Armenia state budget occurred in 1993, when it reached 34 per cent of expenditures and 12 per cent of GDP. Cuts in state budget expenditure led to a proportionate decline in state financing of the social sphere, the share of which in total budget expenditures fell by about half in 1992–6.

The dire economic situation prevailing in the country in its transition period determined the nature of Armenia's economic relations with the outside world. In the international market system, the republic up to now has been considered to be predominantly an importing country with a negative balance of payments. The trade deficit in various years in the 1990s reached one-third of GDP.

Both the domestic complexities and Armenia's weakness in the global market damaged the population's living standards so severely that, in the early years of economic transition, charity became the most important means of support for the Armenian people. Humanitarian aid flowed in from a variety of countries and from international organizations. Even though the deep economic crisis of 1990–3 created a desperate need for the relief of poverty, the dominant logic of the situation forced the government to direct its main efforts towards carrying out structural reforms while also struggling to create macroeconomic stability. The most important economic reforms were in the fields of privatization, the formation of market economic institutions and the fundamental restructuring of the banking system.

Parallel administrative reforms built a national civil service to replace the old Moscow-centred organizations, introduced the concept of local and regional self-governance, and ushered in a new legal system covering both economic and civil matters. The contemporary Armenian economy is based on a variety of property arrangements, and there are now several types of organizational and legal economic entity. The long-term impact of the free-market-oriented economic reforms has been to transform the character of the entire Armenian economy, with relatively few of the Soviet-era institutions remaining, at least in the formal sense.

Positive results became apparent from as early as 1994, and since 1995 economic growth has continued at a moderately high rate, averaging 6.7 per cent for 1995–2002. Armenia got to the windward of the Russian financial crisis in 1998 better than other CIS states and went through it without experiencing a real setback. In 2001 the annual rate of GDP growth rose to 9.6 per cent and in 2002 to 12.9 per cent; then, in 2003, Armenia's recorded growth soared to 13.9 per cent. In the judgment of the International Monetary Fund: 'Economic performance [in Armenia] since 2000 has been impressive, reflecting prudent monetary and fiscal policies, structural reforms, and financial support from the Armenian diaspora.'[1] Armenia also introduced one of the most favourable legal frameworks for businesses and foreign investments to be found in any of the post-Soviet countries.

Nevertheless, the success of the Armenian economy should not be overestimated. However important the macroeconomic restructuring appeared to be for economic recovery and visible growth, the bulk of the resources

---

1   Statement by the Director of IMF, Horst Koehler, reported by Agence France Presse, 10 November 2003.

that made the boom possible were neither domestically produced nor hazarded as venture capital. The growth has occurred mainly on a foundation of external financing from two sources: official foreign and international assistance in the form of grants and credits, and a considerable flow of non-official transfers from people who have emigrated abroad and now continue to support their extended families in the country. For example, by 2004 the Lincy Foundation alone had spent US$ 175 million on road construction or repair and refurbishing cultural centres.[2] As to the development of local production, moderate success can be detected only in the diamond-polishing and jewellery trades, together with the food and alcoholic beverage industries.

A further unpromising characteristic of the Armenian economy is its territorial discrepancy. The development processes are concentrated in the national capital, Yerevan. In 2002 Yerevan accounted for approximately 50 per cent of industrial production, 80 per cent of registered trade turnover, and 76.3 per cent of services. This activity made a major contribution to the reduction of poverty in the capital, but it left the rest of the country in much the same miserable condition as a decade earlier.

Underlying these massive discrepancies in economic outcomes are major policy failures at government level in the fields of economic regulation and redistribution. These have been pointed out both by local politicians and economists, and also by international analysts. The core of the problem, they suggest, is that the process of economic and structural reforms in Armenia was accompanied by several negative phenomena, most notably the expansion of the unregulated informal sector of the economy and the pervasiveness of outright corruption. Together these two problems have thwarted the intent of much of the reform process and created a wide gulf between government and society.

The economic policy debate

From the outset the government's policy of radical reform to achieve a free market economy has had its critics. Among these were some who accepted the goal of establishing a market economy, but argued that the 'shock' tactics of rapid price liberalization and privatization would carry unacceptably high social costs, and that a more gradual and compassionate approach was needed. There were also those on the left of the political spectrum who opposed on principle the switch to a market capitalist economy, preferring to maintain a high degree of state control and public ownership to make the economy serve the needs of society, rather than forcing society to adapt to the needs of the market economy. While both these views enjoyed a considerable

2   The Lincy Foundation was established by the prominent American Armenian Kirk Kerkorian.

measure of support among public and elite opinion, the fact that the government's programme had the backing and resources of the West and the international financial institutions effectively clinched the argument, since, with Russia preoccupied with its own economic crises, there were no other potential means of support for the Armenian economy once the Soviet 'safety net' had been pulled away. This changed, on the one hand because of the firm Russian stance on the development of a free market and the recovery of its economy after the 1998 crash, and on the other hand because of the reluctance of overseas investors to risk their money in the opaque Armenian economy with its obstructive bureaucracy. The Kocharian government had to make a deal with the Russian government to settle part of the accumulated debt through the sale of a number of large enterprises plus some electrical generators. Russian businesses such as banks and services also moved into the Armenian economy with confidence.

Criticism of the government's management of the economy intensified in the latter part of the presidency of Levon Ter Petrosian (1991–8). In addition to the points mentioned above, there were increasingly strident accusations of massive corruption and cronyism, which meant that the profits from privatization and the goods generated by the return to economic growth were overwhelmingly concentrated in the hands of a privileged, and criminal, few. Though some of the most notorious members of this new corrupt plutocracy were removed before or at the time of Ter Petrosian's ouster, similar accusations were levelled at the government of Robert Kocharian.

Another area of economic policy that aroused heated controversy was the relationship of the national Armenian economy to the world economy in an era of globalization. The government of Levon Ter Petrosian laid strong emphasis on the importance of foreign investment to generate renewed economic growth. Ter Petrosian argued further that such investment would not be forthcoming as long as Armenia remained in conflict with Azerbaijan over Karabagh, and cut off from its neighbours and markets by blockade. This explicit linkage of the economy with the Karabagh conflict exposed the president to accusations from nationalists of every hue that he was willing to 'sell out' Karabagh for the sake of foreign investment, and thus contributed to his political downfall in late 1997 and early 1998. His challenger and the future president, Robert Kocharian, argued that the principal obstacles to investment were corruption and the failure to properly implement reforms and laws, and that any political obstacles were secondary.

More generally, the selling off of state and public assets to foreign interests aroused considerable political and public disquiet. The objections raised by opponents of foreign ownership of Armenian assets were similar to those raised by nationalists in other countries: that the ownership and management of strategic industries, such as telecommunications, power generation and transmission, transportation and food and water supply, should not be entrusted to foreigners because maintaining control over these is vital to national security and an integral part of national sovereignty. Linked to such arguments was a more emotional reluctance to see national assets – especially those with a special resonance in Armenian hearts and minds, such as the Yerevan cognac factory – handed over to foreigners. Such feelings were inevitably reinforced in a period when many Armenians viewed the international community, and the West in particular, with suspicion or antipathy, largely because of the belief that they tended to side with Azerbaijan over the Karabagh dispute. These criticisms notwithstanding, post-Soviet Armenian governments have maintained a more or less consistent policy with regard to economic reform in general and attracting foreign investment. Once in office, Robert Kocharian's policies in the economic sphere showed few marked differences from those of his predecessor.

Social costs of the transition period

The transition period in Armenia produced social consequences of a dual nature. On the one hand, the new economic and social institutions and their legal framework are adapted to the objective demands of the market economic system and to basic human rights and freedoms, all of which represents a necessary condition for the integration of the country into the world economy and community. On the other hand, the transition period was accompanied by a drop in living standards for most of the Armenian people and by widespread and acute impoverishment in a population that had been accustomed to a tolerable standard of living in the Soviet period.

Poverty as a phenomenon was recognized in Armenia only in the post-socialist period. When the harsh economic crises of 1992–4 resulted in a drastic social collapse, poverty emerged as the most negative consequence. Both government and society faced the difficult problem of understanding and coming to terms with this new phenomenon, which could be achieved only through conducting special studies.

In 1996 the Ministry of Statistics (today called the National Statistical Service of the Republic of Armenia) conducted comprehensive nation-wide surveys of the living conditions of the population in general and of poverty in particular. This study recorded the following picture: the poor constituted about 55 per cent of the population, and the very poor 28 per cent; more than one in ten people in Armenia was extremely poor. Refugees (mostly from Azerbaijan) and the population in the earthquake zone, especially those living in temporary dwellings (wagons and containers), were more vulnerable to poverty than other segments of the population. Disabled and elderly people living apart from relatives, and orphans, were also highly vulnerable to poverty.

The difficult economic conditions of the population and the high price of basic social services emerged at a time when the government was cutting social expenditure, with the inevitable result that education and health care became more and more inaccessible for the greater part of the population.

About one-third of households mentioned the inaccessibility of education, especially pre-school, vocational and tertiary education. Health care became unavailable for 33–34 per cent of patients for financial reasons.

The failure of the education system since 1990 could be attributed primarily to difficulties connected with government funding. The government expenditure on secondary education had been cut to between a half and a third of previous levels and amounted to less than $40 per student per annum. Moreover, teachers received the lowest salaries in the country, equivalent to a mere US $10–20 per month, which was usually paid 2–6 months late. Inevitably, such swingeing cuts had resulted in a severe deterioration in the quality of education.

After a decade of continuous underfunding of education, 55 per cent of schools needed ongoing or capital repairs, while the condition of 37–38 per cent of vocational institutions rendered them unsuitable for use. Every fifth school lacked a water supply, about half of schools were getting restricted supplies (mainly in the morning and evening hours), and 60 per cent did not have medicines and medical supplies. The biggest problems of educational institutions were basic sanitation, especially sewerage and heating. During the winter months many schools were closed.

The health service network, especially in rural areas, did not possess adequate specialists and medical equipment, which created barriers for access to primary health care in those places. General statistics indicated that during the first ten years of independence the number of visits to clinics per citizen decreased by a half to two-thirds, and the rate of occupation for hospital beds declined by up to a half. Undoubtedly these changes were not indicative of a healthier population requiring less medical care, nor of greater efficiency in the medical services, but show, rather, that the health care system had become inaccessible to a significant proportion of the population. A survey revealed that two-thirds of patients did not apply for medical treatment, with 32 per cent of them choosing to treat themselves (see chapter 12).

A number of other surveys of the labour market conducted in 1996–8 concluded that the level of overall unemployment had reached 26 per cent (which was 2.6 times higher than official registered unemployment), and that 18.6 per cent of the unemployed were so-called 'discouraged workers', who had lost hope of ever finding a job. Poverty is an acute problem for the unemployed, though low wages mean that 21 per cent of the employed are very poor as well (for example, the average wage in public establishments in the late 1990s was less than $22–23 per month, while in educational, health and cultural establishments the figure was approximately $18–19 per month).

According to a 1998 survey, the role of wages in the family budget of the majority of the employed population was insignificant. Even the lowest estimations of minimum per capita consumer expenditure exceed the nominal wage of an employee by 1.5–2.0 times. If we take into account that each employed person had on average no fewer than 2.8 dependants, the insignificance of wages becomes more striking. According to the data from household surveys carried out by the National Statistical Service each year, the share of wages in the overall incomes of families steadily declined in the 1990s. In 1990 it accounted for 72 per cent, while in 1998–9 it represented only 24–25 per cent. Wage earners and others are obliged to supplement wages by taking second or third jobs in the informal economy.

Another widespread problem of the surplus labour force was that of underemployment, and of *de facto* unemployment among the employees of many enterprises. Large numbers of workers were employed at enterprises that were 'temporarily' closed, i.e. were neither producing goods and services nor, for the most part, paying their employees. Many employees were classed as being on 'administrative leave', meaning that their jobs had been suspended, often permanently. Probably about one-third of the 'employed' workforce in the industrial sector could more realistically be considered as unemployed. The analysis of survey data revealed that poverty affected about 60 per cent of the formally employed but non-working segment of the population and 71 per cent of those who were on 'administrative leave'.

In 1998–9 a new Living Standards Integrated Survey was implemented in 3,600 households over a twelve-month period (300 households per month) with technical assistance from the World Bank. Results showed a yawning gulf between the richest and poorest segments of the population. The per capita income of the richest 20 per cent of the surveyed households was thirty-two times higher than that of the poorest 20 per cent. This is solid proof of the obvious income polarization of Armenian society.

In 1999 a special study on the poverty of vulnerable groups in Armenia was made through the survey of 2,000 households (1,000 refugee and 1,000 local) selected mostly from the poorest regions of the country. The survey results indicated that 35 per cent of both refugees and the indigenous population living in the same neighbourhood were below the 'food line' regarded as necessary for minimal subsistence, and that more than 22 per cent of non-settled refugees and 14 per cent of the earthquake zone population were extremely poor, not having enough money even to buy bread.

The most important conclusion of the study related to significant distortions in the demographic structure of these vulnerable groups. Women made up an exceptionally large proportion of the twenty- to thirty-nine-year-old age group, which has a decisive role in both natural and social reproduction. This created a situation in which 20–30 per cent of young refugee women and young women living in the earthquake zone did not have the opportunity to form a family household and, if they had children, were condemned to take care of their children on their own, since their potential or actual husbands were absent. This situation was the result of intensive emigration, especially of young men. Hundreds of thousands of people left Armenia in general, and its poorer regions in particular, to seek jobs, social protection and better living conditions abroad. Emigration was attributed largely to anxiety about the gloomy prospects for the future caused on the one hand by bleak socio-economic conditions and intense competition for jobs, and on the other by the indifference of the state to social problems.

Even starting from such a low base, economic growth had a mitigating effect on poverty. The overall number of poor and very poor people had been steadily decreasing from the 1990s onwards, and by 2003 the proportion of the population who were very poor fell to 14.1 per cent, with the most favourable changes observable in Yerevan. Even so, as the new millennium began, only about half of the population of Armenia could be described as having risen above the poverty level. In order to tackle this continuing problem, the World Bank brought together a number of international organizations, including UNDP, to assist the government of Armenia in mobilizing the best available intellectual resources of the nation. A large team of academics, consultants and NGO personnel then set about the task of drawing up a comprehensive strategy for poverty reduction. They gathered and analysed large quantities of data, and then devoted two years to an intensive debate about policy. Their work culminated in August 2003 with the publication of a substantial programme, 'The Poverty Reduction Strategy Paper' (PRSP), which was approved by the government as an overall framework for action. The document provides an analysis of the causes of the existing conditions and sets out a number of pathways towards the reduction of poverty and inequality. If the schemes are put into operation and if they succeed, they should lower the proportion of the poor in Armenia to below 20 per cent by 2015.

Bibliography

Economist Intelligence Unit, *Armenia Country Report* (London: Economist Intelligence Unit, published quarterly).

Growth, Inequality and Poverty in Armenia, report of a UNDP mission led by Keith Griffin on the Impact of Macroeconomic Policy on Poverty (Yerevan, August 2002).

Iradian, G., *Armenia: The Road to Sustained Rapid Growth, Cross-Country Evidence* (Washington, DC: International Monetary Fund, 2003).

Lampietti, J.A., *Utility Pricing and the Poor: Lessons from Armenia* (Washington, DC: World Bank, 2001).

National Statistical Service of the Republic of Armenia, various statistics, reports and publications available online at http://www.armstat.am/.

UNDP Human Development Reports (New York: Oxford University Press, 2000–2003).

Valdivieso, L., *Armenia: Recent Economic Developments and Selected Issues* (Washington, DC: International Monetary Fund, 1999).

World Bank, *Armenia: Confronting Poverty Issues* (Washington, DC: World Bank, 1996).

World Bank, *Armenia: Poverty Update* (Washington, DC: World Bank, 2002).

World Bank, *Armenia: Public Expenditure Review* (Washington, DC: World Bank, 2002).

12 Society in transition

Marina Kurkchiyan

Society beyond statistics

Statistics about Armenia are likely to be confusing for a reader who has no direct experience of the country. For example, how do people manage to get along, financially? The official evidence appears to make no sense. More than a decade into the transition the minimum cost of living was generally reckoned to be about $35 per person per month, but a monthly pension was a mere $10 and the the typical salary of a teacher or doctor only $20–25. Worse, pensions and salaries often went unpaid for months at a stretch. Given such figures, it was not surprising that half of the population lived below the poverty line. Nevertheless, there was no firm evidence that people actually suffered from malnutrition. It was undoubtedly the case that the health of the population as a whole was deteriorating, but it was not doing so as rapidly as might be expected. And it was generally understood that the average expenditure was actually about $100 per month – much more money than people are officially supposed to have.

To explain these and the many other enigmas in post-Soviet Armenian life, one has to probe below the misleading veneer represented in the anomalous statistics. Doing this exposes the deeper layers of social texture, where ordinary people live their lives from day to day, dealing with their problems as best they can and enjoying whatever privileges they may have. The assumptions that they take for granted about their social interactions and the techniques that they habitually employ together form a set of social institutions – the Armenian version of what is called 'civil society' elsewhere.[1]

Among these social institutions, undoubtedly the one that dominates everyday life in Armenia today is the informal network of kinship, friendship and mutual exchange of favours. These three social bonds together

---

1   The *Oxford Dictionary of Politics* tells us that if we want to find civil society, we should look for 'a set of intermediate associations, which are neither the state nor the family'. Under this generous definition there has always been civil society in Armenia and a great deal of it, before and after the fall of the USSR.

form a web of relationships that ties everyone together. It has supplemented or replaced the functions that might otherwise be provided by the institutions of civil society that are found in other countries: advice and information, personal services, protection, financial and practical agreements, mutual solidarity and even social security in the form of monetary support. An example is the supply of news and information; in Armenia the most reliable way to find out anything is considered to be from friends and neighbours, not from the media. Similarly, to secure advice on any issue, be it legal, business or personal, people would usually not go first to a firm of lawyers or accountants or to an advice bureau; instead they would try to find the 'right' person through the network, and talk to him or her in an informal setting. Faced with an unavoidable visit to a government agency or a big company, even if it is to deal with a routine matter, people will go to considerable lengths to identify the official or manager in charge and then personalize their relations by making contact beforehand through a network link.

This informal pattern of relationships played an important role in overcoming the repeated difficulties caused by the succession of transitional crises after 1990. It was particularly apparent in 1992–5 when Armenians had to survive cold winters without heating and with only a couple of hours of electricity supply per day at best. If at that time anyone could manage to obtain a stove and chimney and fit them into a flat despite the unsuitable Soviet-era design, then typically all the neighbours would be invited to come in and spend many hours sitting in a small room around the only source of heat in the building. In due course, each neighbour would find a reciprocal favour to perform. If anyone experienced a financial crisis, other members of their extended family, and sometimes beyond it, who had a source of income would share whatever they could spare. Borrowing money from neighbours, friends and relatives was the usual way to get through a period of extreme hardship.

In a society that works like this, large organizations and professional institutions do not operate in the Western manner, in which considerable effort is made to ensure that personal services and bureaucratic functions are typically performed in an impersonal, businesslike way. In Soviet and post-Soviet Armenia, all positions were and are personalized. For example, when a patient meets a doctor for the first time, in the eyes of that patient the doctor does not symbolize the medical profession, or a hospital, or the national health service. He represents himself; and he is a neighbour or a relative or a friend, or at least the friend of a friend. If at first the fact is that the doctor happens to be none of these things, then the patient must make sure that he becomes one of them. Until that is achieved, he will feel nervous about the quality of the treatment that he is to receive.

It is tempting for a Western observer to regard this cultural preoccupation with making personal contact as nothing more than influence-peddling, one of many examples of the corruption that has recently taken such a tight grip of most of the post-Soviet societies. That view would be unjustified and simplistic. The habit of asking 'who do you know?' as a way of solving problems can be regarded not as a decayed form of social organization, but as a mature version. In the Armenian case it stems from a traditional scheme of values that evolved far back in history as a way of sustaining communal life during many centuries of repeated military attack, exploitation and persecution so severe that it occasionally lapsed into pogrom or genocide. The attitudes brought to the informal dealings tend to be honourable, and the undertakings are usually reliable. Traditionally, the ethical scheme accorded different weights to each set of human relationships. Commitment to the nuclear family had the highest priority, then came a degree of loyalty only slightly less compelling to the immediate circle of relatives, friends and neighbours surrounding the family. Next were obligations acquired through acquaintanceship within a large network of contacts and people among whom favours were exchanged. Only after those responsibilities were satisfied could the person attend to other calls on his conscience, such as professional duties to strangers.

The seventy years of the Soviet experience strongly reinforced this pre-existing disposition to do things in the established way rather than to adopt the ideas about socialist values that came from the centre. Communism's initial idealism was challenged as early as the 1930s by Stalin's brutality, but the necessary patriotism of the Second World War ensured that scepticism did not become generally apparent until the 1950s. From then onwards a loss of faith developed, both in the formal institutions of the state as a whole and more particularly in the way in which Soviet Armenia was governed. By the time the USSR imploded in the 1980s, its main legacy was distrust. The standard Western literature on the USSR tends to misrepresent this feeling, possibly because of the ubiquity of Cold War attitudes in the two generations after 1950. Descriptions of Soviet society from that period tend to be hostile and mechanical in tone: 'coercive power', 'authoritarian regime', 'Communist Party dictatorship', 'centralized economy', 'arbitrary rule', '*nomenklatura*'. While such terms do have some validity, the image that they convey is incomplete and somewhat misleading. They suggest that everyday life in Armenia, as in the rest of the USSR, was little more than a dreary subjugation to repression. That was not the case at all. For most Soviet citizens, what mattered most in their lives was the element of spontaneous activity.

Ordinary Soviet social and economic life was in fact an astonishingly rich phenomenon, especially in the final three decades of its history. A great deal of it took place beyond state control and often went against Party ideology. It was actually a double life, lived within two contradictory but peacefully co-existing worlds. On the surface, there was the formal life, carried on within the official ideology and distinctive for its many speeches, public ceremonies and performances, and the peculiarly meaningless language used to describe it all by the mass media.

Below the surface, there was the informal life. Its foundation was total cynicism about the ideology, combined with a healthy sense of the ridiculous about the supposed quality and benefits of all the institutions. People understood very well that if they wanted to prosper, they could not afford to place their trust in the formal, planned, legally constituted economy. Instead they created their own informal economy, and it was through that system that the real distribution of income took place and through that system that personal goals were achieved. Simultaneously, everyone took part both in the official world of publicly accountable responsibilities, and also in the networks of informal relations that were legitimized only by the mutual benefit achieved by the exchanges. The informal economy drew out people's creativity, and it reached into all areas of life. The entire population was involved, and their involvement generated and sustained a profound social consensus around the co-existence of the double worlds. Everyone was faced with the choice of either taking part or suffering social exclusion.

When the Soviet Union collapsed, the official institutions of government and economy collapsed like a row of melting snowmen; no one felt any obligation to shore them up. With what remained of the official system paralysed, daily life degenerated. In Armenia as in other post-Soviet countries, it soon became clear that the state had become incapable of providing employment, welfare, security, public services, or predictable life for the population. The early years of transition were years of the highest possible degree of uncertainty: unemployment was widespread, hospitals and schools could barely function, factories and shops had vanished, travel was acutely difficult, and many people had little hope. By the mid-1990s material conditions had been reduced to mere survival level. Each family struggled to make ends meet, searching for a viable means to support a more acceptable life.

In the worst years of the 1990s the only strategy that worked was the complete reverse of official Soviet theory: the practice of self-reliance. Everyone began to engage in informal problem-solving, pragmatically finding a solution to each problem one by one. This they achieved by asking around, sharing expertise, bartering possessions and services, and generally taking steps at the lowest social level of interpersonal relations. Using their local know-how, people would illegally set up an additional electrical supply to their apartment in order to have more hours of electrical power than the official two hours a day. They would do a deal of some kind to gain access to health care. They would arrange elaborately orchestrated swaps of promised favours to ensure education for their children. In the post-Soviet world in which everything useful had suddenly become scarce, they would somehow devise a source of income by finding a market niche hitherto unthought of. At the personal and family level, the early years of the transition gave rise to remarkably imaginative feats of entrepreneurship.

As the century came to an end, it was apparent that the period of collapse had stamped its mark on the social climate in the country. Even in Soviet times the practice of networking to gain access to all kinds of goods and services, and then paying for them informally, had been widespread, but during the harsh 1990s it became the dominant norm in the society. The converse of this was the rejection of authority. Traditionally, the relationship between a Soviet citizen and any public official had been relatively whole-some: distant, often sceptical or even alienated, but also resigned to the need for the state and occasionally teasing and playful. The shock of the transi-tion, however, converted this attitude into one of profound distrust and wholesale detestation. A complete lack of respect and support for govern-ment became the new philosophy of Armenian society.

By the mid-1990s it was becoming clear to everyone that their only hope for the future lay in self-help through the informal economy. The crippling effects of uncertainty began to subside as people learned what to expect, and no longer made false assumptions only to see them contradicted. As the so-called 'transition' turned into a crash course in survival, it strengthened the old Soviet-era techniques of finding ways around, through and even under-neath the formal institutions, with the result that informal exchange became the main force helping to shape the new social fabric. This meant that most of the real economic activity in the country became invisible, because people moved it out of sight of the tax collectors and the regulators. Just a few peaks, in the form of the official economy, were allowed to remain in full view. It was only this group of enterprises, together adding up to a small section of the whole, that was effectively under the jurisdiction of the government. For a substantial period, therefore, the state became irrelevant both to the economy and to the lives led by ordinary people.

Towards the end of the 1990s material conditions began to register a slow improvement, and in response the state tried to reassert its dominant posi-tion by operating the levers of legislation, regulation and tax collection. These efforts met strong resistance, which is not surprising under the circum-stances. Within the single generation leading up to the year 2000 the people had experienced a decaying USSR, a failing *perestroika*, and an exception-ally cruel reconstruction phase. Each person had established a source of income only with the greatest possible difficulty, and therefore tended to consider it a private achievement that the government had very little to do with and would not be allowed to meddle with.

The outcome is that nowadays the bulk of the economy is hidden from official view. It is not reported in the official statistics, and it is therefore not subject to government regulation. The avoidance of scrutiny is systematic and comprehensive. It can take any of numerous forms. The most exotic is purely criminal, where what is often called a Mafia business operates under a code of silence that is enforced by intimidation and open violence. A much greater number of companies, however, are more or less legal except for one significant feature – that they manage by various means to evade most taxes. More common still are unreported business activities. There are doctors who engage in private practice within public hospitals, and builders who 'moon-light' using vehicles and equipment borrowed without permission from a government agency. There are teachers who in the evenings and at weekends give paid tutorials to the self-same pupils that they also see at school in the daytime. There are housewives who deliver home-made cookies to the customer's door. Naturally such activities create an environment in which informal networking, the exchange of favours and the use of cash payments for every kind of service are all regarded as normal. People naturally think of the advantages: the speed and flexibility provide a short cut to getting any job done, the absence of tax and overheads keeps costs well down, and the fundamental importance of reputation within the informal economy (where deals are agreed by word of mouth) provides guarantees of quality and reliability. At the same time, the informal payments and profits are universally accepted as the normal way to bring the pathetically low official salaries into line with market prices.

Social services in transition

Education

Education was one of the greatest achievements of the Soviet Union. Illiteracy was almost completely eliminated within a few years of the Bolshevik Revolution despite the primitive conditions in such areas as rural Armenia, and the universal provision of free education throughout childhood and youth gave all social groups access to higher education. Teaching at all levels was state run and standardized in terms of structure, syllabus and procedures throughout the vast territory of the Union. Children received ten years of general education, all of them progressing from primary to secondary schools. Specialized schools were available to those who wished to acquire specific occupational skills. These offered vocational courses ranging from two years to four years in length, and were open to those who had completed eight years of compulsory study in a general school. The extensive tertiary level comprised a variety of academic universities, technical colleges and professional institutes offering five-year courses.

Educational and research standards achieved in the republic were among the highest in the USSR. By the end of the Soviet era in 1989 adult literacy reached 98 per cent, and 15 per cent had a higher education qualification. In a republic with 3.2 million people, there were 1,371 general schools with 592,000 students and 54,000 teachers. Armenia had 13 higher educational establishments with 57,900 students and 1,059 doctoral students. Gender equality in higher education was also notable, at 45 per cent female to 55 per cent male.

Russian was available as the medium of instruction in Armenia in 15.1 per cent of schools, as well as Armenian (80.5 per cent) and Azerbaijani (4.4 per cent). But whereas Azerbaijani schools mainly served the needs of the national minority, the Russian schools attracted many of the children of Armenian intellectuals and the ruling elite in addition to those from ethnic

Russian families. An education in Russian was thought to improve the chances of admission to a university in Moscow and Leningrad (now St. Petersburg) and thereby to open the door to a better career. This should not be interpreted as an indication that Armenia was subjected to Russification. The dominant status of the national language was never questioned. It was spoken at home and in the street, and outside the classroom even in Russian-language schools. In respect of their distinct identity, Armenians felt secure under Soviet rule.

An account of education in Soviet Armenia would be incomplete without mention of the informal economy that operated alongside the formal one. All primary and secondary schools were open to everyone and completely free of charge, but many parents nevertheless chose to pay private fees direct to teachers in order to secure extra tuition for their own children. The practice was most pronounced as school-leaving approached and students were preparing to take examinations for admission to the higher education institutions. More significantly, the system was not immune from corruption. Networking was incessant and insidious, and it undermined the ostensible commitment of the entire process to fair and open competition between students.

After the collapse of the Soviet Union, the task faced by the government of independent Armenia was unique. Unlike in most countries, its concern was not to increase the enrolment rate and expand capacity to cater for the extra students, or even to improve the quality of the existing system. With a population that was already highly educated, an enrolment rate close to Western levels and an increasing popular demand for lifelong education, the question for the new state was how to sustain its educational system despite the drastic fall in the resources available. In the first few years after 1989 the Armenian GDP shrank by an estimated 70 per cent in response to a catastrophic economic crisis, while the proportion of it allocated to education fell from 8 per cent in 1989 to 4.9 per cent in 1993 and 1.9 per cent in 1994. Therefore the challenge confronting Armenian post-Soviet educational policy was to maintain equity, standards and universal access to general education, while spending only a small fraction of the money that the system had cost before. Inevitably, the challenge proved impossible to meet.

Meanwhile, the new government recognized the intellectual and political importance of setting education free from Communist ideology, removing the many Soviet-inspired distortions in arts, the humanities including literature, and social science subjects like history and economics. The need was to create a system more responsive to Armenia's national requirements. The first steps were taken in this direction in early 1990 and consisted of abolishing all teaching in the medium of Russian and declaring most of the textbooks used in schools to be unsuitable. Unfortunately, the policy was implemented without preparation, so there were no transitional arrangements in place, such as providing new textbooks or arranging for the gradual adoption of the Armenian language for teaching in the Russian schools. The consequences were general confusion followed by a significant drop in standards.

The economic rigours of the transition provoked a predictable and catastrophic decline in general education. The finance available to the schools barely covered even the ridiculously low salaries of the teachers. Many of the qualified staff were forced by poverty to leave their positions and search for alternative means of living. Those who remained lost their sense of commitment to the job and found it hard to devise creative ways to deal with the chaos that was developing in both curriculum and management. Teaching equipment quickly became outdated, and then school buildings began to deteriorate physically. For several years in succession schools were closed for at least three months each winter because heating was unavailable. Contributions from parents became the main support that kept the schools going at all. It became common practice to ask parents to carry out maintenance on the classrooms and to collect money to buy equipment or to cover the cost of fuel during the cold season. As an official from the Ministry of Education remarked during an interview: 'If parents did not help, the school would immediately fall apart.'

Towards the end of the first transition decade, the government decided upon a response to the shortage of resources. It chose to adopt a strategy of 'optimization', meaning reductions in both the number of schools and the number of teachers. The justification put forward for the new policy was that the scale of educational provision inherited from the Soviet period was excessive. It was argued that the number of teachers was disproportionately large in relation to the number of pupils. The system as a whole would benefit, therefore, if facilities were to be shared between schools and at the same time the number of staff was reduced. In this way, it was claimed, the financial pie could be cut into bigger slices. These proposals were enthusiastically supported by the international advisers. But as soon as they were implemented, the negative results became apparent. Many schools were closed down without adequate provision of transportation to the alternative location. Unemployment among teachers rose to unmanageable levels. By the winter of 2003–4, the government was forced to suspend the policy under increasing social pressure.

Despite the troubled history of schooling in independent Armenia, it would be incorrect to infer that a good education is no longer available in the republic. It continues to be provided for many children, especially in Yerevan, the capital city. However, it can now be obtained at either primary or secondary level only where elaborate private arrangements have been set up. Many state schoolteachers have become private tutors for part or even all of their time, and their services within the informal economy are successfully filling the gap that emerged after the collapse of the old system – but only for those able to pay.

An alternative way to obtaining a decent general education is to send children to the newly emerging private 'colleges' or secondary schools.

However, their capacities are very small as yet and almost all of them are located in Yerevan. By 2001 there were 53 such colleges (against 1400 state schools), and they catered for only 2 per cent of the secondary school population. Vocational education barely survives at all, in either the public or private sectors. The old specialist secondary schools do still exist, but demand for the technical training they provide is low because of the paralysed economy and the high unemployment that accompanies it.

Higher education, although also struggling, is in a somewhat better condition. Like the schools, it presented the newly independent government with an unmanageable dilemma about how to satisfy the substantial demand without having the necessary resources. But unlike in the case of schools, the government has extricated itself by a remarkable innovation in policy. Its goal has been to detach itself from the obligation to pay at least the main part of the necessary expenditure, but not to lose control over the institutions because of their ideological and political importance. It appears to have succeeded, although at an educational price that has still to be paid. In the first five years of the transition, the number of students approximately doubled. For the first time the higher education establishments admitted applicants who received low marks in admission tests – provided they agreed to pay. Only a small proportion of all students now receive their education free of charge; the majority pay substantial fees. The fee-paying students study in the same classes as the few state-supported students. Income received from the students covers the main institutional costs together with the salaries of the academic and support staff and related expenses. Effectively, the new arrangements mean that the government has managed to keep the universities and other institutions afloat, while transferring the major financial burden from itself to the population

However, it is not difficult to see that injecting large numbers of fee-paying students into traditional state institutions is not in itself a progressive action. There has been no tangible change either in the hierarchical Soviet management structure or in the authoritarian style used by the rector and his subordinates in their dealings with academics and students. The new funding arrangement has nothing in common with a fully privatized education system that would create autonomous institutions and then encourage them to experiment freely, to offer choices to their students, to compete with one another in as many ways as possible and thereby to stimulate development. The half-reformed system that now exists tends to produce nothing more than an overload of the organizations within a rigidly conservative academic framework.

Meanwhile, the establishment of new, wholly private higher educational establishments was permitted from the earliest years of the transition. By 1999 the number of private universities had reached 81, with an average of 240 students in each. They were set up in classic informal-economy style by enterprising teachers from the state-controlled establishments, many of them working for both institutions in parallel. The new establishments were fee-paying, with virtually unlimited freedom for their managers and with complete responsibility for the quality of the teaching. Students who registered in them were usually among the weakest school-leavers, the ones whose examination results were so poor that they could not even get into the fee-paying quota in the state institutions despite the low requirements there. The legitimacy of the private universities was in doubt for some years. Although they were formally authorized from independence onwards, the certificates of graduation that they issued to students upon completion of their courses were not officially recognized as certificates of higher education until 1999, when a new education law was passed. In other words, for a decade a substantial number of students paid fees to secure a low-quality education and then received a document that was effectively meaningless.

Overall, the trend in educational development has been changing during its second decade of transition to the market. The quality of the state universities and professional institutions has been falling dramatically. These organizations, which commanded such high prestige only a generation ago, are now unreformed and mismanaged. At the same time, the private universities have been forced to engage in competition both with the public sector and with each other in order to survive. As a result of this competition, a handful of private institutions have strengthened their image and have begun to produce graduates of an acknowledged high standard, while the weakest are simply disappearing.

The Education Act adopted in 1999 was an attempt to bring order to the chaotic scene in the entire education sector. The new law introduced a requirement that all private educational institutions must be licensed on the basis of having reached satisfactory standards relating to such criteria as the use of suitable teaching space and equipment, qualified teaching staff and appropriate curricula. With the introduction of these requirements, eighteen universities were immediately closed down. The law also paved the way to legitimizing the certificates awarded by private universities, using a procedure whereby the results achieved by students in their final examinations were to be monitored over a three-year period. A special Committee of Licensing was established within the Ministry of Education to supervise the process. The first five private universities obtained their state accreditation in 2001, and others followed.

The law was also intended to reorganize educational provision generally, and to bring it closer to international practice. General education, including the primary and secondary stages, was extended from a total of 10 years to 11 years. Higher education was henceforward to be organized in a Western manner, with four years of undergraduate study followed by two years of master's degree study and then three years of research or professional training for a specialized higher qualification. Overall, it does seem that by the end of the 1990s the period of chaotic disruption in the educational sector had finally been brought to a close, or at least towards a close, and development is now proceeding in a more orderly fashion.

However, it is clear that education in Armenia has become an expensive commodity that is accessible only to children from relatively well-off families. There are costs at every stage of schooling and advanced study. All schools seek contributions for routine costs. Even in primary schools, families have to pay for supplementary private tutorials if they want a good quality of education for their child. In secondary schools there are semi-formal fees to be paid to avoid stigmatization of the child. Higher education is extensively marketized, with high fees charged formally for nearly all students. This brings an additional dimension of inequality to a society that already suffers from severe economic stratification. The situation is made even worse by the fact that higher education has effectively become available mostly to citizens of Yerevan because most of the institutions are located there, and the cost of living there is too high to be affordable for families from outside the metropolitan area.

The health service

The most noticeable feature of the health care system in the USSR was its comprehensiveness. The country developed an extensive state-financed medical system and was successful in achieving an adequate national health status. Its indicators, for example life expectancy, mortality and morbidity, were lower than Western equivalents but much higher than those found in other nations with similar per capita income levels. According to the authors of a study carried out for a United Nations agency, conditions as the Soviet period came to an end in the 1980s were impressive: 'In terms of living standards and health status, the CEF/FSU countries were close to Southern Europe.'[2]

The Soviet health service was centrally financed and free to the population. The various medical units – local health units, polyclinics, general hospitals and specialized hospitals – provided most drugs free of charge; others were available in pharmacies at a very low price, subsidized by the government. Of course, the ubiquitous informal economy was also prominent in the Soviet system of medical care. Although payment was officially discouraged, in practice doctors and nurses in ordinary state hospitals were given fees by patients on a regular basis. Despite this, it was usually possible to receive service without any payment, although this was less reliable. Usually payment was only for labour. Other necessities were provided free of charge, for example medicines, the bed, and the use of the hospital's equipment and facilities generally. The payments could be made in cash or in kind and although they were nearly always expected, they were not large in amount and the vast majority of patients could afford them.

---

2 *Poverty in Transition*, UNDP report (New York: Regional Bureau for Europe and the CIS, 1998), p. 41.

In the closing years of the Soviet regime, an event occurred that had a significant impact on health care provision in Armenia: the devastating earthquake of December 1988 centred on the town of Spitak, not far from the country's second largest city, Leninakan (now Gyumri). The international community responded generously and in the aftermath several new hospitals were built, equipped and, in a few instances, initially staffed by Western agencies. The experience of operating in them provided opportunities for local doctors to benefit from working alongside and in constant communication with their Western counterparts. These foreign links would later, in the impoverished post-Soviet phase, become one of the principal sources of support for medical care. The support came in various forms (and continues to do so), notably as financial assistance, equipment supply, and training both for managers and for all categories of medical and professional staff.

Overall, Armenia emerged into independence with a well-developed system of health care supported by a large number of qualified professionals. At the same time, the system was bulky, over-staffed and inefficient. The ratio of medical staff to population exceeded international norms.

Very early on in the post-Soviet period it became clear that the new Armenian government could not afford to continue its expensive habits of providing free and universal health care while also carrying responsibility for the elaborate and costly central administrative structure. There followed between 1991 and 1996 a post-Soviet phase of transformation in the provision of health care services that can best be characterized as disintegration. Although the official status of the health care system was not changed until 1997, the reality from the very beginning of the transition period was that government expenditure was sufficient only to cover a small proportion of the total cost.

The financial shortfall caused real if unofficial decentralization, all the way down to the level of each medical unit. Finding themselves at the cutting edge of the funding problem, the front-line providers of health care perforce turned themselves into *de facto* independent agents, each developing its own survival strategy. In most cases this consisted of reliance on funds provided informally from within the community served by the unit. By the mid-1990s direct charges, in the form of cash payments made in return for services rendered to patients, had become a principal feature of financing within the medical system. By the same time patients had learned to perceive health care as a scarce and expensive resource, preferably acquired by first-hand, personal arrangements if the best possible treatment and facilities were to be secured. And so informal contracting and networking became basic norms within the health care system.

The first active response of the government to this uncontrolled transformation of the health care system occurred in 1995, when plans were announced to implement a set of reforms. Changes were introduced to alter the legal status of the health providers. By mid-1997 all hospitals, polyclinics and village units were converted into public/private enterprises, and granted the power to function as quasi-commercial entities. This meant that they were given permission to charge fees to their patients. Another innovation in the health institution as a whole was the privatization of pharmacies. In practice this step has caused a wide range of drugs to become freely available for purchase in Armenia from the many newly established drugstores without any requirement for prescriptions or professional advice.

However, fees at the levels officially announced could not possibly cover the needs of health care. The yield from official charges amounted to much less than the real market cost of the services because of the wide gap between the officially recorded income of the population, which was very low, and the relatively high level of market prices under which the real economy operated. Also, for low-income Armenians even the below-market prices were difficult to afford, which meant that for at least one-third of the population health care had become more or less unavailable in practice.

Following the formal introduction of payment-based services in 1997, the total number of patients dropped significantly. In any case, the number of people coming forward for treatment had already been much lower in the transition years than in the Soviet period, because the poverty that set in between 1989 and 1996 had prevented many sick people from seeking help that they knew would have to be paid for informally. But when in 1997 the customary pattern of informal payments was transformed into, or more accurately certified and extended by, a law-based system of formal payments, the numbers turning to the medical institutions became even smaller and their condition when they eventually presented themselves for treatment became correspondingly more critical. After well over a decade of transition, hospitals in Armenia functioned at only 25–30 per cent of their total capacity. Most of the beds in the hospitals, or in certain departments within a hospital, had not been used for years.

To keep access to the health services open to the poor the government has introduced what is known as a 'social order'. This consists of a decision in principle to subsidize the treatment of certain vulnerable groups of people, together with a set of serious medical conditions. To implement the decision a 'basic package' has been introduced, setting out the rules and procedures governing the application of a subsidy to a particular treatment and/or to a patient from a specified social group. Although the social order has eased the financial problems of the health-providing institutions to some extent, it has failed in its other purposes. It has not enabled the poor to return to the hospitals, and the sums were too small in total to make any impact on the practice of making informal payments. What it has actually achieved instead is to open up space for skilful networking. Would-be system-fixers have appeared and set about devising ingenious schemes under which an appropriate combination of social order subsidies, formal fees and informal payments can enable patients with the know-how to get a better deal.

In 2000 the Armenian government took a radical step towards the privatization of health care: it announced that many hospitals would be put up for sale. Not only did this action fail to solve the problems of health care provision, but it actually achieved the very opposite. It increased the volume of informal payments, and it reduced even further the accessibility of the health services to the greater part of the population.

The net result of Armenian health care's arbitrary mixture of informal practices, practical problems, commercial initiatives and official interventions can be broadly described as follows. In general the patients pay for, or in respect of some items have to provide for themselves, nearly everything that they need for treatment in a hospital. That includes the bed, food, laundry and all the medicines and supplies, from bandages to the use of surgical equipment. In addition, they pay all the fees charged by the doctors, nurses and technical staff. The prices are established only through the informal network and communicated by word of mouth. The amount actually charged to patients varies considerably from case to case. For example, there are large geographical variations in price between the capital city, which is markedly the most expensive, and small towns in the various regions. Prices are affected by the ability to pay, which is usually assessed by a doctor using an informal means test that consists mainly of his own estimate of a patient's circumstances. Prices can be reduced to take account of informal relationships, friends of friends, relatives, past favours and other privileged links.

The main effect of the high cost of professional health care has been de-institutionalization. People try to avoid doctors, clinics and hospitals, and tend instead to retreat to their homes. They draw upon their own experience and knowledge to make a diagnosis and then to administer therapy and medication to themselves, and they do not hesitate to ask for advice from other people – relatives, neighbours, friends and contacts. Self-treatment has become the standard response to any health problem for as long as professional intervention can be avoided, and it has been facilitated by the commercial availability of almost any drug that is on sale anywhere in the world.

This practice is considerably less unexpected and dangerous than it might seem. In sharp contrast to the West, Armenians generally have a self-assured approach to their own health. Partly this is one of several beneficial legacies of their history. In the Soviet period, although people felt fairly confident in the hands of the professionals, they were also aware that they risked coming across an incompetent doctor whose qualifications and rank had been acquired not by merit but by networking. People therefore adopted the habit of questioning and double-checking everything a doctor said, in an attempt to understand the problem and to judge the adequacy of the treatment proposed. As a result, the population in all Soviet countries moved towards the free market already experienced in dealing with health problems and in taking self-prescribed drugs.

Although there can be little doubt that the Armenian population's standard of health has fallen since 1990, it is not at all clear how far the fall has gone, because most people now go unexamined for long periods. The health of the public could hardly have failed to get worse, given the severe deterioration of the Soviet-era national health service, in conjunction with the disastrous fall in real incomes. Some evidence does suggest that the decline is indeed severe. Life expectancy fell from 71 years in 1990 to 68 in 2000, according to World Health Organization data, while the crude death rate increased from 6.2 per 1000 people in 1990 to 9.7 ten years later.[3] Even so, there is no general indication of illness and weakness on a worrying scale. And some indicators fail to show any worsening at all in health status. There even exist a few of them, such as infant mortality, that suggest that a slight improvement has occurred since 1990.

If the majority of the population does indeed enjoy an acceptable, although minimal, standard of health (which is not unequivocally so, but also not unequivocally not so), then it follows that the technique of self-help supported by the informal network must be having at least some beneficial effect. But how could it? The answer appears to be that the cultural tradition of mutual support, acting in combination with certain other factors such as the high educational level of the population, acted as a shock-absorber to help the citizenry to absorb the disturbance caused by the health-care crisis of the 1990s. The spontaneous acceptance of responsibility for health care, shifting from institutionalized professionalism to self-reliance at home with the wholehearted backing of the community, was in no way a reversion to the superstition and irrational practices of the distant past. Rather, the urgency of deciding what to do without professional expertise set in motion an intelligent debate, bolstered by common sense. Usually the decisive role in discussion would be accorded to the most respected and best-informed person who could be called upon for advice. This interpretation is not intended to be an argument for replacing the medical profession with amateurs. An overall deterioration of health in Armenia is unavoidable given the socio-economic crisis, but the decline has not been as severe as might have been expected.

Migration as an alternative way of problem solving

The multiple crises afflicting Armenia since 1990 have induced a great variety of reactions among the people, ranging from mass depression to nationalist chauvinism, and from vigorous dissent to casting a vote for strong-arm leadership. As the argument presented in this chapter has

3   It is necessary to bear in mind that statistics on health in Armenia are exceptionally unreliable. According to data supplied by the Ministry of Health, and used by the World Bank, life expectancy has even improved recently, reaching 74.7 years in 2000; this seems most unlikely.

suggested, the most persistent attitude to be found within the population is a total scepticism towards all political authority. Most Armenians seem to have this feeling and deal with it by abandoning the possibility of trust in an abstract 'system' and instead putting their faith in informal networking that they can rely on. But for some people, the consistently bleak prospect facing the country has persisted for too long. They simply want to leave.

This sentiment has induced a major wave of voluntary emigration throughout the 1990s. It has caused a prodigious decline in the population of Armenia and although there are no statistics that can be relied upon, it is likely that at least one-third of the entire population left the country in the ten years after 1990.[4]

The mass emigration from Armenia was triggered principally by the collapse of the economy during the early stage of independence. For ambitious people especially, migration was the logical response to mass unemployment, poverty, inadequate living conditions, limited supplies of electricity and heating, a high cost of living, and greatly restricted access to educational and health services. There was also the challenge of working out how to function successfully within the uncertain environment of the informal economy.

In this age when many asylum seekers are persecuted and economic migrants are frequently deported or imprisoned, emigration itself has become grossly unpleasant for many of those who attempt it. The fact that over a million Armenians have nevertheless taken the risk is clear testimony to how bad conditions have become for them at home. In common with migrants worldwide and throughout history, emigrants are people who have judged that in order to survive they have to search for a job abroad, even though it means leaving behind their homes, family, friends, language, culture and neighbourhood.

The principal destination for the migration of the 1990s was Russia, together with the other former Soviet countries. About three-quarters of those who have left Armenia are believed to have settled in these Russian-speaking lands. The remainder, certainly a quarter of a million in number and possibly many more, joined the global flow of migrants attempting to make their way to the West. A significant number of Armenians have been attempting to start their new lives in locations that already contain substantial communities of their ethnic fellows, such as the United States (in particular Los Angeles) and France. But nowadays many small Armenian communities are forming all over the world, wherever economic activity is vigorous.

The general pattern is common to all economic migrants. It usually starts with a young or middle-aged member of a family leaving the country to look

---

4   The 2002 census suggests that Armenia's population is around 3 million, 800,000 fewer than in 1989. Allowing for natural population growth in the years 1989 to 2002, this would suggest that perhaps a million Armenians have emigrated. Other estimates put the figure considerably higher.

for work wherever there is a chance of finding it. The intention is to send home regular payments to provide financial support for the family left behind. If the migrant is even moderately successful, the rest of the family follows him, and once the nuclear family is settled in the new country they continue to support members of the extended family still at home. The final step is taken when those members of the extended family in turn follow the original migrant abroad. An indication of the importance of recent migration is the fact that accumulated remittances – money sent home by people working abroad – have come to form a significant proportion of the capital circulating in the current Armenian economy.

Emigration on such a vast scale has had a pronounced impact on the demographic and social structure of the population. Like all mass emigrations, the outward flow from Armenia began with young adult males, leaving behind disproportionate numbers of females, the old and the unfit. It is also the case that the proportion of educated people among the migrants has been notably high. Qualified professionals, especially in the hard sciences of physics, chemistry, engineering and the like, had little difficulty in finding profitable employment for their expertise in the Russian and Western labour markets.

Although socio-economic hardship was undoubtedly the main force driving the phenomenon of mass emigration from Armenia, it was not the only one. A desire for material betterment does not in itself explain why people preferred to leave the country rather than to make an effort to improve it. Nor does it provide a framework for understanding the behaviour of those who stayed. Why is the political opposition so weak and ineffective? Why, under continuously worsening economic conditions, has there not been a massive increase in social tension? Why has there been no organized resistance to the government mismanagement of welfare that is so widely perceived?

An analysis of the psychological climate, in addition to an economic analysis, may offer a deeper explanation of both the mass emigration and the political passivity that now prevails in the country. As recently as the late 1980s things were radically different. During the national movement for unity and independence in the late 1980s and early 1990s the mass public was anything but apathetic, and the expectations engendered by the movement were anything but low. There was a high expectation of a smooth move to prosperity, to an open market environment, and to fair and democratic governance. The expectation was that when Armenians became masters of their own house, they could hardly fail to ensure its growing success.

The reality of post-independent Armenia proved to be a contradiction of all those aims and hopes. Corruption, irresponsibility and incompetence quickly became widespread, visible and corrosive. Politics came to be seen as a circle of self-serving intrigue rather than as a responsible attempt to solve the country's problems. It became obvious that many MPs could not possibly be regarded as representatives of their constituents' interests. The effect of these crushing realizations was not limited to disappointment or frustration. It went deeper, causing a sense of alienation to take root. So deep was the reaction that it can best be regarded as a crisis of national identity. This alienation undermined the motivation to participate in community life and lowered the expectation of success in any collective action. It resulted in scepticism, depression and distrust of all social institutions in Armenia, and it provoked people to abandon the country altogether and to look instead for a new place to settle down in. Each new episode of political turmoil, such as the crudely manipulated elections in 1996 and 2003 or the shootings in the parliament in 1999, produced a surge of outward migration from the country.

To conclude the account of recent Armenian society, it is fair to say that the last decade of the twentieth century was a difficult time for the Armenian people. But it was also a time when Armenians took matters affecting their lives into their own hands and started to learn how to build an orderly society. Although the crisis is far from being overcome, there is a noticeable trend towards positive developments. A better picture has begun to emerge of how institutions may now take shape after a decade of chaotic falling apart and failed reorganizations. There is also a new emphasis on social security issues within the Armenian government. An orderly market economy is beginning to form, slowly pushing the subversive practices of informal exchange and networking out of business firms. Professional skills and knowledge are gaining wider acknowledgement and are in growing demand, especially within organizations and firms that have links or regular dealings overseas. All these factors create a hope that a positive trend can now take hold in the development process and begin to restore the social fabric, providing opportunities and a sense of purpose and meaning for the younger and succeeding generations.

Bibliography

Chaudhury, N., *The Effect of a Fee-Waiver Program on Health Care Utilization among the Poor: Evidence from Armenia* (Washington, DC: World Bank, Human Development Sector Unit, 2003).

Hohvannisyan, S.G., *Health Care System in Transition: Armenia* (Copenhagen: European Observatory on Health Care Systems, WHO Regional Office for Europe, 2001).

Kurkchiyan, M., 'The Transformation of the Second Economy into the Informal Economy' in A. Ledeneva and M. Kurkchiyan, eds, *Economic Crime in Russia* (London: Kluwer Law International, 2000).

—— 'The Illegitimacy of Law in Post-Soviet Societies' in D. Galligan and M. Kurkchiyan, eds, *Law and Informal Practices: The Post-communist Experience* (Oxford: Oxford University Press, 2003).

Perkins, G., and Yemtsov, R., *Armenia: Restructuring to Sustain Universal General Education*, World Bank technical paper no. 498, Europe and Central Asia poverty reduction and economic management series (Washington, DC: World Bank, 2001).

13 Homeland–diaspora relations and identity differences

Razmik Panossian[1]

'Oh, Armenian people, your only salvation is in the power of your collective strength [*Ov hai zhoghovurd, ko miak prkutiune ko havakakan uizhi mej e*]'. This line was cryptically written in a poem entitled 'Message' by Eghishe Charents in 1933. The poet soon disappeared in Stalin's purges, but his message imploring unity became a rallying cry for Armenians scattered all over the globe, and divided along political lines. However, the fact of the matter is that in recent history Armenians have never united as one force. Throughout the twentieth century two main cleavages divided the Armenians. The first was a deep socio-political divide within most of the significant diasporan communities. The second was the even more profound split between the homeland and the diaspora based on political and identity differences (see chapter 7). This chapter will concentrate on the latter dynamic.

The basic argument is that there are two Armenian entities, the homeland and the diaspora.[2] Although these two branches are united subjectively as one nation, they nevertheless fundamentally differ from one another in their collective identity and politics. The first part of the chapter will focus on the political dimension, outlining the major events and issues since 1988. In the second part, the deeper historical and identity factors will be analyzed.

Events and issues

The 1988 to 1999 period can be divided into four stages characterizing the relationship between the homeland and the diaspora:

1   1988–91, when the two entities reluctantly embraced one another
2   1991–2, when there was a 'honeymoon' between them

1   An earlier version of this chapter appeared in Russian in *Diaspori*, vol. 1, no. 2, Autumn 2000 ['Diasporas' is an independent academic journal in Moscow].
2   By homeland I refer to the Republic of Armenia, be it Soviet or independent. By diaspora, I refer to the 'external', mainly 'Western', established diasporan communities of Europe, the Americas, and the Middle East. The 'internal' diaspora (in Russia and other former Soviet states) is a wholly different topic of discussion.

3   1992–8, the period of schism and conflict
4   After 1998, the beginning of reconciliation.

Phase one: 1988–91

The first phase began with the two major 'earthquakes' in Soviet Armenia: the political explosion over the Karabagh movement in February, and the devastating seismic earthquake of December. Both events caught the diaspora completely off guard, and both events placed the Soviet republic at the centre of the diaspora's concerns and collective consciousness. As such, the 'homeland' became the focus of diasporan activities, acquiring a more concrete dimension rather than being an abstract notion in the background of diasporan identity. After 1988 there were unprecedented contacts and possibilities of cooperation between the two entities.

In the months following the physical earthquake of December 1988, the diaspora mobilized massive resources to collect aid and send volunteers to Armenia to assist with the reconstruction efforts. The most important consequence of these efforts was the reversal of the roles of donor and recipient of aid. Whereas the republic had hitherto projected itself as the source of assistance to the diaspora, particularly in the cultural field, from December 1988 onwards the diaspora assumed the position of provider of material aid to the homeland. This dynamic continued throughout the next decade, as Armenia's economy collapsed in the early 1990s. Receiving aid from the diaspora was a blow to the self-image of many Armenians in the republic.

The effects of the political earthquake of 1988 were more complicated. The diaspora, on the whole, supported the Karabagh movement. But, more than anything, it was initially bewildered by it. Diaspora Armenians simply could not envision any view or demand broader than the joining of the Karabagh region to Soviet Armenia. They were always a few steps behind the developments and the thinking in the republic. Meanwhile, the homeland had great expectations of the diaspora, especially of the Dashnaks[3] with their nationalist rhetoric of liberation. For the mass of Armenians in the nationalist movement, the ARF was the embodiment of their ideals. As one commentator put it: 'The feelings of the people toward the [Dashnak Party] in 1988–9 had reached the level of religious reverence.'[4] And, by extension, the diaspora was revered – at least the Dashnak side – for its nationalist ideals. The line between the ARF and the diaspora was blurred in the minds of many Armenians.

---

3   The Armenian Revolutionary Federation (ARF) is usually referred to as the Dashnak Party, the Dashnaktsutiun, or simply the Dashnaks. See chapters 4, 5, 7.
4   S. Melik-Hakobian, 'Establishment of the Second Republic of Armenia and the Dashnaktsutiun (ARF)', *Nor Gyank* (Los Angeles), 28 November 1996, p. 51.

But disappointment was soon to follow. In October 1988 the ARF, along with the other two diasporan parties, the Ramkavars (liberal) and the Hnchaks (social democrat), issued a rare joint statement. While they supported the joining of Mountainous Karabagh to Soviet Armenia, they called for moderation, calm and the ending of strikes and the disruptive protests that would harm the 'good standing' of Armenians in the eyes of 'higher Soviet bodies' – on which they called to settle the dispute. This was a complete misreading of the prevalent mood in Yerevan, and it was interpreted by the movement there as condemnation of its activities and support for the Soviet regime. This statement, nine months after the beginning of the mass nationalist protests, was the first step in delegitimizing the ARF, and the diaspora, in Armenia. Even without their conservative attitude, the Dashnaks (and other diasporan organizations) did not have the material resources and connections, nor the ideological flexibility, to have any significant impact in Armenia.

The ARF, as well as the other diasporan parties, established themselves with much fanfare in Armenia during the summer and autumn of 1990. They began to publish newspapers, to hold meetings and to establish various bodies linked with them. Once it became obvious that the Communists were doomed, the Ramkavar and Hnchak parties came to the staunch support of the nationalist leadership (based on their traditional belief that they should be on the side of any government in Armenia). But they failed to build a mass base for their organizations because in the minds of most Armenians in the republic they were tainted by their collaboration with the Communist regime. The Dashnaks, in turn, set their sights on obtaining power and began to organize for that purpose, antagonizing the leadership of the indigenous nationalist movement.

At this point the homeland was opening up to the diaspora, based on the ideals espoused by the latter, but it was the diaspora which could not accept the independence-minded nationalism of homeland intellectuals, counter-elites, and the masses. The initial contact between them was very much a reluctant embrace, much like distant relations who had become strangers. Nevertheless, the institutional barriers erected by the Soviet regime between Armenia and large parts of the diaspora were demolished in this period. A spirit of openness replaced the partial and regulated relations of the Soviet period.

Phase two: 1991–2

The euphoria of independence in September 1991 ushered in a short-lived 'honeymoon' period. The most visible manifestation of the close relationship between the homeland and the diaspora was a series of high-level appointments of government officials from the diaspora. Three of the most notable were US citizens. Jirair (Gerard) Libaridian had already been appointed as an advisor to President Levon Ter Petrosian in January 1991, assuming more senior positions until his resignation in September 1997. Raffi Hovannisian, a 32-year-old US-born lawyer, was appointed as independent Armenia's first Foreign Minister in October 1991. His youthful energy and commitment made him a popular figure. In January 1992 Sebouh Tashjian of California was chosen as Minister of Energy. Such appointments were seen as a clear signal by the new post-communist government of Armenia that it was reaching out to the diaspora, extending a hand of cooperation to bridge the gap between them. The press and much of the political rhetoric in Yerevan and in diasporan communities reflected this spirit of cooperation between the two 'wings' of the nation.[5]

1991–2 was also the period when some diaspora Armenians went to the homeland either to settle there (a minute number) or to help with the state-building process by volunteering their skills to the country on a short-term basis, be it for weeks, months or even a year. It was seen as a matter of 'duty' for diaspora Armenians to go help the homeland in any way they could. But the floodgates of cooperation did not open and contacts remained limited. Although visiting Armenia is seen as a rite of passage for many diasporans, it remains a passage that only a few undertake. Difficult economic conditions in Armenia are partly to blame, but there is also an implicit realization that the homeland feels too different, too 'foreign', for diasporans – and, of course, vice versa. The other side of the contacts has been the arrival of homeland intellectuals and politicians to diaspora centres to rally support for Armenia and Karabagh. As such, they too have had an opportunity to see and experience diaspora communities first hand.

Phase three: 1992–8

As the two parts of the nation came to know each other more intimately, they realized that the realities of the 'other' fell well short of the ideal images they had. Ironically, open contact meant increased tensions and antagonism as the two bodies did not necessarily like what they saw on the other side. Armenians in the republic came to view the diaspora as more talk than assistance, as condescending and arrogant, eager to dispense advice despite being culturally 'corrupted'. Its limitations did not at all correspond to the high expectations the homeland had of its kin abroad. The diaspora, on the other hand, came to perceive Armenians in the homeland as lazy, opportunist, corrupted by Soviet rule – not at all the 'pure' Armenians they were expecting to find. Both sides soon realized how culturally different they were from each other in terms of values, beliefs and outlook. There was – and still is – much disappointment and even resentment, although many personal relationships within families and between individuals continued unbroken.

---

5   The selective use of diasporan experts in government continues to this day. For example, Vartan Oskanian was appointed Deputy Foreign Minister in November 1994. He was promoted to Foreign Minister in February 1998; as of mid-2004 he remains in the post.

The honeymoon period came to an end symbolically with Raffi Hovannisian's resignation as Foreign Minister in October 1992, a year after his appointment. There were tensions between the homeland and the diaspora much earlier, but Hovannisian's departure confirmed the obvious, especially since it was over policy differences in regard to relations with Turkey. What followed was a six-year period of antagonistic relations between the homeland and the diaspora. At this time, acute political differences emerged between the Armenian government and the Dashnak side of the diaspora. For the latter, opposing Ter Petrosian also meant lack of assistance for the Armenian state. This is not to say that the diaspora as a whole opposed the government, but the most significant political force within it came to work against the leadership of the homeland, and, by extension, against the republic itself. As the diaspora, once again, split over the issue of how to relate to the homeland, relations between the two entities cooled considerably. During the 1990s the political dynamic of the ARF–government relationship overshadowed other aspects of homeland–diaspora relations, as well as becoming a major political issue within the republic.

The first significant showdown was the 1991 presidential election. The Dashnaks, misjudging the mood of the country, put forward their own candidate. Popular local actor Sos Sargsian, a political novice, ran against Levon Ter Petrosian of the Armenian Pan-National Movement (ANM).[6] Sarksian and the ARF – which, incidentally, had emphasized its diasporan links – were humiliated. They received a little over 4 per cent of the vote, while Ter Petrosian received 83 per cent. This major blunder by the Dashnaks lost them prestige both in Armenia and in the diaspora; it also set the stage for the oppositional politics to come.

A few months after the election, the ARF began to agitate for a coalition government. After some discussions between President Ter Petrosian and the ARF leadership, the two could not come to an agreement in the face of increased Dashnak demands. Relations soon disintegrated to the point that Ter Petrosian publicly accused the Dashnak leadership of undermining government policies and activities in relation to the Karabagh war. In June 1992 he expelled Hrair Marukhian, the Dashnak leader (and a Greek citizen), from Armenia. This was also a message to the diaspora according to Senior Presidential Advisor Jirair Libaridian. The President, he says, 'took on the most powerful man of the most powerful [diaspora] organization and it was a message in a way, from my point of view to the diaspora: Know your place! You are not running this republic! ... This is not an all-Armenian government.'[7]

Two years later Ter Petrosian delivered the most severe blow to the ARF when on 28 December 1994 he banned the ARF, its subordinate organizations

---

6   The party is often referred to by its Armenian abbreviation – HHSh. See chapters 6 and 9.
7   Interview with Soren Theisen, 1 September 1992. I have not seen it published, but it did
     appear on *Groong* Armenian News Network.

and its press in Armenia. He accused them of harbouring a secret para-military organization called Dro, which, he said, was responsible for assassinations, drug trafficking and destabilizing activities to undermine the government. In a series of arrests preceding the announcement, twelve Dashnaks were detained and subsequently tried. The charges ranged from murder to possession of false documents. The trial concluded in December 1996, when ten of the accused were found guilty and given sentences ranging from three years' imprisonment to the death penalty. No direct links were found, however, between their crimes and the ARF. Nevertheless, the party remained outlawed. The ARF was officially forbidden to operate because it was a 'foreign' organization controlled from abroad. Another wave of Dashnak arrests followed in the summer of 1995, among them Vahan Hovhannisian, one of the national leaders of the ARF in Armenia. He and thirty other party members were all accused of planning a coup.

1995 was the lowest point in homeland–diaspora relations. Not only was it becoming clear that Armenia, under the leadership of the ANM, was much less democratic than at first appeared, but it was rejecting a significant part of the diaspora which was in opposition to its rule. Even ANM supporters in the diaspora, such as the Ramkavar Party, condemned the outright banning of the ARF on insufficient grounds. The Ramkavars issued a statement criticizing the ban as a dangerous precedent in violation of democratic principles. The homeland leadership wanted a docile and apologetic diaspora to operate in the republic, not a diaspora which had a mind – and an organization – of its own.

The next major showdown between the ANM and the ARF came with the September 1996 presidential elections, and the subsequent events. Most of the opposition, including the Dashnaks, united under the banner of the National Alliance Union (NAU) and put forward one candidate: Vazgen Manukian (see chapter 9). The ARF played an important role in mobilizing against the re-election of Ter Petrosian. The NAU promised dual citizenship for diaspora Armenians, more integration between the diaspora and the homeland, and the lifting of the ban on the ARF.

The antagonism between the opposition and the government reached a new high immediately after the elections, when, amidst justified accusations of electoral fraud, the opposition vehemently protested against Ter Petrosian's re-election with a majority of less than 2 per cent. When a mass demonstration turned violent and became an attack on the National Assembly, the administration cracked down using the army. Once again Dashnaks were accused of fomenting unrest, planning a coup and engaging in illegal agitation to obtain power. More arrests followed, and the ARF once again took a beating in Armenia.

Issues in homeland–diaspora relations

In these years there were a number of issues fuelling the antagonistic relations between the ARF and the Armenian government led by the ANM.

Independence The issue of independence from the USSR before 1991 was the most crucial difference between the Karabagh movement/ANM and the ARF, setting the stage for subsequent opposition. Although the Karabagh movement was not initially advocating independence, by late 1989–90 Armenian intellectuals began to think in terms of separating from the USSR. The ARF – whose motto, ironically, was 'Free, Independent and United Armenia' – was against the country's independence at this stage. The ARF consistently opposed the ANM on this issue and dismissed calls for independence as irresponsible and 'adventurous.'

Relations with Turkey ANM wanted to develop normal relations with Turkey, putting aside historical considerations and rejecting pan-Turkism as a threat. As Ter Petrosian put it in a speech in the Supreme Soviet on 23 June 1989: 'Pan-Turkism, as an ideology, born during the First World War, has presently lost its context as a political factor since Turkish speaking people have taken the path of national development.'[8] He went on to say that seeing Armenia as surrounded by enemies and therefore only capable of safeguarding its existence under the protection of a great power is a 'bankrupt and dangerous' way of thinking.

For Dashnaks, Turkey and pan-Turkism were the real threat to Armenia and the root of the nation's problems. The Karabagh struggle, Sumgait, Azerbaijani policies, etc. were all tied to pan-Turkism and not to the Soviet Union. Hence, there should not be any relations with Turkey without the historical fact of the Genocide being taken into account.

The Armenian 'Question' and the Armenian 'Cause' (see chapters 4 and 5) For the ANM the primary aim of the Armenian 'Cause' was the strengthening of the independent statehood of Armenia and the security of Karabagh. Genocide recognition and land claims were secondary to this. This was a reinterpretation of the 'Question' to suit the needs of the republic. It was argued that policy should be based on realist calculations of the current capacities of the country. Raising wider issues would have been, for the ANM, biting off more than the country could swallow and hence detrimental to its security.

The ARF was much more hardline. It did accept that not all elements of the wider 'Question' could be addressed immediately, but it argued that Armenian policies must reflect the wider issues of Genocide recognition and

---

8   Reprinted in *Droshak*, 5 July 1989 (20:6), p. 18, and in Libaridian, p. 156.

the lost lands in Turkey and Nakhichevan. The first item on the agenda was, however, the reunification of Karabagh with Armenia, followed by Nakhichevan and Akhalkalak (the Armenian region in Georgia). What is more, this was to be done through the Soviet Union.

Karabagh The ANM and the ARF had profound differences on the issue of the solution to the Karabagh problem. Fairly early on, in 1989, Dashnaks began to criticize the Karabagh Committee for 'mixing water in the wine of Artsakh [i.e. Karabagh]', since the Committee was broadening its demands from the attachment of the region to Armenia to wider political issues and independence. Soon the ANM was being accused of 'selling' Karabagh. These accusations emanated from the fact that the ANM always insisted on the security of Armenians in Karabagh, leaving questions of status open. For the ANM, the question of the unification of Karabagh with Armenia or its independence – i.e. of its final status – was secondary to peace and security. The ARF, on the other hand, insisted that Karabagh must be part of Armenia or be recognized as an independent republic, and Armenians must continue the struggle to achieve these ends.

Political ideology The ANM's ideological views were based on liberal democracy, market relations and privatization of state assets. They were openly against any idea of socialism. They also implemented a strong presidential system, and a constitution which centralized power in the President's hands.

The ARF believed in a mixed economy and social democracy. They too, of course, advocated democracy but wanted to put a stop to the unchecked privatization of land and state enterprises. They also objected to the creation of a strong presidency, and preferred a political system in which parliament held more power than the President.

Citizenship Despite a clause on granting citizenship to diaspora Armenians in the 1990 Declaration on Independence, the 1995 constitution rejected the notion of dual citizenship and did not give any special status to diasporans. Foreigners could become Armenian citizens only if they settled in the republic and renounced other citizenships.[9]

The ANM objected to dual citizenship on the grounds that it could be a loophole for young men to dodge military service. In reality, however, the movement did not wish to give diasporans too much political leverage within the republic while their long-term commitment and responsibility to it could not be taken for granted. It was reasoned that diaspora Armenians,

---

9   There are exceptions to the law. Special citizenships can be granted by presidential decree. But, according to the Law on the Legal Status of Foreign Citizens (adopted in June 1994), a foreign citizen of Armenian origin, or others with interest in Armenia, can obtain a ten year (renewable) residency permit (Article 21).

who would continue to live abroad, should not be on an equal footing with the locals, as dual citizenship would imply. Hence, anyone in the diaspora who wanted to be a citizen of both Armenia and their country of residence was effectively disqualified. The ARF attacked the law disallowing dual citizenship. Dashnaks have consistently advocated dual citizenship as a tangible means of linking the diaspora with the homeland.

The diaspora's role Finally, each party's view of the diaspora differed radically, based on their conception of the nation. According to the ANM, Armenia and the diaspora are two different entities, and they should not meddle in each other's internal affairs, especially in politics. In Ter Petrosian's words, 'the concept of national political parties which exist and function outside their country is unnatural. There will always be a mutual lack of understanding and trust, so long as the diaspora leadership does not come to terms with the reality that policy is determined here, on this land'.[10] This mentality was also reflected in the fact that the diaspora was hardly mentioned in the speeches, declarations and pronouncements of the ANM and its members. In short, the diaspora is shut out not only from the internal politics of the homeland, but also from political issues which affect Armenians as a whole (e.g. Genocide recognition). The ANM wanted to limit the relationship between the homeland and the diaspora to the arena of economic aid/investment, cultural links, and the selective use of diaspora experts whose opinions were in congruence with the ANM. Hence, what was required was dialogue and mutual contact, based on the assumption that the homeland and the diaspora are separate and distinct entities.

The ARF's approach diametrically opposed this view. Dashnaks, using the slogan 'one nation, one homeland', blur the line between the diaspora and the homeland. Their mentality is based on the belief that the nation is indivisible and therefore its politics should be a symbiosis between the homeland and the diaspora. It is, therefore, legitimate for diaspora-based 'pan-national' parties such as the ARF to have a direct say in the affairs of the homeland. As Apo Boghigian, a member of the ARF Bureau (i.e. ruling council) declared, 'imposing distinctions between native Armenians and Diasporans when it comes to involvement in Armenia's politics is insulting'.[11]

As these key issues indicate, the division between the ANM and the ARF was deep. Homeland–diaspora relations cannot, of course, be totally reduced to ANM–ARF antagonisms, but the political opposition of these two parties is a fairly good indication of the tensions between Armenians of the republic and Armenians of the diaspora. Needless to say, there were many in the diaspora who supported the ANM and Ter Petrosian, and many

---

10 Interview, *AIM*, March 1994, p. 32.
11 Interview, *AIM*, November–December 1994, p. 39. Boghigian, a US citizen, had just been expelled from Armenia at that point.

in the republic who supported the ARF and the local opposition. But these were not the most visible or significant political forces setting policy or the national agenda. And even when there was political agreement between diasporans and native Armenians, identity differences, as we shall see, remained.

Phase four: reconciliation since 1998

It is only with the resignation of Ter Petrosian and the loss of political power by the ANM that relations began to improve between the Armenian government and the ARF, and by extension between the homeland and the diaspora. The 'reconciliation' period began in February 1998, when Robert Kocharian, the Prime Minister, in cooperation with the Defence and Interior Ministers, ousted Ter Petrosian and some of his key allies. The new leadership of Kocharian seemed to have a more inclusive view of the diaspora and a much more accommodating attitude towards the Dashnaks. In fact, days after he acquired power as Acting President, Kocharian legalized the ARF as a political party (on 9 February 1998). At the same time, almost all of the Dashnaks arrested and convicted during the previous three years were freed. Kocharian even appointed Vahan Hovhannisian, the formerly imprisoned leader of the ARF, as an advisor to him, as well as having two Dashnaks in his cabinet.

There was much overlap between the views of the ARF and Kocharian. Their approach to relations with Turkey, the Armenian 'Question' and Genocide recognition, the solution to the Karabagh conflict, dual citizenship and relations with the diaspora were similar. The diaspora on the whole was enthusiastic about Kocharian's election, and particularly appreciative of his gestures of cooperation and inclusion towards Armenians abroad.

However, the differences between Kocharian's and Ter Petrosian's approach to the key issues for the diaspora proved to be mostly rhetorical. In fact, under Kocharian's presidency, Armenia has made attempts to improve relations with Turkey, negotiations with Azerbaijan over Karabagh continued (albeit sporadically and from a less compromising position), and dual citizenship has not yet been adopted (although it was part of a wider constitutional reform package defeated in a referendum in May 2003). Kocharian has made important symbolic gestures to reach out to the diaspora in the form of two Armenia–diaspora conferences held in Yerevan in 1999 and 2002.

Diasporan Armenians have recognized and responded to the more careful and balanced policy towards the diaspora. The wealthier donors have rewarded the Kocharian administration with substantial investments in the impoverished economy of the homeland. Their contributions have helped to renovate the Armenian road infrastructure, to develop business firms in the tourism industry and to improve services related to it, and to construct buildings, particularly in the area that suffered from the earthquake in 1988.

Yet it is too soon to conclude whether or not the reconciliation between the homeland and the diaspora will prove lasting. There is no doubt that the current leadership in Armenia is genuinely interested in strengthening the country's links with the diaspora because it sees in the diaspora a material as well as a political asset which it can use. Of course, the moral argument of 'we are all one nation' permeates all discourse on the issue. As President Kocharian put it in his Inaugural Speech on 9 April 1998:

> Our generation is here to shoulder one more responsibility. That is the unification of the efforts of all the Armenians and the ensuring of Diaspora Armenians' active participation in the social, political and economic life of our republic. A constitutional solution to the issue of dual citizenship will also contribute to the issue. Armenia should be a holy motherland for all the Armenians, and its victory should be their victory, its future, their future. We have to realize that a nation, understanding the value of its combined force, can never be defeated.[12]

These are indeed lofty words, paraphrasing Charents' call quoted at the start of the chapter. But the reality remains that, despite closer relations between the homeland and the diaspora, fundamental divisions persist in the realm of identity.

History and identity

After a decade of contact and interaction between the homeland and the diaspora, it has become clear that 'Armenianness' has acquired a different meaning for each of these entities. Perhaps the most important lesson of the last few years has been the realization by Armenians of how different the two branches of the same nation are, despite the rhetoric of unity. National identity in the diaspora has become far removed from the homeland, particularly from the idea of 'return' to it. Armenia is seen not only as geographically distant, but also as culturally foreign to most Armenians living abroad.

The differences between the homeland and the diaspora are much more profound than political disagreements. Rather, they have deep historical foundations rooted in the nineteenth century, when Armenian collective identity was metamorphosed from an ethno-religious sense of belonging to a modern nationality. There were two parallel trends in this process, which is generally referred to as the period of national 'awakening' (see chapter 4). The division between the homeland and the diaspora can be traced back to these developments: on the one hand, there was the Western trend based in Constantinople (Istanbul) and diasporan centres in Western Europe; on the other, the Eastern trend based in Tiflis (Tbilisi) and diasporan centres in the Russian Empire and Eastern Europe.

---

12 Quoted by *Armenpress*, 9 April 1998, as posted on *Groong* Armenian News Network.

The theoretical, ideological, and sociological sources of each of these two trends had separate origins which influenced intellectuals and subsequently the masses. The Western component of the awakening evolved around the liberal reform project, influenced by French and Italian thought, constitutionalism and 'Western' nationalism. The Eastern component was influenced by Russian and German thought, radicalism and 'Eastern' nationalism. By the end of the nineteenth century both of these trends co-existed in Armenian national identity, and in the nationalist and revolutionary programmes of the Armenian intelligentsia. But there was tension between the two approaches, both in identity and in politics, even though they were part of the national movement of the same nation.

What emerged by the beginning of the twentieth century was a triangular relationship, with the two ideological sources of 'imagining' the nation based in diasporan communities: the Western point, embodied by Constantinople, but also including Venice, Vienna, Paris, etc., and the Eastern point of Tiflis, including Moscow, St. Petersburg, Dorpat (now Tartu, Estonia), etc. The third point of the triangle was the actual homeland, the 'raw stuff' of the local realities and developments in Armenia itself.

But Armenian national awakening was also a totalizing experience in so far as it transformed, or at least affected, all the crucial elements of identity: language, literature, political ideology, religion and social class. Each of these domains was affected by the East/West divide, and in each case parallel developments took place. For example, the vernacular that emerged was divided between the Eastern and Western dialects; literature was influenced by the realist school in the West, whereas the romantic school was more prevalent in the East; political ideology centred on reform, liberalism and constitutionalism in Constantinople, whereas activists were pursuing revolutionary goals in Tiflis; religious jurisdictions were administratively divided between the Ottoman and Russian empires as well. All of these factors had profound effects on the parallel emergence of Armenian national identity. Herein lie the main roots of the homeland/diaspora division.

After the 1915 Genocide, and the emptying of Armenians from the Ottoman Empire/Turkey, the Western point of Armenian identity was dispersed in the diaspora, whereas in the East, Armenian identity came to be rooted in the surviving part of the homeland, transformed into a Soviet republic within the USSR, and therefore guided by Communist principles. These two entities lived and evolved more or less separately from each other throughout the twentieth century. Contacts between them were limited, highly regulated and usually on the terms set forth by the sovietized 'homeland'. Tensions and antagonism – especially between the ARF and the Communists – were interpreted strictly in terms of political opposition. In short, seventy years of Communist rule had frozen the possibility of cultural and identity synthesis between the diasporacized West and the sovietized East. When this freeze began to thaw after 1988, the tensions and clashes between the two sides came to the fore and were visible to all. However, these differences are not yet fully recognized by Armenians, and there is no substantive discussion on such issues of identity between intellectuals of the homeland and of the diaspora. More than anything, they talk past each other.

It is essential to add a few words here on the nature of diasporan identity and its perception of 'homeland'. On the whole, this unique identity is based on a hybrid and hyphenated sense of belonging and dual loyalties to the homeland and to the 'host land' (see chapter 7). The Western diaspora is no longer connected in any meaningful way to a specific homeland (least of all to one that was sovietized). It is not the diaspora of a concrete or 'existing' homeland but of an idealized homeland – a 'spiritual' diaspora of a 'spiritual' fatherland. For this community, with its hybrid identity, 'Armenia, Soviet or free, lies in the realm of the spirit. It is an emotional link,' observes Anny Bakalian.[13] This leads to the possibility that diaspora Armenians can have more than one 'homeland' which can alternate between, or simultaneously be, the *host*-land, the current home-*land*, the *ancestral*-land, or the diaspora condition itself as *home*-land. These answers are highly personalized, and differ from community to community, and from individual to individual. Moreover, the answers are not fixed, because identity is an evolving phenomenon.

Despite such profound divisions, differences and competing identities, a sense of belonging to the same nation – of being, or feeling, Armenian – still prevails. There is a thread which ties the diaspora to the homeland and vice versa, and connects all the diasporan Armenians together. This thread is the subjective sense of belonging to one particular nation despite real differences. More than anything, this thread is an emotional bond. In the absence of 'objective' factors making up a nation on its own land, or in its own nation-state, the diaspora replaces them with a subjective sense of belonging.

The tangible expression of this subjective sense is active practical commitment to the Armenian nation (however defined). This is what makes communities abroad a diaspora and not only a minority ethnic group. Such commitment is often expressed in terms of involvement, as Armenians, in political activities in pursuit of the national cause (e.g. lobbying for Genocide recognition, etc.). It can also be expressed through support for Armenian cultural activities in the host society, in terms of mobilization on behalf of other Armenian communities and/or on behalf of the home-state, through economic aid, etc. The subjective sense of belonging to the same nation, despite geographical dispersion and differences, underpins all such efforts.

---

13 A. Bakalian, *Armenian-Americans: From Being to Feeling Armenian* (New Brunswick: Transaction Publishers, 1993) p. 161.

Conclusion

The Armenian diaspora has historically played a crucial role in the formation, strengthening and maintaining of national identity – in some ways
replacing the role of the state in the nation-building process. It is undeniable
that much of the initial learning, research and publication about and by
Armenians in the eighteenth and nineteenth centuries, as well as political
activism, was done in diasporan centres, from the Mekhitarists of
Venice/Vienna to the merchants of Madras. A similar process was carried
through by diasporan organizations after the Genocide, when the mass of
the Armenian refugees were forged into a relatively coherent diasporan
nation (particularly in the Middle East). A parallel dynamic took place in
the other part of the nation, in the Armenian Soviet Socialist Republic,
which played the key role in maintaining and augmenting a strong sense of
'Armenianness' (especially after the mid-1950s). In the twentieth century,
and even earlier, Armenians have experienced a dual-track nation-building
process.

Given that there were, and still remain, two fundamental entities which
make up the Armenian nation, the logical question to end on would be:
what should be the relationship between the once again independent homeland and the diaspora?

One side argues that the republic and the diaspora should stay out of
each other's affairs, especially politically, and that only loose cultural and
economic ties should bind the two together. This was the position of the
former President Ter Petrosian. The other side rejects this approach, and
insists on the unity of the homeland and the diaspora, suggesting that the
politics and policies of the former should reflect the interests and views of
the latter. The ARF position is the clearest manifestation of this argument.
The current President, Robert Kocharian, is trying to take the middle road
between these two positions. But the balancing act is a difficult one to maintain. At the heart of the debate lies the question of legitimacy.

The President of Armenia is elected by the population of Armenia, and
on what grounds can he claim to represent, or speak on behalf of, the entire
nation, including the diaspora? Some in the diaspora would accept that the
President should be regarded as the leader of all Armenians. For example,
Dikran Voskuni, the editor of the popular *Nor Gyank* newspaper based in
Los Angeles, has said, in relation to the former president, that 'Ter Petrosian
should be, feel and act as the president of *all* Armenians [world-wide]'.[14] But
others insist that the diaspora is a separate polity in its own right, and
cannot be represented by the leadership in Yerevan.[15] However, so far the

---

14   *Nor Gyank*, 7 August 1997, p. 42.
15   Krikor Beledian makes this point, along with Khachig Tololyan, in a stimulating discussion
summarized in the report 'Fresh Perspectives on Armenia–Diaspora Relations', *Armenian
Forum*, no. 3 (Autumn 1998), pp. 61–6.

Armenian diaspora has been unable to create a unified body which could represent its interests as a whole. More broadly, national unity – including both the homeland and the diaspora – has been even more elusive throughout Armenian history, despite constant calls for it. At the end one must ask: will one side of the equation making up the Armenian nation prevail? That is, will the republic's (the nation-*state*'s) agenda come out on top? Will there be a fusion of interests? Or, will the diaspora eventually succeed in articulating a clear agenda on its own and deal with the homeland on such terms, effectively making the relationship between the two one of relatively equal partners? There is also the ever-present reality that the diaspora will eventually succumb to assimilation and wither away as any kind of serious entity. All of these remain open questions as Armenians enter the fourth millennium of their existence.

Bibliography

Bakalian, A., *Armenian-Americans: From Being to Feeling Armenian* (New Brunswick: Transaction Publishers, 1993).

Dekmejian, R.H., 'The Armenian Diaspora', chapter 13 in R.G. Hovannisian, ed., *The Armenian People* (New York: St. Martin's Press, 1997), pp. 413–43.

Libaridian, G.J., *Modern Armenia: People, Nation, State* (New Brunswick: Transaction, 2004).

Panossian, R., 'The Past as Nation: the Evolution of Armenian Identity', *Geopolitics*, vol. 7, no. 2, Autumn 2002.

—— 'The Diaspora and the Karabagh Movement: Oppositional Politics Between the Armenian Revolutionary Federation and the Armenian National Movement', in L. Chorbajian, ed., *The Making of Nagorno-Karabagh: From Secession to Republic* (Basingstoke: Palgrave, 2001).

—— 'Courting a Diaspora: Armenia–Diaspora Relations since 1998', in E. Ostergaard-Nielsen, ed., *International Migration and Sending Countries: Perceptions, Policies, and Transnational Relations* (Basingstoke: Palgrave, 2003).

—— *In Search of a Nation: Armenian Identity in History, Diaspora and Soviet Rule* (Hurst Publishers, forthcoming 2004).

Index